BRIGHTWORK

The Art of Finishing Wood

*W*e brought back these reliefs of a humble art.
I woke with this marble head in my hands;
it exhausts my elbows and I don't know
where to put it down.

It was falling into the dream as I was coming
out of the dream
so our life became one and it will be very
difficult to separate again.

What are they after, our souls, traveling
on the decks of decayed ships . . . ?

Giorgios Sefiriades
Mythistorema (1935)

BRIGHTWORK

The Art of Finishing Wood

REBECCA J. WITTMAN

International Marine
Camden, Maine

Published by International Marine

10 9 8 7 6 5

Library of Congress Cataloging-in-Publication Data

Wittman, Rebecca J.
Brightwork: the art of finishing wood / Rebecca J. Wittman.
p.   cm.
Includes bibliographical references.
ISBN 0-87742-984-7
1. Wooden boats—Maintenance and repair. 2. Wood finishing.
I. Title.
VM322.W57   1990
623.8'207—dc20   90-5979
CIP

Questions regarding the content of this book should be addressed to:
International Marine
P.O. Box 220
Camden, ME 04843

Questions regarding the ordering of this book should be addressed to:
The McGraw-Hill Companies
Customer Service Department
P.O. Box 547
Blacklick, OH 43004
Retail customers: 1-800-822-8158; Bookstores: 1-800-722-4726

Imageset by High Resolution, Camden, Maine.
Design by Sherry Streeter.

DEDICATION

Old paint on canvas, as it ages, sometimes becomes transparent. When that happens it is possible, in some pictures, to see the original lines: a tree will show through a woman's dress, a child makes way for a dog, a large boat is no longer on an open sea. That is called pentimento because the painter 'repented,' changed his mind. Perhaps it would be well to say that the old conception, replaced by a later choice, is a way of seeing and then seeing again.

—Lillian Hellman

When I was in my youth I spent a couple of very enlightening years working in the garment business. It was during this tenure with Seattle-based Brittania Sportswear that I served as assistant to a wonderfully bright designer named Kathy Brown. Brittania had hired Kathy to create a women's line, and she immediately brought into this otherwise prosaic business a poetic breeze of inventiveness and foresight. After a few hours of meetings her first day, it was announced that she had named the new line "Pentimento." This was a word with which I was not familiar, but I was fairly certain it shared no kinship with the red vegetable commonly found nestled inside green olives. One day I got up enough nerve to ask her what the name meant.

Kathy responded, in her trademark nasal drone, "Read this," and, handing me a dog-eared copy of Lillian Hellman's book of the same name, pointed just inside the book's cover to the paragraph quoted here. She went on to explain that this concept mirrored her own philosophy of the cyclical traditions of clothing design, and that this was her reason for embroidering it on a label.

What, one might ask, does all this have to do with a book on brightwork? Two things, really. First, and foremost, the essence of this "folk art" is found in the direct effect each phase of refinishing has on the next laborious pursuit. The element of time has an unswerving way of exposing every change of heart, every lapse of energy, every omission of thought in the commission of our refinishing tasks. Like skins of an onion, the layers of our refinishing efforts can be peeled back to betray our degree of commitment, or lack thereof.

The second reason I offer this lesson in art terminology is that brightwork is a true artform, and over the years I have found that every person has at least some potential to express himself in this medium. Some people are more impassioned in their tapping of those artistic reservoirs than others —and their boats reflect the degree of that passion —but it seems every boatowner, crewman, owner's spouse, and owner's kid has within him the capacity to make some statement on this canvas. Even if some never acquiesce to that creative alter-ego they are still affected by it, if only in the form of a keen appreciation of another's well-varnished rail.

This is a book for those people, the artisans who take a certain pride in what they do and in what they have. It is not for the refinishing expert whose first priority on the job is the making of money, nor obviously is it for the boatowner who is so taken with his capacity to amass possessions that he is content to leave his toys in shambles, until it's convenient to hire some expert to come along and clean up the mess.

And it is definitely not a book for people who place a greater value on the saving of time than on the investing of it.

This is a book for people who understand the intoxicating feeling that comes with accomplishing something creative and challenging, something departing from the easy and the familiar. It is meant to be a companion to these adventurers when they are confused or exhausted or needing reassurance after a mistake or two. Like an old salt patrolling "his" dock, it will be there to answer questions, impart courage and sometimes most importantly, provide a salvo of humor through what can often feel like mundane or sobering tasks.

This is a book for people who, seduced by that glistening varnished rail, cannot resist running their hand along its sensual surface. It's for the romantic who believes, as do I, that within every neglected boat there lies a weeping soul. It is for the souls of those boats that long to be touched.

The pentimento phenomenon has not only touched, but seems to have become elemental to my life as I've watched my own resume develop into a collage of artistic pursuits: clothing design, music, yacht refinishing, writing. I realize that I have been able to do all these things because at one point I had a guide, a mentor: a person who at the start of my professional life gave me reasons to tap my own resources and believe in my own ideas. It's only fitting that the very person who brought the term "pentimento" to my attention should be the one who set my life on a course of professional artistry.

This is a book for the artist in all of us. Kathy Brown taught me not only that such a spirit existed within me, but to respect and celebrate that spirit. I have wished many times since her death in 1983 that we could touch bases just once more. This book is dedicated to her memory with deep gratitude and love.

ACKNOWLEDGMENTS

*T*he ideas contained in this volume, while perhaps original in their collective presentation, were culled from twelve years of access to a community well of thought. Without the generosity of hundreds of people, from boatowners to materials manufacturers, this book could not have happened. The following people in particular deserve a special note of thanks.

Jerry Husted, Doolie Pierce, Lee Knudsen and the gang at Doc Freeman's, Henry Hellieson, and Greg Allen and Northwest Yacht Repair for making my years in the business of refinishing boats more than monetarily rewarding.

All my clients, for allowing me to use their boats as my floating laboratory, and especially George and Mary Davis for their generosity and unflagging moral support.

Carol Broom, University of Washington School of Forestry Library; Bob Picket, Flounder Bay Lumber; Donna Christianson, U.S. Department of Agriculture Forestry Products Lab; Jack Hickey, International Paint Company; Bob Simonet (and all other helpful individuals), 3M Company; Herb Paulson, Daly's; Rick Schmidt and Kim Thompson Park, Porter Cable Company; Reese Kennedy, Easy Time Refinishing Corp. —for generous assistance with research; and Debora Erickson and Paula Ness, for years of help and moral support.

Kay Walsh, for giving me space in *Waterlines* magazine to find my reading audience; Jon Wilson and the very supportive staff at *WoodenBoat* for helping extend that audience beyond the Northwest; and Jonathan Eaton, for believing that that audience would enjoy seeing these ideas contained in book form.

Dr. Fay Van and all the participants in the 1989 Lake Arrowhead Antique and Classic Boat Show, for their cooperation while I photographed their boats; the staff of the California Yacht Club; Dan Dewes, Alan and Marcia Rosner, for leading me to some beautiful subjects to shoot; John T. Turner, my photography mentor; and Marshall Nelson, a very nice lawyer, for his legal guidance.

To Chris Eden, Marty Loken, and Neil Rabinowitz for their willingness to contribute works of art to this book; to Jennifer Elliott for her insightful participation in the editing; to Molly Mulhern for her patience with my mother-henning; and to Sherry Streeter for contributing her artistic talents to the book; and again to Jon Eaton, whose patience was, I'm sure, put to its greatest test: to this group especially, a very BIG thank you.

And finally, some very personal thanks to: My mother, whose sense of humor taught me that everything goes a little smoother with a smile and a little background music; my dad, whose passion for wood, strong work ethic, and sense of perfection set the tone for my own professional endeavors; Kristine Wittman Marvich, my first business partner and co-"Teak Twin," and John Wittman —both people of superior refinishing talent, without whose collaboration on many projects I would have been lost; Garth Julian L'Esperance, my finest creation, without whose tireless sorting through my office wastebasket I might have accidentally lost something important; John J. L'Esperance, the one person without whose support, encouragement, faith, partnership, and love I could not have finished this book.

CONTENTS

PREFACE:
HOW TO USE THIS BOOK

*I*f you find yourself leafing through this book because you were drawn to the pictures, with no plans to refinish a boat, I would simply say, "Enjoy!"

If, however, you *are* planning to use this book to assist in your refinishing efforts, I offer one simple suggestion: Read the entire book first, from beginning to end—and then go back to the chapters specific to your project to do the work. If you skip reading the whole book, you will miss out on the most important point behind its being written, which is to provide a grasp of the whole picture—all the options, good and bad—that makes successful refinishing possible.

Materials and tools referred to throughout each how-to chapter are discussed in detail under a separate section. I did this because I felt such information would be disruptive in the course of the how-to text. But knowing how to best use each item makes its application to any project that much more fruitful.

And finally, please don't leave this book to languish on your coffee table or library shelf. Take it to your boat or shop—or wherever you do your work—and *use* it. While it may be a beautiful book, it is meant to be treated like any other tool in your bag. Mess it up, splash varnish on it, cover it with teak dust. Allow it to reflect its role in your refinishing journey.

When you've come to the end of that journey, you'll be able to recall where you've been by looking at those tattered pages.

Part One

AN INTRODUCTION

1

THE HEART OF IT

The woods are lovely, dark and deep.
But I have promises to keep,
And miles to go before I sleep,
And miles to go before I sleep.
　　　　　　　　　—Robert Frost

A few years ago the enterprising folks who run Seattle's famous Pike Place Market decided to defray the cost of reflooring by inviting anyone with $35 to underwrite (so to speak) a granite tile, with the offer that said patrons could then immortalize themselves or whatever vital sentiment they deemed appropriate by having twenty letters etched into that tile. I was feeling flush at the time, and it seemed safe enough to proclaim for all eternity (or at least until the Market should go sliding into Elliott Bay) the feelings that I held for my husband, so I paid my money and took my chances. Now, in front of the old Hasson Brothers Fruit Stand, there is a granite tile inscribed "Rebecca loves Luther." This particular sentiment wouldn't likely catch your eye unless you were standing in line right over it, passing the time with a study of the hundreds of names and messages at your feet. But it's there, stuck to the floor for all time.

The Hasson Brothers are no longer in the fruit business, Luther and I are divorced, and I am blissfully invested in a new marriage complete with offspring.

This little vignette about etching things in stone is the perfect analogy for the danger inherent in publishing a book about brightwork. By the time the ink dries someone may come up with a more enticing way of doing things, perhaps even relegating the earlier information to obsolescence. But I think it's important to document what we know to be true while it is true, in the event it might benefit those involved at that juncture.

Love affairs notwithstanding, varnishing boats has been my primary passion for a number of years. Over the course of those years a potluck of opinion on this humble craft has been served up and documented in every marine publication. With the emergence of each new strategy, readers (myself included) have often been seduced by the notion that new is better. And sometimes new *has* been better — heat guns being a perfect example of a slicker variation on an old theme. But sometimes new has been nothing more than a fleeting seductress unable to replace the timeless strategies we've known and loved for years. If nothing else, I've learned

The hull is mahogany plywood with teak trim and spruce oars.

that it's important to keep an open mind to these things, tempered with a clear understanding of what we're trying to accomplish.

What I'm trying to accomplish in this book is a presentation of brightwork as an artform within the grasp of the average Joe or Josie. I had a friend years ago who believed very firmly that you don't have to be Renoir to create a masterpiece, you simply have to have a vision of what is beautiful to you and a simple plan for reaching your creative goals. Anyone who has strolled down a dock or two has undoubtedly seen a beautifully varnished boat and so has the ability to visualize the masterpiece. As for the plan, the

one I've been using continues to work, and despite its ever-changing components is still simple after all these years. This is the direction I take with this book —a simple, time-honored plan that consists of five basic components: Commitment, Organization, Understanding, Energy, and Realistic expectations. For the acronym junkies I suppose that spells COUER, which is French for heart, a word wholly appropriate as a bottom line to the equation. If in our refinishing affairs we set out to create a work of art that, once completed, we think will never require another whit of attention, we set up ourselves—and our boats —for a broken heart and an empty relationship. So, if there is any component more important than the rest, I would say it is commitment. Be true to this love and she will reciprocate your affections. Cheat on her and she slips quietly away from you, sometimes irretrievably.

Organization needs little definition. The key is that this concept extends beyond the actual doing of a project into the way one approaches the entire brightwork program on a boat. For example, if you don't have time to refinish all the trim on the boat in one season, and you can't abide the bare wood option, you can organize the boat into manageable sections to be refinished season by season. If you complete one area and refresh previous efforts within each refinishing interval, a wholly varnished boat emerges gradually and on workable terms. Organize your schedule of finish maintenance on the very day you give the boat its final stroke of varnish, not the day you notice the first sign of lifting. This is a classic circumstance where failing to plan is planning to fail.

The foundation of commitment, of course, can only spring from one's understanding of the subject as well as the medium. Certain woods on a boat require less attention and protection than others, and knowledge of their intrinsic tenacity gives one the option of fussing over them slavishly or leaving them completely bare. The term brightwork is meant really to encompass *any* wood on the boat that is not coated with an opaque finish, so the sun-silvered teak toerail can be every bit as honorable as the proudly varnished one —possibly more so if it rests this way because the owner realized and acknowledged his limited available maintenance time. If you don't have the time —or the energy, physically or financially —to keep after a varnish finish (or oil, since a properly applied oil finish re-quires a significant outpouring of labor, too), learn what it takes to keep your sweetie happy and protected without an uptown pelisse. In many cases this requires little more than good old salt water and a bucket.

The part about realistic expectations involves an understanding of the basic purpose as well as limitations of any brightwork finish. Whatever goes on in the way of varnish or oil ultimately comes off, and keeping it on is possible only to the extent that you keep it refreshed and tend to the owies as they happen. I swear (and many *have* sworn at this subject), ask a can of varnish to do *your* job, which is to make it last, and it will flatly refuse.

Brightwork finishes have a natural lifespan. They get old and start breaking down at the foundation, just as we do. Everything in life has to be replaced eventually. If you find yourself being sucked into the vortex of claims put forth by some manufacturers that a particular finish or product can forever withstand Mother Nature's best shots —with inane slogans such as "makes varnishing obsolete" —stop and ponder the simple fact of erosion. If entire coastlines comprised of stone cannot win the battle, common sense dictates that a thin, transparent membrane stands little chance of being but a fleeting memory in the grand scheme. Acknowledge a tired, worn-out finish and give it respectful passage.

Know what you're dealing with, enjoy the brightwork you see, and, as you reach out for a touch, allow the beautiful brightwork around you to touch you back. It makes being part of the creative process a very rewarding experience.

2

SAD AND SORRY BRIGHTWORK

In its widest possible sense, a man's self is the sum total of all that he can call his, not only his body and his psychic powers, but his clothes and his house, his wife and children, his ancestors and friends, his reputation and works, his lands and horses, and yacht and bank account. All these things give him the same emotions. If they wax and prosper, he feels triumphant; if they dwindle and die away, he feels cast down.
　　　　　　　　　　　　　　　　　　　　—William James

*E*ver heard that famous line once uttered by J.P. Morgan, "Any man who has to ask about the annual upkeep of a yacht can't afford one"? The steam yachts of J.P.'s day boasted a lot of brightwork, and no self-respecting robber baron would do his own refinishing.

Buying a boat is not much different from entering into a marriage; all the same emotions come into play. But too many people make the mistake of thinking of boats as inanimate objects, out there floating on an anonymous sea of expectations. Brightwork upkeep is the most salient point of boat reality that people gloss over in their zealous courting. The siren's song pulls them blindly into precarious waters, and they can't hear the varnish gods shouting, "Teak on starboard!"

If you're drawn to a boat with even a moderate degree of brightwork, you are obviously so attracted because you appreciate the aesthetics of

Bare teak deck, varnished teak covering boards and toerails, all in need of attention.

wood. Teak butterfly hatches and cockpit coamings don't make the boat sail faster or more efficiently, so the ultimate motivation for owning them is found in the way they look to you. You think they enhance the beauty of the vessel. You might also be telling yourself that owning a boat on which you could do some varnishwork would be nice, because it would give you a creative outlet in your spare time, when you feel like communing with your yacht instead of taking her to sea. You're thinking a couple or three hours every so often with a brush and a can of spar varnish would be a nice escape from life. Or, you may be wanting a boat for ocean cruising or living aboard that has a certain homey feeling below, and it just happens to come with teak decks and a full range of exterior teak appointments integral to the design of the boat. They look nice on the boatshow floor, and don't seem likely to be too great a burden in the general scheme of owning the boat.

The gleaming finish you see at a boatshow or in a dealer's showroom is not a permanent one, and in the case of new boats, usually not what is delivered to you as part of a commissioning package. That finish you're looking at, all shining and new, is what the brightwork is *capable* of looking like. But that finish, like the time and money it takes to keep it there, does not grow on trees along with the wood. It comes from you, the owner —in the form of a maintenance program you set up from the day you take delivery. If you buy the boat because these appointments are beautiful to you, then you defeat your purpose if you allow them to slide into an unsightly state—a condition that doesn't take long to arise when things are neglected.

When you buy a new boat, it's typically delivered to you with exterior brightwork that is lightly sanded and, unless ordered to stay bare, wearing some type of wood sealer —one or two coats at most. This is not a long-term finish, and it is seldom applied over wood that has been meticulously prepped. Most people doing commissioning brightwork have less than two years' experience in the business, and their training is rarely at the master's knee. The finish is applied by these summertime pros as a part of the presentation package, courtesy of the dealer, and will last at the outside about three months. There is the rare exception to this practice, of course, commensurate with the value of the boat. The exterior brightwork on such luxury yachts as Feadships and Hinckley sailboats gleams with a professionally applied Epifanes finish as a standard feature. Unless you've purchased a boat at this end of the price spectrum, though, it's likely your new yacht will sport a less exacting finish when you assume the role of skipper. There are then two basic options available to you.

You Can Do the Finishing Yourself

If you decide to "do" your own brightwork, you can take one of these approaches in caring for your new charge:

1) If the brightwork is teak, ask the dealer to deliver it to you bare but finish sanded (which means devoid of factory flaws such as deep sander scratches and rough edges or a significantly raised grain). They might balk at the sanding, but if they're selling quality boats I don't think they will, as it isn't that much trouble —especially if you're not asking for anything in the way of an oiling or sealer. If you aren't confident of your dealer's grasp of the brightwork issue, don't hesitate to specify that such sanding should be done with a watchful eye to adjacent surfaces. Most dealers won't need such babysitting, but on rare occasions you'll run across one who hires careless greenhorns to do the commissioning finish work and doesn't keep a close eye on things.

After you take delivery of your bare teak, you could just leave it bare. Period. No oiling, no varnish, no fuss no muss. Just bare, to elegantly silver with gradual exposure to sun, salt, and fresh air. However, "bare" is *not* Swahili for neglected. Leaving the wood bare means keeping it clean by regular washdown with a "no bristle brushes" policy (cellulose sponges or soft nylon tile scrubbers are the only way to go, contrary to the popular misconception that bristles are the only means to a clean wood surface). Swabbing every other week or so (depending on exposure to the elements) with a simple mixture of water, Lemon Joy, and a tablespoon of TSP (trisodium phosphate) per five-gallon bucket will do the trick. This keeps the grain of the wood intact, the mildew from setting in, and the boat in top condition for exercising future options of more elaborate treatments. This is the best initial plan for the owner who isn't absolutely sure what he wants to do with the wood, or whether keeping the wood finished is something he has the time or extra money to do, or whether the intended use of the boat will be compatible with a varnish finish.

2) If it's a boat out of Taiwan —or anywhere, actually —and you're not sure how long the teak

was allowed to cure before it was cut up into the little pieces you now see in the shape of handrails and winch pads, you may be concerned about leaving the wood unsealed as it seasons. In this case, you could make the same request of the dealer regarding the finish sanding and then saturate the wood with a linseed or Tung oil-based sealer (one that is not primarily solvents), applying a fresh coat of this oil every two months for the first year. After you feel the wood has stabilized, bleach off the oil, give the wood a good sanding, and leave it bare or varnish.

3) If your boat's exterior brightwork is not teak, you have little alternative but to varnish. Given the requisite free time to prep, apply, and maintain a proper varnish finish (which for exteriors involves about eight initial coats and refresher coats, at least twice a year every year thereafter), by all means go for it. You don't have to be a pro, you just have to know that this approach requires a true commitment. If you've never done this work before, this book can teach you the basics and your boat will be your campus. Varnishing can be done, and done well, by anyone who approaches it with the right attitude.

You Can Have the Finish Done For You

If you want that gorgeous varnish finish but you know you don't have time to do it, your only remaining option is to delegate the "doing" to someone else. That someone can be a spouse or your children or the next-door neighbor or a professional, the choice depending in part on what you are willing to pay and the quality of job you can call satisfactory. If you want your boat varnished like a Feadship, prepare yourself emotionally for that luxury by walking into your bathroom and flushing a pile of C-notes down the toilet. You now understand that good brightwork is a no-monetary-return investment. Just like your boat. Now, ask around until you get three identical answers to the "who does the best brightwork in town?" question, and then call that company. If they say they are too booked up to take your boat for at least three months, you know you have the right place. If they say they can take you tomorrow, you know they have a lot of relatives around town doing their PR work. Move on. I've seen some pathetic things happen to boats because new owners thought an inexperienced varnisher couldn't hurt anything. If someone hands you a pretty little business card, ask to see something they've done before you let them board your boat. Even then, before you hire someone who sounds like the right person, ask to see their best-looking brightwork job; then ask for that boatowner's number and verify that this person did the job according to contract, on time, or indeed at all. (I was *so* shocked the first time I found someone taking credit for one of my boats; I wondered why I'd never thought to be that clever!) The bottom line here, once you've committed to spend any amount of money, is that the investment doesn't end when the initial job is completed. It continues as you spend "refresher dollars," and if you don't have followup work done you are wasting the original investment. The happy compromise, if possible, is having someone do the more time-consuming initial finish, after which you do the maintenance coats.

If you choose the complete professional service route, and money *is* an object, you might be able to save yourself some billable hours by delivering the boat to the brightwork company cleaned and stripped down—freshly washed, fittings removed, butterfly hatches dismantled, stanchions down, etc. I know I was always happy to get my hands on a boat in this condition, and I'm sure most true professionals have a busy enough schedule that they'd be happier investing their time on the wood itself.

The qualifiers to all these brightwork options are several, including but not limited to the type of moorage you enjoy (whether you're in a covered slip on a remote freshwater lake or tied up next to a freeway with its relentless grit and pollution), how often and how carefully you use the boat, whether you put a canvas cover over it in the winters, and so forth. You can cut down on overall brightwork time by avoiding the temptation to commit "varnish overkill." Choose to finish only certain parts of your brightwork and leave the balance to silver out—an option that is as lovely to look at as it is practical.

If you have your eye on a pretty little brokerage boat, understand that the same principles of upkeep apply. In this case, however, it's probable that the boat is already wearing a finish of some sort. If its varnish appears to be in good condition (no obvious breakdown or checking, pretty color, and well adhered to the wood) or recently done, find out what the previous owner used and how old the present finish foundation is. To me this is akin to getting the service records on a used car. If he or she has refinished it from fresh wood within the previous three years and has kept it up with a good-quality product, you should be able to pick up where he left off with a regular refresher schedule of your own. A used boat that comes with brightwork nicely done and in good condition offers an asset that you'd be crazy not to protect. I always encourage people who bring me in as consultant under these circumstances to make their first purchase a set of canvas covers.

If you are buying your first boat, don't let brightwork maintenance come as some kind of surprise to you after you get your floating dream home. Preventive maintenance from the beginning is the key to a healthy, long-lasting brightwork finish and ongoing enjoyment of your boat. Too many people fall out of love with their boats because they didn't plan a brightwork program from the day they took delivery, and then when it was too late didn't have the resolve to retrieve the once-beautiful finish. Don't allow your dreamboat to become a nightmare.

3

CHOOSING FINISHES

And God said to Noah, "I have determined to make an end of all flesh; for the earth is filled with violence through them; behold, I will destroy them with the earth. Make yourself an ark of gopher wood; make rooms in the ark, and cover it inside and out with pitch."

—Genesis, 6:14

Noah did as God said, building that ark according to His specifications. But the nature of gopher wood remains a mystery today among the dendrological set. There are those who speculate that it was from the family of trees known as Cedars of Lebanon, while others insist it had to have been a cypress. The riddle seems destined to remain as such, but one thing is certain: Given what we know about the evolution of coatings, the finish on that floating barn had to be bright, since the Bible tells us it was a pitch concoction. I would also bet my kneepads that while Noah tossed about in that forty-day squall, the last thing on his mind was whether the finish was holding up, much less whether it was beautiful.

Whether your boat is an ark or a dinghy, the finish can function not only as its guardian but as its flatterer. Differences in emphasis spring from the type of wood being finished. Teak, for example, needs little or no protection. It maintains its own storehouse of protective oils and if left without a finish can survive relatively unscathed for decades. If we want to see the teak's original color again, we simply bleach off the oxidized

A bright-hulled Concordia yawl.

surface oils and *voila!* there it is. Putting a finish on teak is something we do for ourselves. We are Professor Higgins, and teak is Eliza Doolittle. We dress it up and groom it to be what we think of as refined and elegant, when all the while it is respectable in its natural guise.

Some woods are not so blessed. They beg not only your flattery but the protection afforded by such fussing. African mahogany, while considered a hardwood, is not as dense as teak or so imbued with natural oils and as a result is predisposed to permanent staining from prolonged exposure to moisture. It looks absolutely gorgeous all varnished up, but the foremost reason for applying such a finish is to protect it.

Some of the woods you can encounter in your brightwork adventures are recounted in this excellent paragraph from *The Proper Yacht* by Arthur Beiser. Perhaps he's describing your boat:

Different functions aboard ship call for different materials, and it is, in fact, quite remarkable that such a broad range of properties exists in wood that a proper combination can take care of nearly all the requirements. The stem, keel, and frames require great strength and durability, together with an ability to hold fastenings securely, which makes white oak the best choice. Planking needs a stable wood, not too heavy, that can be given a smooth finish and that is available in long, defect-free lengths, specifications that eliminate oak but lead directly to mahogany. Clamps and bilge stringers require a strong, fairly light, straight-grained wood, making fir the logical candidate. A wooden deck must be very stable and durable —in fact, capable of being left bare for the life of the boat—and no better wood than teak has been found for this purpose. A tiller must be strong yet limber enough to take up some of the shocks that the rudder produces, and ash is good on this score. A light but durable wood is needed for ceilings, for which cedar is excellent. Wooden spars must be both light and strong, and the wood they are made from must be available in long lengths and have a straight grain, with hardness unnecessary, and for this spruce invariably is the selection. Cabin soles of teak are best constructed with thin, raised, alternating strips of hardwood to improve slip resistance, and now the finger points to holly. Eight different woods, yet this number is far from being unusual in a wooden boat.

The Bright Finishes

The remarkable thing about the wide variety of woods mentioned above is the fact that any and all of them can be—and from one boat to another have been over time—finished bright. There is no law that says any particular wood in any certain part of the boat must be painted, and as a result bright finishes have found their way into every nook and cranny of vessels since the time of Noah.

What prompts the choice of a bright finish? Aesthetics? Tradition? Romance? Masochism? Or a combination thereof?

What tempers the bright choice? Experience? Pragmatism? Aesthetics? Laziness? Doubtless a combination thereof!

Frankly, a bright finish isn't necessarily superior to its opaque counterpart. Varnishing everything in sight can be nice on some boats, but on others it's gauche and irresponsible. "Because it's there" may be a good reason for climbing Mount Everest, but it's hardly the apt motivation for varnishing a trim on your yacht. Judicious employment of bright finishes is the mark of a classy boat and an owner's grasp of what's best for the wood underneath that finish. What is best under certain circumstances, say a foray into tropical waters, might just be a close encounter with a can of white marine enamel.

Learning how each wood responds to a bright finish, as well as how that bright finish responds to the elements, is vital to a successful finishing campaign.

All wood swells when it absorbs water and contracts when it dries out. This causes cracking of any finish at the joints, regardless of the quality of construction that went into the boat. The best shipwrights I know still fight the annual battle of broken varnish over their scarf joints. It is a simple fact of life on any boat, and no finish has ever been invented that has the elasticity to span those joints without breaking (despite some products' preposterous claims to such fame). Some oilier woods, such as teak, reduce the trauma of this by their reluctance to drink in the water at those joints, leaving only a break in the varnish itself and minimal problems at the surface of the wood. But most others, especially woods such as mahogany, permit wholesale moisture penetration at exposed joints. The moisture travels by capillary action in dark streaks along the grain of the wood and, given time, clear into the flesh of the wood, causing permanent discoloration at the depth and breadth of those spots in addition to lifting the varnish above. Wood in general is much more porous and vulnerable to moisture penetration at open grain ends than at right angles to the direction of the grain, which is why water stains are more readily removed from uncut

surfaces than from joints.

There are three basic bright finishes for consideration on marine wood surfaces—varnish, oil, and bare —with many possible variations on the first two themes. You need to formulate your ideal finish program by considering the fundamental behaviors of these finishes as they relate to the woods they adorn.

VARNISH

Varnish brings out the beauty in a wood and is the strongest protector of all bright finishes. This is especially true of the newer varnishes made with polyurethane resins. As an exterior finish, varnish can look beautiful after three coats but requires substantial buildup—no fewer than eight coats from bare wood—in order to function properly as a protector. This foundation must be refreshed periodically to

Veneer like this mahogany plywood must be protected immediately with varnish.

maintain its integrity as well as its beauty. Varnish is not only appropriate but recommended over other finishes for use on exterior brightwork areas that will not be left bare, chiefly because it gives a greater return in tenacity on the same investment, prep-wise, as that required by so-called easier finishes. It is also appropriate for interiors in its various sheens, but there requires less maintenance and buildup than for exterior surfaces. Varnish can be applied to almost any wood, the very few exceptions being those of such high oil content as to contaminate and render undriable any varnish applied. The one wood that should *always* be varnished, especially on exteriors, is a veneer of any type. Most hardwood veneers these days have such a thin skin that more than one light sanding causes an instant exposure to plywood. It's better to protect this thin membrane at the beginning, and then through the years refinish the finish and not the wood.

OIL

A true oil finish also brings out the beauty in a wood but affords it little, if not completely transient, protection from the elements. The combination of sun and moisture acts to break down even the highest-quality oil finish within a couple of months of its application, and for this reason oil should be reserved for interiors. As an interior finish on most woods, oil is not only acceptable but can look and feel positively sublime if applied properly, offering years of beautiful protection in exchange for relatively easy maintenance.

Certain oil products that are free of added resins and solvents can be used on teak decks if the owner is hell-bent on having brown decks, though even this is inadvisable for reasons given in Chapter 14. Many oil formulas or other sealers and "dressings" (which typically comprise an oil or silicone formula heavily diluted with solvents and inundated with synthetic resins) are disastrous to seam compounds and can, after repeated application, shrink and destroy them. Even if the seam compound is not destroyed, the constant bleaching and reoiling that ensues when such finishes start to go bad can compromise the woodgrain over time. For these reasons, the following program is often the most intelligent.

BARE WOOD

If you like, and if you know the wood on your boat has had adequate time to cure, you can elect to use the fabulous "no-finish" finish, also known as "scrubbed wood." It requires proper wood preparation and judicious care but is the best approach for areas such as decks—for reasons of safety, practicality, and aesthetics—or on

boats that have an overabundance of teak trims, the varnishing of which in their entirety would be a burden. Boats that fall into the "acres of teak" category, such as Hans Christians or Bob Perry's Panda sailboats, actually look prettier, I think, with a thoughtful combination of finished and unfinished surfaces.

There is a science to leaving any wood bare on a boat, and it boils down to a balance of regular care and prudent cleaning techniques. It also requires that a wood be able to take care of itself, which usually means it has a generous supply of natural oils. Teak is the granddaddy of self-sufficient woods, with a terrific supply of natural oils to keep it from reacting adversely to prolonged exposure. Ironbark, another hard, oily wood, is often found acting as bodyguard to topsides in the form of a rubrail, and in this capacity frequently sports the "silvered" look. Other woods that are sometimes left unfinished include fir, Port Orford cedar, iroko, pitch pine, and Queen Island beech. Typically these are left bare when used as deck planks, though occasionally they can be found in the buff as small trims, protective railings, or backing pads beneath hardware. But given their propensity for staining, rotting, and lack of resistance to wear, all these woods are stable to a much lesser degree than teak and require more tender loving care and protection from the elements (as in the use of covers) to keep healthy. The safer approach on all exterior woods save teak is the protected one—which translates to varnishing.

One important thing to ascertain before choosing to leave brightwork bare is the degree to which the wood has cured, or was allowed to cure before being cut up into the pieces that now adorn your boat. If you are not sure of its seasoning, it's best to help the wood stabilize for about a year by keeping it oiled with a heavy linseed or Tung oil-based formula, thus preventing serious changes in the moisture content of the wood. After a year's time, such an oil buildup can easily be bleached off and then the "bare program" commenced with greater assurance that the wood won't be disposed to dramatic splitting.

The Ubiquitous Bright Woods

TEAK

Here is a bit of background about a wood that today's boatowner has come to take for granted, from Herbert Edlin's *What Wood Is That?* (1969):

Long before the first European navigators had reached India, Eastern people had realized the unique properties of teak, which grows in southern India, Burma, Thailand and Java. Teak timber had been used for the building of Arab dhows and Chinese junks, and Portuguese, Dutch, and British seamen soon applied it to the repair of their oaken craft, damaged by the seas on the long voyage round the Cape of Good Hope. It was found to be remarkably strong and naturally durable, resistant to both insect attack and fungal decay, and even to termites and marine borers. Teak is so hard that ordinary nails cannot be driven into it, and it is therefore pre-bored, or fastened with wooden pegs or screws. In contrast to oak, it does not corrode iron fittings. It is exceptionally heavy, and freshly felled logs sink in water.

Teak grows as a magnificent tree in monsoon rain forests with a marked dry season, as revealed by its clear annual rings. It may reach 150 feet tall by 40 feet round, but it is seldom found in pure stands and must be sought out in mixed woodlands. Seedlings are easy to raise, and extensive plantations of teak have been made in India and Indonesia, to ensure future supplies more profitably than those from wild trees scattered through remote jungles. Most teak, however, is still harvested from naturally grown trees. After felling and cross-cutting, the huge logs or baulks of timber are hauled to the nearest waterway by elephants. These powerful beasts have been captured from wild herds and trained for haulage work. They will also, when instructed, lift and stack logs with the aid of their great

trunks. The timber is floated for great distances downstream along broad rivers like the Irrawaddy and then landed at the seaports for shipment to North America or Europe.

Teak is one of my favorite woods to varnish, possibly because over the past twelve years I have refinished more teak than any other kind of wood. Comfort in this life comes from familiarity, and if nothing else I am certainly conversant with this oily hardwood that smells of leather when freshly cut or sanded.

Rumor has it in many published accounts of brightwork technique that teak does not take well to a varnish finish. I have to wonder how such slander ever sprang forth. Not only does teak accept a varnish finish, it can wear the original foundation quite grandly for many years with proper maintenance and some simple TLC. The trick, if there has to be one, is understanding the relationship between the oily wood and the finish you want to dress it in.

Some "experts" have suggested that the only way to get varnish to stick to teak is to strip the wood of its surface oils by way of a solvent bath before you apply the finish. There's an official term for that treatment: it's "hogwash!" This concept may sound good on paper, but it just isn't true in the real world. Anyone who has bothered to read the label on a can of varnish will know that one of the primary ingredients in varnish is oil, so what logic is there in pretending that one oil won't penetrate and anchor itself in another?

In Chapter 11 you will find not only that you can leave the teak's natural oil intact, but that you can use as a sealer, prior to your first varnish coat, a rubbed-in oil treatment, wet-sanded and mixed with the wood's own *oily* sawdust to fill the grain. Trust me when I tell you that the varnish does stick—for a long time, if you take care of it.

The other popular finish for teak is simply oil, usually a commercial preparation of Tung or linseed oil combined with other less expensive oils and some resins and solvents for enhanced

durability and drying. While an oil finish on teak is wonderful to touch as well as to gaze upon, it is not a practical exterior finish because it does not hold up longer than a month or two when exposed to the elements and, as discussed previously, it is likely to attack seam compounds if used on a deck. This type of finish should be reserved for interiors, where if properly applied it can give teak a wonderfully touchable quality you don't get even with rubbed varnishes.

Teak "dressings," which include a wide variety of products made from oils, petroleum-based silicone formulas, et al., are usually referred to by their promoters as "revolutionary"; these are not really finishes but rather temporary coatings that wash away or dissipate rapidly from exposure to the elements. Even though they might last a little longer when used on interiors, they do not afford the protection that you would get from a good Tung or linseed oil formula or varnish, nor are they even remotely comparable in final appearance. When planning your brightwork program, these products should not be considered as serious finish options, as in the end they are usually a waste of money and your precious time.

MAHOGANY

Again, from Mr. Edlin's fine tome, here is a little narration on this species of wood that has comprised the better part of many a vessel over the centuries:

> As soon as the first Spanish explorers reached the West Indies they began to examine the timber resources of their New World. They needed wood to repair their ships, battered by the long Atlantic crossing, and they also sought something valuable to load into their holds as a return cargo. They soon discovered the won-

derful red-brown timber that they called 'caoba,' which we know as 'mahogany.' As early as 1514, it was being used in the island of Santo Domingo. Cortes, the conqueror of Mexico, used it for shipbuilding. By 1584 Philip II of Spain was employing it to decorate the Escorial Palace in Madrid.

At that time it was easy to get the large planks the cabinetmakers preferred from Cuba, Jamaica and other West Indian islands. As large trees were cut out, the loggers turned to Honduras, on the Central American mainland, which now gives its name to all mahogany cut in this region. During the present century shortages in Central America have made exporters look to South America for supplies, and much mahogany, of this or closely allied species, is now felled in Colombia, Venezuela and along the upper reaches of the River Amazon in Peru, Bolivia and Brazil. Plantations have been established in Trinidad, India, and British Honduras.

When freshly felled, the heartwood of mahogany is bright pink, with a thin zone of colorless sapwood. On exposure to the sunlight, the heartwood rapidly darkens to the rich coppery-red shade that we know so well. Mahogany is rather a light timber and also quite soft. Its great virtues are ease of working and stability; once a piece of seasoned mahogany is shaped it does not shrink or warp. It is naturally durable, and has long been favored by shipbuilders, from the Amazonian Indians, who carved it into canoes, to the modern designers of luxury yachts.

Honduras mahogany shows no marked structural features. It is an even, deep coppery-brown colour, with obscure rings and only slight grain, but its rays can be seen clearly on radial-cut surfaces as smooth plates which reflect light.

The value and at times the scarcity of Honduras mahogany have led timber-importers to seek similar woods in other lands. Africa has proved the most productive source, and the botanical genus 'Khaya' which is closely related to the true Honduran mahogany genus yields acceptable substitutes as large-sized logs and in

Clockwise from top left:
A fiddle block with bronze sheaves and ash shell.
Varnished planking of Port Orford cedar. The stem is probably gum and the sheerstrake is mahogany.
At the forward terminus of a teak handrail, a decorative monkey's fist rests on a varnished teak toerail.

considerable quantities. Several species grow in the rain forest belt along the West African coast, from Sierra Leone east to the Congo, and all alike are marketed as African mahogany.

In appearance and working properties, African mahogany is a close match for the nearly related Honduras kind. It is generally held to be a little less stable, and is rarely so beautifully figured, but it has been applied with success to the same range of uses. The two timbers are far from easy to distinguish, but a useful pointer is that the pores or vessels of African mahogany are usually grouped in clusters, rather than being evenly spread.

The "true" mahoganies, African and Honduras, are expensive woods, found on older vessels more than on newly manufactured craft, and are absolutely the most beautiful of this arboreal family. The mahogany "wanna-be's"—including Philippine mahogany, Sapele, and lauan, among others—while pretty in their own way, do not have the intensity of color or the dramatic pattern of grain markings of a true mahogany and can only hope to measure up to the elegance of their more legitimate cousins. Regardless of lineage, though, mahogany of any type accepts a wide range of finish options, the common theme of which is a protective varnish coating.

Exterior mahogany appointments, with rare exceptions, cannot hope to survive the onslaught of moisture at joints and fastenings with the minimal protection of an oil finish, and it is almost a jailable offense to allow a wood as intrinsically gorgeous as Honduras or African mahogany to lie ungraced by any finish at all. Varnish is, for these and a multitude of other reasons, the only "topcoat" advisable for exterior mahogany. An additional possibility that comes to the average boatowner's mind, when considering a total finish program for his mahogany-laden vessel, is usually a staining treatment of some sort. This is fine, certainly when the wood has some problem that needs solving, but is not always the best way to capitalize on the beauty of the wood. Mahogany, when simply sealed with oil and varnished to a deep gloss finish, will smile back at its admirers with a three-dimensional gleam that can make your heart fairly ache with joy.

If you have a more exotic strain of mahogany on the interior of your boat, a well-rubbed oil finish can look and feel wonderful and because of the more protected location will endure with faithful maintenance. Under such circumstances, you could also choose to leave the better-quality wood bare—but again, this seems a crime to me, as the true wonder of the wood only comes out with a finish of some kind. The cheaper woods really must have the protection of a hard finish, and overall the best option for interior Philippine, lauan, Honduras, or African mahogany is a rubbed-effect varnish, which apes the look of a rubbed oil finish while affording the permanent seal and protection of varnish. This finish can enrich the color of mahogany and its satin sheen gives warmth and lends a terrific cozy feeling to interiors. Philippine mahogany left bare *anywhere* on your boat is an eyesore waiting to emerge.

IRONBARK OR IRONWOOD

Typically found on boat exteriors in the form of caprails or rubrails, this is as hard a wood as it sounds, and it can either be varnished or oiled. If it has seasoned sufficiently before construction, it is successfully left bare, but oiling brings out the natural beauty of this almost purple-black wood. If it is a rubrail, definitely finish with oil, not varnish; otherwise you'll forever be repairing dings.

COCABOLA

The boat that wins the prize as the most remarkable in my refinishing career would have to be an Ingrid 38 named *Kingsblood*. Built by Jerry Husted's crew in Woodinville, Washington, she was launched and commissioned in Seattle after being finished out in the Midwest. For reasons that can be discovered in various parts of this book, this boat was a marvel of lessons learned at an early point in the refinishing careers of two sisters from Idaho. One was the volatility of the precious metals market. (The owner offered to pay us the value of our bill in gold bullion; we declined, thinking it would be too great a hassle to make the exchange for real cash; three days later, feeling secure with American dollars in hand, we watched the gold market soar to a point that would have doubled our take!) Another lesson learned was the fact that some woods simply will not take a varnish; their oily character is so dominant that no finish requiring the oxidation of oils to harden has a snowball's chance in hell of setting up, because the oils in the wood will contaminate the finish.

Kingsblood had, among other pieces of furniture constructed from exotic hardwoods, a white oak and cocabola cabin sole. The first time we laid eyes on that cabin sole we nearly shed a tear at its magnificence. The owner wanted it varnished, and we happily commenced to oblige. But a day, and then two, and then three, and finally four days (in the warm summer with ample ventilation) after the first coat of varnish was applied, the floor of that blessed boat was still as wet as it had been the moment we brushed the varnish on. We wiped the whole mess off with lacquer thinner and tried again. The same thing happened. This time we called the manufacturer of the varnish, and lo and behold, we were informed that although the oak was certainly a candidate for varnish, cocabola, with its surfeit of natural oil, would never in a million years abide such a finish. Not only that, but any wood that had the audacity to abut this gloriously maroon wood could count on contamination from its oily neighbor to such an extent that no varnish could hope to dry there either. Our final approach to this ill-advised marriage of timber was to sand it to the finest finish possible and then lightly oil it with a tung oil sealer that we were careful to rub off to the point of assuring that no residual undried finish remained.

In general, most other hardwoods that are being left bright on a boat's exterior should be varnished. Spruce, ash, oak (red or white), fir, and red or yellow cedar are best served by a varnish finish on interiors as well as exteriors, as they are inclined to wear poorly without a finish and require more maintenance with the minimal protection of oil.

Port Orford cedar decks can be oiled or left bare; for safety considerations the rare and expensive decks made of this wood should not be varnished. Interior appointments can be varnished but look and feel nicer when oiled.

Before you have your carpenter head off to the Hardwoods Emporium, make sure he knows how you plan to finish the wood, and how that particular piece of furniture *should* be finished, and whether the woods you've specified will cooperate with the program. The wood you've chosen could just be one that will only tolerate the "no-finish" finish.

4

ABOUT VARNISH

Little shall I grace my cause
In speaking for myself. Yet, by your gracious patience,
I will a round unvarnished tale deliver
Of my whole course of love.

—*Othello*, I, iii, 88
William Shakespeare

*I*t would seem that a book about brightwork could not be considered a complete survey without some historical account of the life and evolution of its brightest star. Though there is a chapter on brightwork materials later in this book, wherein types and brands of varnish are duly discussed, this material among all others begs a chapter of its own. Through all the years I've spent slathering the sticky, amber-colored liquid onto acres of wood, I've wondered who first dreamed up varnish. It's the same curiosity I experience whenever I eat an artichoke: Where did this come from and who was the first person to figure it out? Writing this book gave me an excuse to find the answers to these questions — about varnish, at least.

Varnish—The Name

When I was a freshman in high school my mother thought I had a pretty singing voice, so she signed me up for voice lessons with the neighborhood vocal pedagogue. One of the first songs I had to learn, from a book of *Art Songs for High Voice*, was a little Schubert number called "Who Is Sylvia?" Lesson after lesson I strained to warble with a straight face, "Who is Sylvia? What is she, that all our swains commend her? Wholly fair and wise is she; the heavens such grace did lend her that adored she might be" —lyrics first penned by The Bard himself. To this day, "Who Is Sylvia?" is still so ingrained in my subconscious that it filters up through the recesses of my brain whenever I start wondering at the identity of something, and in recent years the etymology of the word "varnish" became trapped in this bizarre pattern of pondering. Time and time again I would be leafing through the card catalogs at the library on a varnish snooping mission, and my brain would be serenading me like some twisted sound track, "Who is varnish, what is she?. . ."

After considerable dredging I discovered that this seemingly inconsequential term was inspired by a lady every bit as fair as our mysterious Sylvia. From A.H. Sabin's 1903 volume *Technology of Paint and Varnish* comes this wonderful account of the origin of the word we've come to regard as the grande dame of the wood finishing world:

In the middle of the third century B.C. Berenice, whose grandfather was a half-brother of Alexander the Great, a very beautiful golden-haired woman, one of whose descendants was the famous Egyptian queen Cleopatra, was Queen of Cyrene and wife of Ptolemy Euergetes, King of Egypt. Not long after her marriage the king, her husband, engaged in a long and highly successful campaign in Asia, during the time of which the queen offered up prayers for his successful return, vowing to sacrifice her beautiful hair on the altar of Venus if the King should come back in safety. This she accordingly did; but the shining and jewelled tresses disappeared during the night from the altar, and it was found by the astronomer Conon that the deities had carried them to heaven, where they form, in the Milky Way, the constellation still known as the Coma Berenices, or Berenice's Hair. The poet Callimachus celebrated them in Greek verse as 'The consecrated spoils of Berenice's golden head'; and Catallus, telling of the rivalry between Venus and Juno, says that

> The winged messenger came down
> At her desire, lest Ariadne's crown
> Should still unrivalled glitter in the skies;
> And that thy yellow hair, a richer prize,
> The spoils devoted to the powers divine,
> Might from the fields of light as brightly
> shine.

When to the Greeks was brought from the far-off shores of the unknown Northern Sea the yellow translucent mineral we know as amber, they likened it to the sacred yellow locks of the beautiful Grecian woman, the first queen in her own right of the Macedonian race, and called it by her name, Berenice, and by this name it was known both to the Greeks and Romans for several centuries.

The word Berenice is equivalent to Pheronice, literally meaning 'bringing victory.' Ph is changed to B in some Greek dialects, even in classic Greek, and B was in some dialects pronounced like our V, as it now is by modern Greeks, and as it was in the middle ages. Hence the word Berenice, meaning amber, was often written Verenice in Latin. . . . and when we get down to the twelfth century we find in the Mappæ. Claviculi the word spelled in the genitive verenicis and vernicis. This is probably the earliest instance of the Latinized word nearly in its modern form, the original nominative vernice being afterward changed to vernix, whence comes our word varnish. The German name for amber is Bernstein, or Berenice's stone, and the Spanish word for varnish is Berniz, nearer to the Greek than our own word, which comes through the later Latin. . . . In the Lucca manuscript (eighth century), Veronica is often mentioned as an ingredient of liquid varnish, and this latter word, Veronica, is the modern equivalent of the name Berenice. Saint Veronica, however, had nothing to do with Berenice, but perhaps she might be adopted as a patron saint by the varnish-makers.

Such is the origin of the word varnish.

Varnish—The Medium

Now, for the answer to "what is she?" In essence, varnish is defined as a substance that is applied as a liquid, and on exposure to air—through the absorption of oxygen, the dissipation of its solvents, or both—hardens to a thin, transparent film. The simplest varnish comprises an oil and a resin. Solvents, in later centuries, were added to accommodate conditions of application. The evolution of varnish over time has followed an interesting course of variations on these themes, but today's best varnishes remain faithful to the basic formula.

The oldest known varnish is that on wooden mummy cases from Egypt, figured to be around 2,600 years old. According to Professor J.F. John of Berlin, this varnish was a compound of resin and oil, possibly a solution of resin in an essential oil such as oil of cedar, that being an oil Egyptians were able to make in early times.

The varnish on these mummy cases is pale

yellow, surprisingly free of cracks (I'd love to see a varnish label today claiming its ability to last 2,600 years without cracking), and apparently hastily and roughly applied, as though smeared on with a flat blade or with bare fingers. (I *have* seen varnish that looked as though it had been applied in this manner, though not on mummy cases.) Carthaginian sarcophagi of about 1000 B.C. were sealed with a varnish made from sandarac, the resin from North African sandarac trees that has been available through modern times. Phoenician mummy cases reveal the use of varnishes made with amber, the valuable resin that at times itself came to be referred to as varnish.

During the classical period the materials used by the Greeks and Romans did not, according to any writings of the age, include varnishes, but pitch was used for tarring ships, and pitch and wax for protecting ships' bottoms. Resins and oils were used only for therapeutic purposes.

After the Renaissance, greater interest was shown in oils. The use of rosin and sandarac in linseed oil as a varnish for armor, crossbows, and harquebuses has been documented from the 16th century, the varnish again being thick and applied by sponge, finger, or stick after it was warmed. Artists the likes of Leonardo da Vinci and Rembrandt are said to have used amber varnishes as vehicles in some of their paints.

In what is considered be the earliest important treatise of the Middle Ages on technology, *The Schedula Diversarum Artium,* the monk Theophilus Presbyter described the principles of varnish making by means of incorporating molten resin in hot oil. The following is his method; if you find yourself stranded on a desert island with no chandlery and only this book, and your brightwork is looking a little shabby, you could be in business:

> Put some linseed-oil into a small new jar, and add some of the gum which is called fornis [varnish], very finely powdered, which has the appearance of the most transparent frankincense, but when it is broken it gives back a more brilliant lustre; which when you have placed over the coals, cook carefully so that it may not boil, until a third part is evaporated; and guard from the winds because it is dangerous to a high degree and difficult to extinguish if it takes fire from the top. Set up four or three stones which are able to stand the fire so that they lean apart; on these place a common pipkin, and in this put the above-mentioned portion of the gum fornis, which is called Roman glassa [amber], and over the mouth of this pot set a smaller pipkin which has in the bottom a middling-sized hole. And around these put luting so that nothing may get out of the crevice between these pots. You should have, moreover, a slender iron rod set in a handle with which you may stir this mass of gum, with which you may feel that it is entirely liquid. You must have also a third pot set over the coals, in which is hot oil, and when the interior of the gum has become liquid, so that with the end of the iron rod it may be drawn out like a thread, pour into it the hot oil and stir it with the iron rod, and at the same time cook it so that it may not boil, and from time to time draw out the rod and smear it properly over a piece of wood or stone, that you may find out if there is separation; and see to this that in weight there be two parts of oil and the third of gum. And when in your judgement, you have cooked it thoroughly, removing it from the fire and uncovering it, cool it out of doors.

From the 11th to the 18th century, practically no progress was made beyond this general formulation. Many variations emerged, especially in the oils and resins employed, but when a really good varnish was desired artisans resorted to this recipe, which was handed down from one generation to another.

The solvents of antiquity were the more common essential oils—oil of turpentine, for example—and were prepared both by Egyptians and Greeks before the invention of the still. One of the earlier methods of this preparation was to put crude turpentine —which is the gum from longleaf pine trees —in a pot and lay over the top some sticks that supported a fleece of wool. When the contents were heated, the essential oil condensed in the wool, from which it was squeezed out. The first written account of the use of thinners in varnishes is found in Alberti's collection of formulas, penned in 1750. The use of thinners soon became general practice.

In 1772 a Frenchman by the name of Jean Felix Watin wrote the definitive tome on the subject, *The Art of the Painter, Varnisher and Gilder*. This revered text became the varnish maker's standard and endured as such through its fourteenth edition in 1906. Much to my chagrin, in all my years of research I have never once been able to get my hands on a copy of Watin's opus. Perhaps Santa Claus will help me out someday. Until then I must content myself with vignettes quoted in others' volumes on the subject to sample some of the more endearing moments in Watin's book:

It is forbidden by various regulations to make varnish in the middle of towns. This is prudent policy. The resins are so combustible, they are able to cause serious fires; besides which, their odor is so penetrating that it is noticeable at a distance and is disagreeable to the neighborhood; so that varnish-makers are obliged to work outside the city limits and in the country.

It is necessary to use spirit of turpentine, without which the varnish will never dry. The quantity is commonly double that of the oil. We use less turpentine in summer because the oil, drying more quickly by the heat of the sun, becomes thick more rapidly and the work dries from the bottom. On the other hand, in the winter, when the heat is less, and often only artificial heat, we put in less oil so that the varnish may dry more quickly, but we also add more spirit of turpentine, which evaporates more easily.

It is important that one's attention should be constantly on the work, and to take every precaution against accident. If the operator, working in an obscure place, should wish to bring a wax taper or a lighted candle near the work, the vapor of the resins, the spirit of wine, or the oil may take fire and cause a conflagration. It is necessary, in case of accident, to have several sheepskins or calfskins, or cloths folded in several thicknesses, always kept wet, to throw over the vessels which contain the varnish materials, to smother the flame.

Artisans and artists did not depend on manufactured products, each producing for himself all that he needed in the way of varnish and paints, thereby assuring good quality. Varnish factories per se didn't come into existence until 1790, when they appeared in England. This signalled the beginning of the varnish industry in Europe, with France and Germany following in 1820 and 1830 and Austria in 1843. The first varnish factory in the United States appeared around 1815 in Philadelphia. The varnish and paint industry in all these countries remained strictly an art, however, technological progress moving at a snail's pace.

During the 19th century, progress consisted largely of finding new and more favorable combinations of known materials, and of small variations in the methods of cooking them. Varnishes were made from linseed oil, natural resins, rosin, lime, lead, manganese, and turpentine. They were slow drying and of moderate durability. Varnish manufacturing was a secret art, and all information pertaining to it and its raw materials was jealously guarded. Published accounts of current methods were practically nonexistent. Hence progress into the 20th century continued to be slow, each new idea bordering on a major revolution in the industry. In the early 1900s, manufacturers finally began to hire chemists to find out how to produce genuinely good paints and varnishes.

In the 1920s, China wood (Tung) oil and ester gum came into wide use. Tung oil presented new problems because it was tricky to work with, even though it was favored over other oils for its extraordinary drying properties. Ester gum found ready favor because of its solubility and neutral character. These products and the synthetic resins that came into the market soon thereafter became important just as manufacturing was expanding into the modern phase of large-scale production. Each advance seemed to fuel another, and skillful merchandising and capable servicing of those products increasingly became the rule. The paint and varnish industry finally arrived at the point of being much less an art (though that was not completely lost) and more a practiced science of far-reaching importance to a broad segment of the civilized world.

What's in Varnish Today?

The generic descriptive term for the typical modern varnish is "oleoresinous." No, these are not varnishes made from margarine! The oleoresinous varnishes of modern formulation are composed of resins, both natural and synthetic, which are cooked with any number of drying oils and thinned to proper viscosity with hydrocarbon solvents. Usually the solvent used is mineral spirits but, depending upon composition and use, other solvents are also used. In addition to resins, oils, and hydrocarbon solvents, oleoresinous varnishes contain metallic driers added in the form of manganese and cobalt or other metallic salts of organic acids, which speed the drying process by catalyzing their oxidation. Many of the best varnishes have added pigments whose purpose is to absorb and refract the damaging ultraviolet rays from the sun. These are referred to generically as ultraviolet absorbers, or "UVA."

RESINS USED IN OLEORESINOUS VARNISHES

Natural resins are exudations of trees of many different genera. I came into contact with natural resins long before I opened my first can of varnish—indeed, long before I laid eyes on my first boat. My grandfather, Orbie Lee Herndon, was not only a consummate tomato grower and my introduction to stoic sensitivity in a man; he was also a fiddler of considerable talent. Whenever he opened the lid on his flawlessly kept violin case and pulled out that exquisitely varnished instrument, a current of excitement shot through the room. But the concert would wait, just for a moment, while Grampa rosined up the bow. A hard chunk of powder-covered rosin inhabited a purple velvet-lined compartment of that case, and when he brought it out I always wondered if it would taste as much like candy as it looked.

Modern varnishes have over the years obtained their film characteristics from many different natural resins with such beautiful names as Dammars, Boea's, Congo, Pontianak, and Kauri copols—even my grandfather's rosin, which originates as sap from the longleaf pine tree. However, the majority of resins used in varnishes today are synthetic, and there is available such a wide variety of these that the formulating chemist can choose from literally hundreds to give his varnish the particular properties and characteristics he seeks. The great bulk of marine varnishes are made with such synthetic resins as the following:

Pure phenolic resins. Phenolics are among the oldest and most widely used of the synthetics. Dr. Leo Baekeland was granted a patent in 1909 for the discovery and invention of the resin, which ultimately came to be named Bakelite after its inventor. These are either heat reactive or non-heat reactive condensation products of formaldehyde with phenolic compounds such as alkyl-substituted phenols. They promote alkali, chemical, and alcohol resistance of the film, fast drying, toughness, water resistance, and good durability. They fail eventually, in exterior varnishes, by erosion rather than by checking and cracking. Phenolic resins are used in the best spar varnishes on the market today, and account for great strides in the varnish industry as a whole.

Modified phenolic resins. These are like the

pure phenolics described above except that they contain on the average around 75 to 85 percent rosin, esterified (reacted under heat so that the acid is neutralized) in the manufacturing operation with glycerine, pentaerythritol, or both. Used in varnishes they promote fast drying, good water resistance, and fair chemical and alkali resistance. In exterior varnishes they fail by erosion but may show some checking and cracking, depending upon the resin used and the type of varnish produced.

Alkyd resins. The term alkyd resin, which has become common in paint use today, generally refers to the reaction products formed by combining a drying oil, glycerine, and phthalic anhydride chemically. These three ingredients occur in different ratios in different resins. Alkyd resins would be solid at room temperature if they were not thinned at the time the batch finished cooking, so that alkyd resins as they are usually thought of are really alkyd resin solutions and are already much like varnishes in this respect. They contain oil-resin solids dissolved in solvent, and so does a varnish. Some are marketed as varnishes after being thinned to the proper viscosity and receiving a drier. Some very good marine spar varnishes are clear alkyd resin solutions. They are excellent in adhesion, gloss, and gloss retention, and very durable on exterior exposure, but ultimately fail by checking and cracking rather than erosion and hence present an undesirable surface if allowed to fail before recoating.

Epoxy resins. These recently developed resins are outstanding in many respects. They are thermosetting, yet some are sufficiently flexible that they can be used alone, without either oil or plasticizer. They are excellent in alkali and chemical resistance, but unlike the phenolics, do not yellow significantly with age, thus providing good color and color retention. They form hard, tough films of unsurpassed adhesion. Epoxy-resin varnishes are difficult to apply successfully, however; they require ideal application conditions, and most are better sprayed than brushed.

Subsequent maintenance of surfaces coated with these varnishes is also complicated. You do not need an epoxy resin-based varnish for beautiful, lasting brightwork, and in short I do not recommend them save for certain professional applications.

Polyurethane resins. The newest technology in synthetic resins includes these oil-modified resins, which form tough films highly resistant to chemicals and abrasion. The aliphatic-modified polyurethanes aid varnishes in maintaining greater clarity and gloss. They generally combine with high-quality oils such as Tung and oiticica to produce a varnish lighter in color than the conventional phenolic resin varnishes. It is becoming standard for companies to include at least one polyurethane varnish with their lineup of conventional varnishes, and this type of varnish is expected to ride a wave of popularity well into the future.

Oils Used in Making Varnish

Oils used in making varnishes and alkyd resins are refined grades of such vegetable drying oils as linseed, Tung, soybean, oiticica, and dehydrated castor oil.

Tung oil, often referred to as China wood oil, and oiticica oil are vegetable oils containing what the chemist calls conjugated double bonds in their fatty acid chains, and consequently they produce varnishes that dry rapidly. (Double bonds are points at which oils react to polymerize and dry.) Oils with this characteristic form varnish films that are hard and tough, and hence are regarded as hard drying oils. They have excellent water resistance, good chemical resistance, and are durable, particularly when cooked with high-quality resins.

Tung oil. Tung oil, also known in the trade as "pure Hankow Wood oil," is obtained from the Aleurites fordii tree, once grown almost entirely in the hills near the Yangtze River in the Chinese province of Hupeh. The fruit of this tree is about the size of an orange, and the seeds found inside resemble a chestnut when hulled. In very early methods of oil production in China, the fruit was gathered at maturity and then stacked in heaps to ferment or roast until the husks were partly decomposed in order to aid in the extraction of the seeds, which hold the oil. The pods were stripped of their seeds (five to seven in each pod), which were then placed in a large circular stone trough and ground into meal by stone rollers pulled by oxen. After being roasted for a short time in shallow iron pans, the crushed mass was thrown into wooden vats with open-work bottoms, over cauldrons of boiling water, and steamed. The oil was expressed by filling a hollow log segmented by wooden spacers with the crushed, steamed seeds. Wooden wedges were then driven between adjacent spacers, providing the necessary pressure for squeezing a small amount of oil from the meal. The crude oil was then sent to the coast for refining, which consisted of heating the oil slightly through steam coils and permitting impurities to settle out.

These unsophisticated methods of oil production, altered but slightly, are still practiced in some parts of China and India. In the American process the fruit is taken to the mill immediately after it is cultivated; there the husks are removed and the cleaned seeds cracked by machinery. The meats are then crushed to express the oil.

Mature Tung nuts generally contain about 50 percent oil. If Tung oil is used in its raw state it will dry with a matte or shriveled appearance; it must therefore be refined before use in varnish production.

American production of Tung oil has increased dramatically since the early decades of this century, with cultivation of China wood trees in Florida, Alabama, Louisiana, Texas, and Georgia. The higher quality controls over the production of this domestic oil, while perhaps not as romantic as earlier Chinese methods, have prompted more consistency in the oil and ultimately the varnishes.

Tung oil in its processed form causes varnish films to dry without the surface tack characteristic of other drying oils, such as linseed. When surface tack is present, a finger pressed to the film or in many cases simply allowed to rest lightly and momentarily on the surface imparts a decided suction, stickiness, or "tack" when withdrawn (this allowing, of course, for appropriate drying time). Tung oil is often used in combination with softer and less reactive oils in making varnish; it aids those oils in giving up their surface tack and encourages better adhesion and harder drying. It is one of the few oils that will make a good varnish with rosin. With the possible exception of oiticica oil, and that with great reservations, there is no substitute for Tung oil. Perhaps its most endearing quality, apart from its wonderful drying property, is its ability to retain its original color. Other oils, especially linseed oil, have a marked tendency to darken as they age on a wood's surface, leaving glaring contrasts in color from one area that is more exposed to the sun to another that might be sheltered.

Oiticica oil. Oiticica oil is obtained from the seed of the tree *Licania rigida,* native to the northern regions of Brazil but found in other parts of South America. The fruit of the oiticica tree contains about 60 percent kernels, of which 60 to 65 percent is oil. This oil was considered of minor importance until World War II, at which time, due to a shortage of Tung oil, it helped take up the slack and was found to be a reasonably good substitute.

Oiticica oil is similar to Tung oil with respect to drying, water resistance, etc., but is not generally considered to be of the same quality.

Linseed oil. Linseed and soybean oils are among the so-called soft drying oils. They dry to softer films, having few conjugated double bonds in their fatty acid chains. Linseed dries harder than soybean, but it also tends to yellow more on exposure. In alkyd resins, however, these soft oils dry about as fast as do Tung and oiticica in oleoresinous varnishes, with the result

again that shortages of Tung oil during World War II induced a shift to the use of varnishes comprising linseed oil and alkyd resins. The Tung oil market took awhile to recover from this, because it was found that alkyd varnishes have certain advantages over Tung oil varnishes that are desirable and attainable at a significantly lower costs.

Certain oils, by virtue of their ability to dry from liquid form into a hardened film without the addition of a resin, have themselves been considered a type of varnish. Linseed is one such oil. If you spread linseed oil over a nonabsorbent surface such as a piece of glass, you will find after time, at most within a few days, that the film is no longer a greasy fluid but has changed to a tough, leathery substance. This new material is formed by the absorption of oxygen into the oil, and it is this quality that has made linseed oil a valuable material in the manufacture of paints and varnish. It is not a quality found in many other simple oils, such as lard or cottonseed oil.

Linseed oil has been the most important raw material in paint and varnish production since early times, and it continues to be one of the most popular oils in the industry, primarily for its versatility and cost. This oil is obtained from the seeds of the flax plant, *Linum usitatissimum.* It is widely felt that ancient Egyptian cultures did not discover linseed oil, but we do know that they used linen—mummy cloths were always made of linen—and the flax plant was cultivated widely. Theophilus, whose treatise on varnish making is excerpted previously, gave instructions for pressing linseed oil with an olive press. Since the Egyptians had for thousands of years been familiar with flax and with the olive press, it is still a matter of speculation as to whether they put two and two together and had use of this valuable oil in their manufacture of finishing materials.

In his 11th century recipe for producing linseed oil, Theophilus's treatment of the seed and method was almost the same as it is today:

Take linseed and dry it in a pan, without water, on the fire; put it in a mortar and pound it to a fine powder; then replace it in the pan and pouring a little water on it, make it quite hot. Afterward, wrap it in a piece of new linen, place it in a press used for extracting the oil of olives, or walnuts, or of the poppy, and express it in the same manner.

In summary, the seed was subjected to four operations: drying, crushing, cooking, and pressing. With the exception of drying, which is now deemed unnecessary, the operations involved today are much the same. In early European times, the linseed oil required for each project was produced by the artist in small quantities, usually in his own studio. In many cases the ground seed was pressed entirely without cooking. Oil made in this manner was called "cold-pressed" oil and was beautifully light in color. However, because of the small yield of oil that results from cold pressing, the cost is considered excessive, and very little is now produced in this fashion.

As the oil became more popular and found more markets, the crudest of mechanical apparatuses were devised for its manufacture. The first attempt at producing linseed oil in quantity was by the ancient screw-and-lever press, a modification of the cider press. After pressing, considerable oil, known as oil cake, remained in the dry residue. These cakes weighed about 25 pounds each and were about 18 inches in diameter and 8 inches thick, resembling a round of cheese in shape. Hence, the device was known as a "cheese box" press.

Cheese box presses were used as late as 1848, when the Dutch mill or wedge press came into vogue. In this greatly improved press, hinged partitions of wooden plates were erected on edge in a heavy rectangular framework of oak or iron. The ground seed was shoveled by hand into woolen bags, and these were hung between the plates. The pressure needed for the expressing of the oil was obtained by driving wooden wedges between the plates by means of wind- or water-powered sledges.

There are now more modern devices for pressing, such as hydraulic presses. U.S. manufacturers are credited with the greatest advancements made in linseed oil machinery in the last century. Today in a large, modern mill both hydraulic and expeller-type systems (mechanical presses that operate continuously and automatically) are employed.

All in all, linseed oil is probably the most versatile of the drying oils available in large quantities. It makes excellent varnishes either alone or in concert with other drying oils, especially Tung and oiticica oils. Its principal disadvantage lies in its tendency to yellow and darken and in its comparatively slow drying properties.

Varnish Oil Length

Varnishes fall into different "oil-length" categories depending upon the degree of hardness, flexibility, and toughness required by the job they are to do. This rating system is based on the number of gallons of oil per 100 pounds of resin used in making the varnish. As the proportion of oil to resin increases, the film tends to be softer, higher in water resistance, slower in drying, and more flexible. As the oil content decreases relative to the resin, the varnish film dries faster, gets harder and tougher, is less flexible, loses water resistance, and is less durable on exterior exposure.

Spar varnish, which was specifically designed for exterior use and meant to be subjected to the ravages of weather, is a relatively "long oil-length" varnish. It may contain from 50 to 70 gallons of oil per 100 pounds of resin in the varnish cook. There are exceptions to this general rule, of course, depending on the resin used, but the basic principle is that spar varnishes are high in oil content because of the durability and water resistance demanded of them.

Interior varnishes (which include many of the

"rubbed-effect" varnishes packaged by marine coatings companies) for use on surfaces that are not subject to hard wear, scuffing, abrasion, or direct exposure to exterior elements, are "medium oil-length" varnishes. Interior varnishes run from 22 to 35 gallons of oil per 100 pounds of resin. The result is a harder film than that of spar varnishes, yet one that has sufficient flexibility, good water resistance, and the ability to last for years.

Floor varnishes have to be harder, but not brittle, drying to a film that can take the heavy wear of foot traffic. Such varnishes are usually made in an oil length of around 18 to 20 gallons. On an interior floor this varnish will do a good job, but on exterior exposure the finish would be relatively short lived, not having the flexibility and durability to stand up under the expansion and contraction of surfaces subject to sharp temperature changes and the ravages of rain, storms, and ultraviolet light. Such varnishes are not typically manufactured for marine application.

Furniture and true rubbing varnishes must be shorter still in oil length, ranging from 8 to 15 gallons of oil per 100 pounds of resin. And the so-called all-purpose varnishes sold in some quarters are usually around 25 gallons in oil length. These short-oil varnishes should never be used in marine finishing: All-purpose varnishes are "good for many things, but best for none" — especially on a boat.

Ultraviolet Absorbers

Ultraviolet light rays come, of course, from the sun, but they are not in the visible range. UV rays are short wavelength energy waves that are most intense in the summer months. They are not as short as X-rays, which can pass through almost anything, but they can penetrate a lot of things that longer light waves cannot. Whereas visible light waves falling on white lead pigments, for example, are reflected (so that we see white),

ultraviolet waves are neither absorbed nor reflected by white lead but go sailing right through it. A varnish pigment that has the ability to absorb ultraviolet light protects the vehicle (or the rest of the varnish) in which it is dispersed from disintegration and breakdown. Such a pigment has a crystalline structure that refracts all of the ultraviolet light that falls upon it, essentially reducing the waves to a lower level of heat or fluorescent energy.

Solvents Used in Varnishes

Turpentine, made by distilling gum from the longleaf pine tree (hence the name "gum turpentine"), has been the favored solvent from the early days for use with oleoresinous varnishes made from natural resins and oils. Turpentine is a natural essential oil obtained by steam distillation, which accounts for its freedom from rosin oil and other products resulting from the direct decomposition of rosin by heat. It is a member of a wide class of essential oils, the terpenes, to which some of our most expensive perfumes belong. A particularly interesting characteristic of turpentine is its preservation or antiseptic properties, which it shares with oil of clove, juniper, and other oils of the same class. As such, it is also a great preventer of mold and mildew, and will even destroy such growths in the pores of some woods. Turpentine is a slow-evaporating solvent and facilitates excellent brushing and flowing. It has been especially beneficial as a thinner in linseed oil varnishes because of its compatibility with the natural resins and oils and its drying properties. It speeds the drying of this type of varnish by absorbing oxygen from the air and conveying it to the drying oils.

With the advent of varnishes produced from synthetic resins, however, petroleum solvents have assumed prominence in the industry, virtually supplanting turpentine's starring role in the finishing drama. Petroleum thinners, including mineral spirits, benzine, and naphtha, are distil-

lates derived from those fractions of petroleum in the upper end of the gasoline range and the lower end of the kerosene range. The typical solvent used to facilitate brushing in today's better varnishes is steam-distilled mineral spirits, which has a very high boiling point. This enables a varnish comprising phenolic resins and Tung oil, for example, to flow on and be worked for a reasonable time before it begins to set and show brush marks or lap lines. Many varnish manufacturers package high grades of mineral spirits as "brushing liquids," to be used to guarantee ease of application of their paint and varnish products under less-than-ideal conditions.

Characteristics of A Good Varnish for Exterior Marine Use

BODY AND CONSISTENCY

A good varnish should not be thin or terribly runny, as thinner varnishes do not afford the protection or film buildup of heavier-bodied varnishes. "Quick-dry" varnishes often give the impression of being more efficient in application, since drying time is shorter, but in reality they are often just dilute versions of their manufacturer's slower drying, full-bodied standard varnish.

FLOW AND WORKABILITY

The length of time a varnish can be worked before it exerts a characteristic "pull" on the brush is indicative of its oil length. If it permits sufficient time for thorough brushing before beginning to set, it is likely a "long-oil" variety, typical of good spar varnish formulations. If it begins to pull almost at once, it is considered a short-oil varnish and inappropriate for use as a protective exterior coating, especially in a marine environment. (These are the extreme ends of the spectrum, and many varnishes fall somewhere between.) The flow of a varnish is judged in its full-strength configuration. Under less-

than-ideal conditions of application, an otherwise excellent flowing varnish can still require the assistance of added brushing solvent.

DRYING TIME

A good spar varnish, because of its higher oil content, should take up to twelve hours to dry sufficiently to be sanded in preparation for the following coat. A varnish that dries hard within four to six hours usually contains a high ratio of aromatic solvent and does not ultimately give a coat equal to that of a slower drying varnish. One important factor in the drying time of any varnish is the number of coats that have preceded it. The first coat always dries far more quickly than, say, the eighth, due to the continued escape of residual solvents from previous coats. Some excellent varnishes have the ability to "skin over" within one hour but then continue to dry throughout the depth of the coat over about a twelve-hour period to an even hardness. Such varnishes can be dented easily with a fingernail in the early hours of drying, but resist such impression after drying is completed. A varnish that takes longer than twelve hours to dry (when it has been applied under proper conditions) may be a "long-oil" formulation but is not practical for use in marine refinishing — unless you have the rest of your life to wait for it to dry. At the turn of the 20th century, the best oil varnishes were considered to be those used on carriages (the ones drawn by horses, not pushed by nannies) and were reputed to take several days to dry to the touch, reaching their ultimate hardness only after twelve months. Definitely l-o-o-o-o-o-n-g-oil varnishes!

WATER RESISTANCE

A varnish film of proper spar formulation should be completely resistant to discoloration by water, even when water sits undisturbed on it for a number of hours. A varnish containing cheaper resins will, under such circumstances, more or less badly corrode and will remain permanently white or discolored. (This is not to be confused with the darkening or discoloration of wood *beneath* a varnish surface when moisture attacks through a break in the film.)

TOUGHNESS AND ELASTICITY

A varnish that is brittle, though it may possess the desired hardness, will easily crack or be crushed by a moderate blow. Therefore, a truly satisfactory varnish for marine application must have a degree of elasticity along with its toughness. This is indicated by the behavior of a dried film when scratched with a sharp instrument such as a small pen knife. A first-class varnish will show a smooth, even scratch with no apparent "dusting" or scaling and should produce a small, uniform ribbon of varnish. If the varnish is deficient in elasticity it will scale away under the knife point, exhibiting a ragged, irregular scratch, and will often dust up, splintering away from the knife in the form of a fine powder. Elasticity is sometimes diminished by a paste-formula wood filler used beneath the varnish to fill or seal the pores of the wood.

RESISTANCE TO ULTRAVIOLET LIGHT

The inclusion of an ultraviolet absorbing pigment is pretty standard in good varnishes formulated for exterior use. If a varnish does not contain such a component, it could still be a good varnish but would not have the lasting power of one with the UVA additive.

In summary, a good spar (marine) varnish should be of medium consistency, should brush on and level with ease, should be tough and elastic and not easily scratched, should dry sufficiently to withstand sanding the next day, and should contain ultraviolet absorbers to prolong the life of the film as it is exposed to sunlight. Probably the best test of a good spar varnish is how it holds up through a year of continuous exposure to the Florida sun —a practice used by many varnish manufacturers in testing their newest "bright star."

I am struck by the fact that varnish has endured through so many ages in its relatively original form. And yet, the reaction to varnish has often been frustration and impatience with what some perceive to be its futility as a usable and lasting finish. Typically, somewhere along the line, those people have been traumatized by a bad varnish experience, and they cannot abide even the idea of this type of finish. Their minds are made up; they don't want to be confused with the facts of new technology. Varnish phobia reminds me of a similar neurosis I developed as a result of one of my great childhood traumas— *snake sandwiches*. This is a true story that I think begs to be told in the context of this discussion, because it shows how irrational fears can spring from incorrect assumptions about otherwise noble entities.

My siblings and I were day students at St. Joseph's Children's Home, a parochial grade school located in a little corner of the Nez Perce Indian Reservation in Idaho. The place was run by (who else?) the Sisters of St. Joseph (I guess he was too busy to do it himself), an order of well-educated, well-intentioned Catholic nuns out of California. Each one of these blessed women had her specialty. Sister Michaeline was the resident jock, not afraid to roll up her wide sleeves to swing a bat or to hike up the fullness of her long black skirt for a better whack at the kickball. Sister Cecilia Marie taught first and second grades, and made you glad you were old enough to go to school. Sister Anthony Xavier was into discipline; Sister Edward Clare, practical jokes. And so forth. All the sisters excelled at what they did. Except Sister Georgia.

Sister Georgia was the cook.

With eight children, my mother did not feel her mornings would be wisely spent packing little lunch pails. So, each day at noon we joined the boarders in the refectory (a word not in the vocabularies of any of my friends who were schooled "on the outside") to share what could generously be called a meal. The fare never varied much. It usually consisted of a mystery soup and mystery sandwiches. The soup was edible, if a little reminiscent of dishwater *after* the pots and pans. And for years the sandwiches, though unidentifiable, were at least on a par with the soup. Something happened, though, the year I was in the seventh grade. From the first day of school the sandwiches looked different; they smelled and tasted dangerous. Then one day, after much discussion and to our extreme horror, we realized what it was we had been eating: *ground-up snakes.* Some days pink ones, other days white ones with black flecks. Any way you sliced it the fact was inescapable: Sister Georgia's specialty had become ground-up snake sandwiches. We could only wonder if she was trying to drive home a new point about the devil with this allegorical fare.

Anyway, there would not be a story here if the refectory had been like any other school cafeteria, where unpopular menu items could be scraped into the trash bin along with the empty milk cartons. But this was first and, in the food budget, foremost a children's home. My parents may have paid for our right to dine alongside the orphans and army brats, but they had not purchased for us the privilege of setting an example of wastefulness. Lunch—every scrap— was to be consumed, and gratefully at that. One of the nuns was even posted in the middle of the room (to this day a maitre d' dressed in black and white makes me a little paranoid) to ensure that we all complied with the rules.

For weeks my sister and cousin and I convened to endure this vile repast together (misery loves company), sometimes tearfully now that we had identified it, often feeling a little sick the rest of the afternoon. Finally, when the ringing of the noontime bell started triggering fantasies of anorexia, we swore ourselves to action and devised a plan that would deliver us from this noontime torture. Each day, when the food gestapo had her back turned, we would cut the offending canapes into quarters and, so as not to arouse suspicion, stuff them one quarter at a time down our blouses. We then calmly ate the mystery soup of the day, drank our milk (which itself had chunks of old cream floating on top), and immediately upon our escape pitched our contraband into the nearest sidewalk heating grate.

For several weeks we enjoyed these happier low-calorie luncheons, until one day Sister Margarita Marie—whose specialty was being short— happened to look down as she stood over that grate. Instead of decomposing as we had expected, our mini-sandwiches had petrified and were stacking up like a small pyramid.

Despite earnest grilling, no one ever owned up to the felony—there are some things even a Catholic can't confess—but from then on *two* food constables stood guard, and we were searched at checkpoint St. Charlie as we left the lunchroom. It was back to tormented lunches for us all. Luckily for me, I got rheumatic fever and missed the last three months of the school year, and when I returned in the fall Sister Georgia had found another, less revolting specialty.

To this day, even if Julia Child herself were in the kitchen, you could not get me to eat a deviled ham or deviled chicken sandwich. I am permanently scarred and have no interest whatsoever in the redeeming qualities of what to my mind will always taste, smell, and *look* like macerated reptiles.

Some people's varnish encounters have been equally horrific, and while I can appreciate the weight of a traumatic experience, I hasten to point out that varnish is integral to most refinishing programs. I can survive without deviled ham sandwiches, but most brightwork cannot survive without varnish. Dispelling the myths about what's *in* varnish is vital to understanding how to use it, and once that is accomplished, artisans in this medium should be on their way toward successful and phobia-free use of this very noble substance.

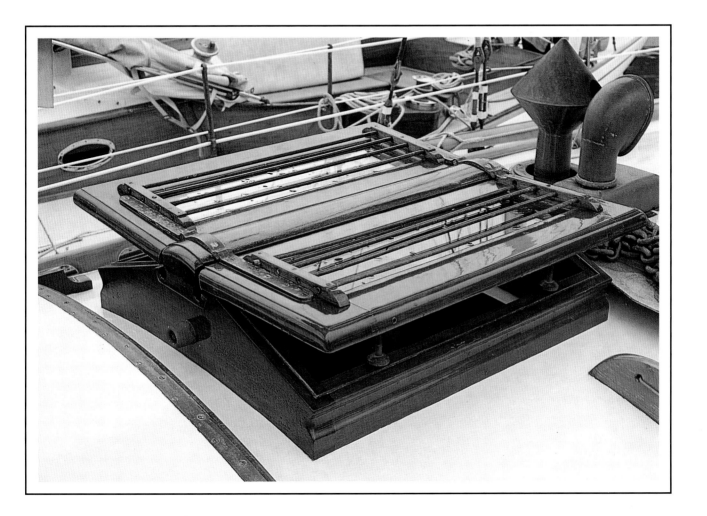

Part Two

THE
REFINISHING
PROGRAM

5

THE YACHT REFINISHING COMMANDMENTS

The season of ships is here
The west wind and the swallows;
Flowers in the fields appear,
And the ocean of hills and hollows
Has calmed its waves and is clear.

Free that anchor and chain!
Set your full canvas flying,
O men in the harbor lane:
It is I, Priapus, crying.
Sail out on your trades again!
     —Leonidas of Tarentum

*B*rightwork! What is it about this part of a boat's makeup that reaches out and grabs every boatowner —and ogler —by the collar demanding, like some toddler, to be played with? What is it about a smooth glistening rail that makes us want to reach out and stroke it, in the same way we would touch the warm coat of a fine Arabian? An acknowledged truth around any dock is that spring fever itself would not enjoy official status without brightwork mania. When the tulips are up and the robins are poking cockily about the garden, the boatowner's muse stretches with her annual yawn from a long winter's sleep and in ritual fashion wanders immediately, if not a bit reluctantly, down the mind's dock, brushes and varnish in hand. The season of ships is indeed here, and so is the season of brightwork; a season that, for all intents and purposes, never ends.

Beautiful brightwork is proof of civilized boat ownership, and in every aspect of civilization there are precepts that help maintain the cultural balance. Brightwork, too, comes with its own set of principles, "The Yacht Refinishing Commandments." I submit them here as a guide for our collective conscience in the often stormy pilgrimage toward brightwork Mecca.

HONOR THY YACHT

The cost of the average boat far exceeds the cost of the above-average car. Would you leave your Lamborghini out in the acid rain, uncovered, with a seagull's recycled breakfast drying on the hood? Would you scrub your BMW with Ajax or leave a chipped spot to rust out? If you had the panel on your Jaguar varnished, would a sloppy job, with drips down the dash and grit dried into the finish, be OK? The common retorts to these questions are, "Boats aren't meant to look like pianos, they're meant to look like they've done battle with the sea," and "All the TLC in China won't maintain that showroom appearance anyway." Horse pucky! If you think of your boat as a yacht, even if it's only nine feet long, and keep it looking like one, it will pay you back in more ways than you can measure at the bank.

THOU SHALT NOT TEMPT MOTHER NATURE

Realize the effects the weather has on your refinishing efforts and plan accordingly. A can of varnish does not come with a barometer on the side, so reading the air and clouds becomes your responsibility. If you don't know *how* to read the clouds, then learn. It makes the difference eventually between coats of varnish that are keepable and ones that must be removed and redone. The trickiest parts of the weather to read are the ones you can't see: That late afternoon dew that takes over and with no warning creates clouds in freshly applied varnish. An informed varnisher expects these natural idiosyncrasies and works with them. Do your weather forecasting homework and you won't have to blame Mother Nature for your mistakes.

BE NEAT IN THY WORK

Many dockside artisans go through all the preparatory steps in refinishing only to pull out a can of varnish and proceed to brush away — oblivious to the mess of sanding dust and grit surrounding their work. The result, especially if the wind kicks up, is what I call "spontaneous nonskid." Do not open a can of varnish or paint until you've cleaned and vacuumed the entire mess posing a breezy threat to the impending finish. It really doesn't take that much time to do, and in the long run it cuts down on the time you must spend building up coats that are so full of muck and grit they must be half sanded off before subsequent coats can be applied.

UNDERSTAND THY CHOSEN FINISH

Choose your brightwork program on the basis of two items: practicality and aesthetic value. Sadly enough, the latter of the two counts for only about 10 percent in making your decisions. A hand-rubbed exterior oil finish is lovely, even romantic to some, but unless one has little more to do with his days, it is a career all its own to keep looking lovely. Understand the actual function of each type of finish before you jump wallet first into a particular course of finishing. Do some finish "soul searching": How practical is this finish? What is the correct preparation for this new coating? What type of climate might affect the application? How many coats help guarantee that you won't have to repeat the entire process literally from scratch every year? What is the best kind of varnish for your level of expertise? And so forth. And for heaven's sake, when choosing any finish, ask yourself, "Do I have the time required to do it right?" I promise you, if you don't do it correctly the first time, you will have to do it over—removing the old finish, cleaning up the wood, and building the finish back up from coat one.

DO THY PRODUCT RESEARCH

Get accurate information about products you've heard about before you ever walk into the chandlery. Don't let some clever marketing whiz do your thinking for you; once you've been bombarded with all those miracle claims and seductive packages, it's too late. Choose your varnish the way you would hire an employee: on the basis of recommendations from someone whose opinions you trust. Walk the docks and see which varnish job wins the "most beautiful" prize, and then ask the owner how long it has been there and what it requires in upkeep. This is where you'll get the truth about varnishes, not from the back cover of your favorite boating magazine. And once you decide a certain product is for you, realize that its manufacturers do not know your boat or the circumstances surrounding its particular upkeep needs the way you do. The responsibility for determining how to make that product work best is yours alone.

KNOW THY HARDWOODS

The fraternity of boatowners on a dock often resembles a refinishing club, every member of which shows up with a different idea of what's best. The president is usually the owner with the best-looking brightwork, and his or her word is considered gospel. This is fine, except when mahogany owners are scribbling down advice that comes from a teak owner, or cedar owners are transcribing tips from the ironbark man. What's good for the goose of mahogany is not necessarily right for the gander of teak. If you own a boat trimmed in any of the myriad of wonderful hardwoods, take the time to learn about that wood. Chapter 3 offers some pointers. Teak is very dense and oily, mahogany is sometimes dense but never oily; oak is very hard, never oily, but will absorb a thinned varnish readily, whereas ironbark is so hard it is advisably left unfinished or at best lightly oiled. Teak throws off a bad case of mildew with a moderate bleaching; fir and oak take on mildew stains for a lifetime and virtually no bleaching will take them asunder. The variations go on and on, and knowledge of the qualifiers is vitally important to the refinisher if a sane program of brightwork is the goal.

NEGLECT NOT THY DETAILING

In my little book, no brightwork (or any refinishing) job is truly "finished" until the detailing is done. If there's a varnish splatter or an oil drip or a stretch of masking tape glue or a paint bleed, tend to it. This is the purpose for which man had the good sense to invent single-edged razor blades and a host of other handy gadgets and products to assist in post-project cleanup. People who do not detail after a refinishing job should have a hard time sleeping at night.

KEEP THEE SAFE AND ALIVE

This is a three-part directive. It demands, first, the thoughtful execution of a project such that you promote safety for yourself and others as you work on the boat and around the dock; second, the intelligent and responsible handling of flammable and caustic materials to ensure not only your own well-being but the security of the vessel as well; and third, the making of decisions regarding treatments of various surfaces of the boat that promote non-hazardous enjoyment of the boat. A bowsprit protruding forth across the dock; a pile of oil-soaked rags left on board after a cabin rubbing; a hard gloss finish applied to teak decks: these are just a sampling of disasters waiting to claim victims. Be cautious; be smart; be alive —and have a boat still floating when you return to it.

KEEP THE PREVENTIVE MAINTENANCE CREED

Which goes like this: I believe that the work I do on my boat has great value because I am important and my time is worth more than money. I believe that once I have poured great labor into my yacht it would be an insult to me and to my yacht to knowingly allow the fruits of my labors to fall back into a state of disrepair when I could have prevented such decline. I believe it is my ethical duty as the guardian of my yacht to maintain its dignity year-round, whether it is yachting season or the middle of the snowy winter. And I believe that, in dollar terms alone, I will spend one heck of a lot less money over the long haul keeping my yacht up on a regular maintenance regimen than I will if I allow it to fall into periodic ruin. Amen.

THOU SHALT LOVE WORKING ON THY YACHT

Boats are like children; you might not *say* to them, "You're a pain in the ass," but if you feel that way, they pick it up in a hurry. If you hate varnishing, your boat will show that fact in its brightwork, and you may as well go golfing instead of wasting your time with the brushes— or better yet, just own an inflatable raft. Brightwork is a labor of love: first, last, and always. No amount of est can help you circumvent that very real fact, so if you are the type of person who cannot participate in the passionate process of this art, do yourself and your boat a favor and have someone else—some hopeless romantic—do the brightwork for you.

6

ORGANIZING YOUR BRIGHTWORK THOUGHTS

Let all things be done decently and in order.
—I Corinthians 14:40

*I*t's the weekend, the sun is shining, it's a perfect opportunity to run down to the boat and do some varnishing. Yes?

NO! Or at least, maybe not!

Have you considered the other projects that might be calling out to you, and that there might be a certain order in which those projects need to be done? You'd better, or your impromptu varnishing adventures could turn out to be wasted efforts by the time you finally do address the full slate of jobs ahead.

From the looks of that opening quote, I'd guess the Corinthians discovered what happens when you bleach the decks *after* you wax the topsides (or whatever it was they did to their topsides —slathered them with pitch, most likely). Destroying one improvement with another is a pitfall many amateur refinishers tumble into. It is best avoided by learning what effect each undertaking can have on the precedent condition of the boat. Minimize wasted labors by keeping a seasonal checklist of refin-

Sometimes a boat is most beautiful when just a small portion of it is left bright.

ishing tasks and then organizing all the phases of those tasks in what I term "D.D.O.": Deductive Destructive Order.

To illustrate, consider this hypothetical situation: If spring automatically means refresher varnishwork, and this year you'd like to bleach that ugly blackened Deks Olje off your teak decks, plus the bottom is due for a new paint job and you've promised your son a new skateboard in exchange for polishing all the bronze ports, you *could* do things in this order: ports first, then the varnishwork, then the bleach job, then wrap up with the bottom.

But only if you want to lose your mind.

For all your efforts, you would end up with streaked ports, possibly scored or softened varnish, and decks with a dusty red hue from bow to stern. The bottom, however, would look lovely.

Here's a basic list, in Deductive Destructive Order of the tasks you may be facing at any one time on your boat and a brief explanation of the threat each step poses to the ones following.

1) **Bottom sanding and painting**

Bottom sanding dust is so pervasive it can set

back the glistening spirit of the entire boat, plus this is one of the nastiest jobs on the list and good to get behind you as soon as possible. Make a bottom project Job No. 1.

2) Repainting or varnishing spars

Whether done from a bosun's chair or with the stick pulled, this exercise can wreak its own distinctive form of havoc on the rest of the boat. When a mast is unstepped, the dangling web of shrouds rarely leaves the brightwork unscarred, and in many cases the decks are filthy by the

Detailed areas must be completely dismantled before the refinishing begins.

time the spar is set back in place and the boat is rerigged. And unless you've been successful in shrouding the entire boat with drop cloths, even the most valiant efforts to be neat cannot eliminate a degree of spattering from above.

3) Sanding painted areas to prep for repainting

I prefer to do this if possible before I strip any brightwork, as the opaque dust that results from sanding paint tends to get into the pores and especially the seams of bare wood and often shows up later, despite the most thorough preparation, under the new brightwork finish. In addition, if a deck bleaching is to follow, the sanding dust that settles in to the deck grain

is easily discharged in the bleaching process.

4) Deck and brightwork bleaching to remove oil

This requires the use of Te-Ka A&B, which can score paint and varnish as well as bronze, brass, and waxed fiberglass.

5) Stripping brightwork with heat, dry scrapers, or sandpaper

These procedures don't necessarily harm anything that follows, but they are best done prior to bleaching with Teak Wonder (see Step 7) in order to take full advantage of that product's ability to remove mildew stains often found beneath old finishes.

6) Chemical stripping of varnish or paint above decks

This can be a very messy process and is best done while you aren't so panicked about what lands on the decks or areas surrounding your stripping work. It is also the perfect time and means to cleaning old varnish encrustments off hardware (cleats, for example), making them easier to polish later.

7) Bleaching to clean up bare decks and weathered trims

This type of bleaching will clean a deck that has not been previously oiled, and can at the same time eliminate a fair amount of mildew where the wood beneath a broken down brightwork finish has weathered. This saves sanding time and preserves the integrity of the wood's design.

8) Sanding, oiling, and varnishing brightwork

The obvious liability with this process is the mess that can accrue by the time it is completed —especially in the form of drips on adjacent surfaces. At this point detailing can still take place without harming what might have been freshly painted or waxed surfaces.

9) Painting topsides and above decks

Doing this *after* you've finished the brightwork creates cleaner boundaries between the two coatings.

10) Sanding bleached decks

I save this half of the deck rescuing job until I've completed all brightwork and paint restoration work, simply because it's a great way to clean up any materials that may have wandered unwittingly away from my brushes —more specifically, spills. Sanding is the Godfather of detailing. It can forgive many transgressions. And since it has to be done anyway (if you've bleached), why not make the exercise doubly worthwhile?

11) Waxing topsides

If you're a woman, you know that you never put on lipstick until you're finished dressing. Waxing gelcoat follows the same premise. Do it after you've finished putting on all the other coatings.

12) Polishing bronze or other metal fixtures

This is just a good spot in the grand order for this type of work. Sooner is too soon, because your polished fixtures can be slopped up with varnish or oil or paint; at any point from here on, the fruits of your polishing labors are not really at risk. Of course, if you have a bag of fittings that have been removed from their place of residence and are waiting for another project to be completed before they return home, you are welcome to polish them up any time that's convenient. Just don't put them back in place before the proper time.

13) Painting decks

The one project that, upon completion, bans you from the boat —for a little while, anyway— so save it for last.

Once the finish program is settled on and the calendar finally says "go," there are a few little details to getting started that can help to keep the refinishing project from wasting valuable time. These are:

1) Shopping for the whole project (or complete phases) all at once;

2) Reading the weather (by looking upward as well as listening to your favorite version of Willard Scott);

3) Prepping the boat for the work.

To Market, to Market

Shopping once for a project means having a firm grasp on what type of finish you're planning, what type of stripping the old finish will dictate, how much you will need of everything, and —most important —what you will need in order to accomplish each phase. With luck, by the time you've read this entire book you will be able to answer all those questions with complete confidence as you begin your brightwork rescue mission. But if you can't anticipate everything, don't worry. Buying as many as possible of the materials you will need before you head off to the boat can save you untold wasted hours running back and forth from chandlery to vessel. In some cases, it can also save you money, since buying things in bulk —sandpaper, for instance —is often less expensive. I liken this to shopping for a dinner party. You wouldn't pick up the ingredients for the appetizer, run home, cook it up, serve it to the guests, and then run back to the market for the salad fixings—not if you expected to return to any guests. At the very least, if you buy your refinishing "groceries" per course, make sure that course will take up the whole weekend.

One big reason for having the fullest possible inventory of materials is that it gives you flexibility during the project to shift to another phase if something torpedoes the original plan. Let's say you had wanted to finish heat-stripping everything, but it looks like a big thunderhead is moving in without an engraved invitation. If you have your Te-Ka A&B on hand, you can stop stripping but continue working, bleaching the oiled cockpit grates that were slated for that treatment, because bleaching and rain go together like corned beef and cabbage. This is the brightworker's version of "effective time management," and it helps prevent an otherwise simple project from turning into a series of false starts.

Learning to Read the Weather

Probable nor'east to sou'west winds, varying to the southard and westard and eastard and points between; high and low barometer, sweeping round from place to place; probable areas of rain, snow, hail, and drought, succeeded or preceded by earthquakes with thunder and lightning.

—Mark Twain

The fog comes
on little cat feet.
It sits looking
over the harbor and city
on silent haunches
and then moves on.

—Carl Sandburg

Once, early in my brightwork career, one of the salty old pretzels holding forth on the Shilshole docks chastised my sister and me for wrapping up early when we figured those big clouds overhead meant impending rain. "Girls," he squawked in his crusty busybody voice, "quitting so soon?" "It's gonna rain!" we shouted back. "Rain!" he howled. "Don't you see that pair of Dutchman's pants a-flyin' in the breeze?" We looked at each other, rolled our eyes in tandem, and braced ourselves for what we figured would be another of his typically baroque chestnuts.

Captain Geezer-buckets went on to enlighten us with an old superstition that dictates "as long as there is a pair of Dutchman's pants flying overhead, you will not be rained upon." A pair of Dutchman's pants, for you humorless cads, is a patch of true blue sky, usually surrounded by —but peaking stubbornly through —a storm of ominous-looking clouds. The captain told us the size didn't matter —those pants could belong to a midget, for all he cared. They just had to be blue. What came across as a bit of fancy that day bore out as the afternoon wore on and the sun eventually came through those clouds. From then on, Dutchman's pants became our daily barometer, and nine times out of ten, as long as there was a patch of denim overhead, scheduled varnishing, sanding, or whatever project we might otherwise have postponed went on as planned—without a dousing.

Hang your hat on this one, folks. It's more than a figment of some sea dog's imagination. It is refinisher's gospel. And anyone who knows the truth of the tale will shame-shame you for ducking out early on a feeble "it's gonna rain" alibi. If you can't place your complete trust in the Dutchman's pants, a more official weather guide is an excellent book entitled *Instant Weather Forecasting* by Alan Watts. It teaches you how to read the heavens under all conditions and to determine what the clouds hold in store for the near future.

Learning to outsmart the weather is a must when planning any refinishing project, especially if you aren't planning to refinish your entire boat in the shop. Knowing ahead of time about impending rain doesn't necessarily make you feel better, but it does eliminate needless frustration brought on by surprise downpours. It also forces you to be creative about the way you organize your work on the boat. A refinishing project often has portable components: a helm, a tiller, cockpit grates, perhaps a cabin sole that comes out at the turn of a screw (or fifty screws). Unless you live in the sunbelt, plan on a few days of rainout and through each phase of the project save the "portables" for last. In other words, strip the whole boat for as long as the weather allows, and when the only thing remaining to be stripped is the helm, strip that. Quite likely the rain will intervene, forcing you into basement or garage for a day or a weekend you had meant to devote to your brightwork project. Take the helm with you. If the torrents continue even after it is stripped, start sanding it. If you're down to 220 grit and the rain is *still* coming down, proceed to the varnish. If old Noah approached *his* refinishing project in this

manner, he undoubtedly had a pretty good-looking helm by the time the sky cleared.

Preparing the Boat

The last "getting started" item is the one that finally lets you get your hands on the project. Prepping the boat means turning your floating dream, just for the duration of the project, into a theme-park of efficiency and organization. You do this by stripping off every possible fitting that stands in the path of your actual work, and dismantling brightwork areas that can either become "portables" or will respond more quickly to your refinishing efforts in component form. Your best friend during this operation is a cordless power screwdriver or VSR drill and a range of driver bits. Your second best friend is the map you make of the boat—on which you very quickly chart the source of each piece of hardware as you remove it. Drop each piece and its fasteners into a small Ziploc bag and label the bag with a number corresponding to the place on the map from whence it came. (If it's a fairly simple configuration of hardware I usually dispense with the map and make the labels self-explanatory.) Don't combine several pieces in one bag just to save on Ziplocs; it's not worth it. If your project encompasses a fairly ambitious spread of brightwork, and if you think this is too much trouble and you choose to toss everything into a bucket, telling yourself that you will remember where it all goes, I need not chastise you here. I will simply assure you that when you die, you will not go to Hell, because you will have known Hell on Earth in your attempts to reassemble the boat from that bucket. I know whereof I speak.

You're organized; you have a new finish in mind; you've shopped; you've checked the weather. The boat is one big, bare expanse of brightwork bacchanalia. Get to work!

7

STRIPPING OLD FINISHES

God, if this were enough, that I see things bare to the buff.
— R.L. Stevenson

All this will not be finished in the first one hundred days. Nor will it be finished in the first one thousand days, nor in the life of this Administration, nor even perhaps in our lifetime on this planet. But let us begin.
—John F. Kennedy

*I*t is a little-known fact that JFK, in this portion of his inaugural speech, was referring to the refinishing project slated for the presidential yacht. What boatowner has not stood before a Twilight Zone of peeling varnish and asked himself whether he has the strength of purpose even to begin? All this thick, worthless membrane needing to be peeled off before one can begin to entertain thoughts of a new finish. And this stripping process itself prompts such confusion. How does one go about it? Can it be accomplished without depleting the national treasury, and within the complement of weekends allotted a mortal lifespan?

So many questions. Do "let us begin."

If you aren't quite sure you should bother taking off your present finish, ask yourself this question: Will the integrity of a refresher coat be greater than that of the original finish? If the answer is "yes," you are wasting your time and money by not wooding down. Of course, ex-

hausted finishes have their own charming way of nagging one into finally choosing to strip— they come off by themselves. Just not in an efficient or pretty manner. For some specific clues to your best course of action, see the list of symptoms and their cures on page 104.

Old varnish is only one of the several types of finish that may need to part company with your brightwork. Oil, silicone sealers, paint, clear epoxy, and polyurethane finishes all fall under the "need to be stripped" heading at one time or another, regardless of their manufacturers' claims. The refinisher can face any combination of these coatings in one restoration project, and it behooves one to understand the differences among them when selecting a method of removal.

There are two basic types of coatings, hard and penetrating, and there are five basic methods for removing them: heat, chemical (solvent) strippers, dry scraping, acid bleaching systems, and sanding.

In the old days, "heat" as a means of finish removal meant propane torches. The flame was directed at the offending finish, just closely

A Port Orford cedar deck with mahogany king plank and covering boards. This type of deck can be oiled or left bare rather than varnished.

enough and long enough to soften (and usually bubble) the finish. Then this seared coating was scraped off with a steel scraper (presumably by someone wearing asbestos gloves!). The problem with this system was that along with the finish, and probably several fingers, an awful lot of wood was coming through the experience with third-degree burns. Amazingly enough, the propane torch is still the heat instrument of choice, especially in many boatyards around the world. But today there is a far superior method of applying heat to soften a finish, and that is using a heat gun.

Chemical or solvent strippers are usually formulations of methylene chloride with a cellulose and paraffin additive to keep the solvent from evaporating or running off like water. These "semi-paste strippers" function by working their way into and literally melting a finish. They are very toxic to use and are the messiest system of finish removal known to man, but they can be quite effective and in certain instances are the only means to a properly stripped surface.

Acid bleaching systems are the only course to pursue when you have an oil, silicone, or other surface-penetrating finish gone astray. They work chemically, destroying the binder and releasing the residual oils and resins after the oil formula has dried, stripping all the natural surface oils in the process and killing the mildew those oils foster. The bleaching part of the system is a caustic formula neutralized by a companion acidic formula, which then must be rinsed to absolute oblivion or the wood can suffer chemical burns and betray such torment in the form of darkened blemishes. Proper use of an acid bleaching system can net you such pristine wood you'd swear the boat was just off the assembly line.

Dry-scraping is a method of finish removal reserved for the strong of heart—literally. It requires but two simple tools: a scraper and a file. Wholesale dry-scraping necessitates a few

months' collaboration with a Nautilus machine to prepare for the task. But if you're up to it, scraping can be the least expensive mode of stripping off a finish. If cost isn't the dominant factor in choosing your weapons, I would steer you toward other methods for the bulk of the job, but there are circumstances where dry-scraping isn't as physically taxing as one would think, and believe it or not, instances where it is advisable.

Sanding off a finish is for the birds. Actually, I wouldn't condemn even a seagull to such punishment. This method needs no definition; as a wholesale means to bare wood, it just needs a proper burial. But under rare conditions it, too, is a necessary way to bare wood. Thankfully, those conditions do not usually entail a very grand scope of the work.

To determine which method is most appropriate to the project at hand, walk mentally through the list of options in deductive order. If you need to remove a hard finish, your options are all but the acid bleaching system. A heat gun should be used whenever and wherever possible to remove the bulk of, if not the entire, finish. If there are delicate areas of detail work, or if there remains a thin layer of residual finish in the pores of the wood after you've used a heat gun, a chemical stripper is the logical approach. If you want to remove a layer of wood along with the finish and you feel up to the physical challenge of dry-scraping, be my guest. If you are feeling extremely guilty over some unspeakable wrong you have committed, and there are no sackcloth and ashes at your disposal, you could sand off the entire finish.

If you are removing an oil or silicone or almost any other penetrating-type finish, the acid bleaching system is the only sensible option.

Heat Guns

Heat guns have stirred up flak in refinishing quarters, I suspect for no other reason than that they are the new kid on the block and the old bullies expect them to pay dues before they join the club.

Don't be afraid of heat guns! They can be the quickest, cleanest, easiest means to a bare stretch of wood. Sure, they take practice. Every worthwhile pursuit takes patience, time, and some degree of repetition before it moves along without a hitch or two. But trust me when I tell you that a dedicated stab at learning the ins and outs of heat-gun stripping will bring you to a happier plane of yacht refinishing. Heat guns will free you from the hours of drudgery attendant to "wooding down" by way of hand block sanding. They also save you gallons of chemical stripper on a big project by removing the greater part of a varnish buildup first, leaving but the tiniest amount of finish behind for chemical consideration. Any remaining varnish in the pores, along with residual paste fillers or stains, can then be chemically removed with minimum chemical exposure, both to you and the wood, and even less damage to the budget.

To allay any fears you may still have about these modern agents of finish dispatch, indulge me on a couple of points. The only way you can burn the wood with a heat gun is by aiming the gun at the surface and keeping it there *past* the point of softening the finish. If you pay attention to what you are doing and you remove the stream of heat once the spot has softened (evidenced in the extreme by a bubbled finish), then you will not burn the wood. And glued joints will not be damaged by the modicum of heat required to soften the finish. Again, if you train the heat on such an area and leave it there until the wood has begun to resemble a briquet, yes, the joint will suffer, but by that time the joint is the least of your problems. When you buy your heat gun, take it home and practice burning an old dresser or chair you found at a garage sale. See how long it takes to soften the finish, and then see how long it takes to burn up the wood underneath. Get a feel for timing, and

then when you feel you have more than a cursory acquaintance with the heat-and-scrape process, escalate to your intended subject —the boat.

When stripping with a heat gun you will need:

A good heat gun
Scrapers
A fine mill file
A vacuum
A dust mask
A source of electrical power

Before you commence stripping anything, take a few moments to learn how to sharpen your scrapers. The best heat gun in the world is useless if it is supported by a dull scraper. The scraping process continually smooths off that "burr" you put on the blade at the start, so prepare yourself mentally for periodic (every ten minutes or so) swipes with the file to restore the burr and bring the scraper back to working condition. If you can't seem to get the hang of sharpening your scrapers, I suggest asking a respected cabinetmaker for a sharpening lesson. You could offer to strip something in exchange for the invaluable tips imparted. If you can't find a sympathetic cabinetmaker, find a copy of *Planecraft*, Woodcraft Supply Company's excellent and inexpensive book on sharpening *any* cutting edge. Their address is 10 State Street, Box 4000, Woburn, Massachusetts 01888.

Incidentally, while we're on the subject of sharp scrapers and keeping them that way, one of those universally-held-but-bears-repeating truths is the absolute importance of sharpening scrapers downwind and away from the boat. Titian freckles might be charming on Charlie Brown's little red-haired girlfriend, but they have no place on your decks. Rust spots are the guaranteed byproduct of onboard filing of scrapers, and are a sign of blatant carelessness during sharpening exercises.

Here are a few pointers for using the heat

gun (other than the big one, which is to *practice* with it). Get comfortable! Don't force yourself to work from contorted angles unless that's the only way to reach something. If you plan to be on your knees, wear kneepads. If it's possible to do a rail from the dock in a standing position, don't opt to lean over and do it hanging off the boat. And while it's nice to start on a fun spot, discipline yourself to use your most productive hours, which are the ones at the beginning of the day, stripping the more challenging pieces—the underside of a long handrail, for example—saving the pieces of cake for that time in the afternoon when you're running low on energy. Easy spots can be looked upon as rewards for doing the hard stuff early on. Arranging things in this way gets the stripping job completed in a timely manner, for you are managing your energy as well as the job in an intelligent fashion. Another good reason to get the nasty work out of the way in the beginning, especially in a big project, is that by the time you've scraped for six or seven days straight, your dedication to the whole idea of nicely stripped wood may begin to wane. If you've put off the more unpleasant tasks as you've gone through the boat, they ultimately become the enemy, and you will likely end up doing your worst work on them when they finally demand your attention.

To do the stripping, hold the heat gun in your secondary hand, aiming the nozzle at the wood at a 45-degree angle and about an inch from the surface, and heat for about five seconds or until the finish begins to bubble, whichever comes first. Then flip the heat gun up in the air and immediately, with the scraper in your primary hand, begin scraping. If the finish does not scrape off, repeat the five seconds/or bubbles/then scrape routine until it does. Heating the finish just to the point of being soft enough to scrape away is the key to skillful stripping. You shouldn't need to produce blisters in the finish before it reaches that stage, though

certain finishes can be that stubborn. If you've allowed the finish enough time to heat up, and you've scraped firmly enough, you should reach bare wood. Of course, any varnish residing down in the pores will remain, as will any stain or other pigment that has penetrated the wood, but the surface should be fairly clean and devoid of its hard finish.

If the grain was reasonably open when the present finish was applied, there will probably be quite a lot of old varnish embedded in that grain. Do not attempt to excavate such areas with your scraper, and definitely don't start scraping across the grain to try to get the varnish out of the recesses. That's a good way to start ripping the wood. Plan a second stripping step with a chemical stripper, or if the piece calls for reshaping, sand those areas to the point of literally planing them down with a heavy grit of sandpaper. In the case of woods that sport filler, stain, or both under the old varnish, the chemical second-strip is almost indispensible. Do not use sanding as a method here (unless the wood really deserves a good sanding anyway), since your goal is to leave as much of the wood in its original shape as possible.

Until you become proficient at a continuous heat-and-scrape process, you should make a deliberate point of flipping the nose of the heat gun into the air as you scrape, as this is when most beginners absentmindedly burn the wood. They become so enamored of the amazingly wonderful results of the gun that they forget that 1,200 degrees of heat is still aimed at the wood in front of them. Once you get the hang of heating the next area while you scrape the softened one, one after another, you can stop worrying about flipping the gun up, as the requisite amount of heating time, along with the time it takes to burn the wood, becomes engrained in your subconscious, and the proper technique of working with the heat gun becomes second nature.

Mahogany coamings with mahogany cap and oak trim, and a cedar seat.

Use some imagination when choosing scraping tools for use with a heat gun. Do not, however, use a putty knife, chisel, or any type of scraper that requires a pushing motion, as invariably the wood will be gouged. Use only pull-type scrapers, and as the finish softens, remove it by scraping toward you. Besides the standard assortment of commercially manufactured scrapers, I have a collection of specialized instruments ranging from dental picks to antique penknives. The more you have to choose from as you work, the more thorough you can be in your stripping.

Don't bear down on the scraper any more than is necessary to bite into the finish. Using too much pressure dulls the blade quickly and can gouge the wood. If you find this happening, you are probably not allowing the varnish to get hot enough before you begin scraping, or the blade is too dull to cut the hot finish quickly. Scrape with the direction of the grain unless absolutely impossible. Be very delicate if you do scrape across the grain, since it is easy to tear out chunks of wood. Be very careful, too, when scraping around bungs. The blade can catch at the edges and chip out pieces, forcing you to replug those spots.

When heat-stripping an area adjacent to a painted surface or *any* surface that you do not want to destroy, affix a very thin wood batten (about 1/8 inch thick) over the surface flush with the area you're heating. If you have a helper, have that person hold the batten in place as you work, and then slide it along for uninterrupted stripping. You can create a similar protective boundary with a taping trick: Mask the "at-risk" surface with 3M Safe Release masking tape, then mask again over that strip of

Marine plywood dropboards, beautifully varnished. Louvers such as these are best stripped chemically, while surrounding areas will respond quickly and easily to a heat gun.

tape with regular masking tape (one-inch widths for both). This only works if the heat gun you're using has a non-fanned direction of heat flow (such as the Easy Gun listed in tools section), since you'll need good control of the heat in order not to burn the tape or surrounding surfaces. When you've used the tape method of protection, allow the surface to cool completely and then pull the tape up very slowly.

If your project is outdoors, stripping with a heat gun can be hampered, and even rendered moot, by a moderate to strong breeze —especially a cool one. If you must work under such conditions, set up a windbreak; otherwise you'll find your efforts slow and frustrating. In some situations, it is better simply to postpone the work until a calmer day.

Protect yourself when you work with a heat gun. Just because you have circumvented the chemical route does not mean the process, though less messy, is free of physical risks. I wear nitrile gloves, which keep my hands from chapping from the prolonged exposure to warm air and prevent the occasional roasting of fingers. I wear a mask to keep from breathing air full of little particles of varnish dust that fly about during this type of stripping. And if I am scooting along on my knees during the project, I always wear my kneepads.

Keep a vacuum or a whisk broom and dustpan handy for collecting piles of shavings that accumulate, as they can become something of an impediment to your work and could catch fire if in the direct path of the heat flow. And please, don't be tempted to sweep such debris into the waterways. Varnish flakes are not biodegradable, nor are they recommended as part of a fish's balanced daily diet.

Chemical Removers

Louvered doors are the bane of my existence. I don't mind telling you I would just as soon make kindling of them as see one hanging anywhere on a boat I have to refinish. But that isn't often an option available to me, so the next best thing is to make them as painless as possible to refinish. A step in that direction is using a chemical remover to strip louvers of old varnish. Any piece that sports a particularly intricate bit of detail is a likely candidate for chemical stripping, because you don't disturb the shape of the wood itself, and the chemicals ensure a thorough strip if used properly. Chemical removers are also, on occasion, the only way to remove certain epoxy-type finishes that don't respond readily to the heat gun. And, as mentioned above, chemical strippers are often the "second stripping step" on certain projects, when varnish, old stain, and pastewood fillers remain in the pores of the wood after a heat gun has removed the varnish buildup.

The best chemical stripper is one that stays wet, which means its solvent doesn't evaporate quickly and so is able to soften and penetrate the finish below. Think of the action of a chemical stripper as the varnish curing process in reverse. As varnish dries, the solvents dissipate and the remaining solids form a hard membrane. When you cover that membrane with a good semi-paste stripper, the solvents (more powerful this time than they were originally) are reintroduced into the varnish, rendering it a liquid once again. The better your chemical stripper is at turning the varnish back into a soup, the more effective it is as a finish remover.

Granted, this method is the messiest and potentially most hazardous of the lot to use. But with the employment of a few clever tricks and a survivalist mentality, it can be invaluable as a means to a necessary end.

When stripping with chemicals you will need:
A good air-supplied respirator
Neoprene-coated gloves
Safety glasses or eyeshields
Proper, protective attire (no swimwear!)
Disposable chip brushes
A good chemical stripper

Lacquer thinner
Soft-medium Pepsodent toothbrushes
Nylon-bristle scrub brushes, varying sizes
A large, hard plastic tub (two, if possible)
Large paper buckets
Clean baby diapers
Hardwood scrapers, varying widths
3M Solvent Resistant masking tape
Waxed paper or Saran Wrap

Always before I address the how-to's of this medium, I try to impress upon people the importance of seeing to one's own health in handling chemical strippers. Peter Spectre and Mary Lou Dietrich's article in *WoodenBoat* No. 79 (Sept./Oct. '87) gives a fine rundown on self-preservation measures for this and other boatyard projects, and I recommend that every would-be refinisher have that copy of the magazine in his library. Solvent intoxication —especially —is nothing to be brushed aside as a transient joke. While it may not seem that breathing methylene chloride and other such vapors is truly dangerous in the short term, I would encourage even the most cavalier refinishers to consider the cumulative effects of such exposure. They are serious, and unnecessary when you consider the availability of products designed to intercept such real and truly immediate dangers. Do yourself a favor: Wear an air-supplied respirator, or at the very least wear a good vapor mask with fresh cartridges (the charcoal in these cartridges has a limited lifespan—take them off the mask between uses and store in an airtight container to keep them from becoming ineffective). And wear proper gloves and eye protection when working with chemical strippers or refinishing chemicals of any nature. If you won't do it for your liver, kidney, and central nervous system, do it for your future offspring; you can never be too sure what these things are doing to your gene pool.

Now for the how-to:

Though there is a standard way of doing things, the art of good chemical stripping is found in several nontraditional tactics. Most people think a chemical stripper works best if they brush on a marginal layer, let it sit a minute or two, and then at the first sign of bubbling or lifting start pushing at it madly with a putty knife. Wrong. Here's a variation on the theme that you won't likely find on the backs of the labels. If the piece can be taken off the boat, remove it. Substitute a large, hard plastic tub for the usual layer of newspapers. Lay the item flat in the tub and pour a liberal but not wasteful layer of stripper onto the piece, spreading (but not stroking) with a cheap bristle brush as you pour, getting into all the nooks and crannies. Make sure you have a somewhat thick, even coating of stripper over every square inch. Now cover the piece with a sheet of waxed paper and let it sit. Go call your mother —do anything that will keep you from fussing with the stripper for at least ten minutes. Then come back to it, remove the waxed paper, and anyplace the stripper has begun to dry out (which is evidenced by dryish-looking, yellow, crinkled patches), gently apply another layer of stripper. Continue in this fashion until adding stripper seems like spreading peanut butter over jelly. The coated areas should be completely sodden with no sign of yellow patches, an indication the varnish is completely inundated with solvent through all layers down to the wood.

Just to make sure this is the case, pour a little lacquer thinner in one spot and, with a soft- or medium-bristle Pepsodent toothbrush (this is the only brand I've found that doesn't melt in stripper right away), scrub gently. What you should discover beneath the soupy layer of goo is clean, unadulterated wood. If that is indeed the case, repeat this lacquer thinner scrub, on a grander scale and with a larger, nylon-bristle scrub brush for very large areas, over the entire piece. Scrub the stripper off the piece, gently, scrubbing just enough to dislodge the stripper and spent varnish from the pores of the wood, and adding more lacquer thinner to facilitate a washing process. Empty the melted dregs from the tub (cleaning it completely) into large paper buckets and repeat the lacquer thinner routine to clean all varnish and chemical residue from the woodgrain. If you're fortunate enough to have a second tub for the lacquer thinner bath, great. You don't have to waste time cleaning the first one, especially if you have more pieces to do. When you're finished, wipe down the piece with a lacquer thinner-soaked rag, preferably a prefolded baby diaper (clean, of course). If raising the grain is not a problem (I try, whenever possible, not to, as it requires a greater degree of sanding later on), and the stripper has a water-neutralization option, I rinse the piece in water instead of wiping down with the solvent-soaked rag. This results in the cleanest possible surface. When you do this type of rinsing, it doesn't hurt to go over the nooks and crannies with the toothbrush again to ensure that all the residue is indeed flushed from the recesses.

You may have noticed that I have not once mentioned using putty knives or scrapers. If you are within at least mail-order range of one of several good chemical strippers on the market, and you follow the above process, you should not need these cumbersome instruments, as they serve no purpose except pushing aside the slime that rests on the wood's surface. It is extremely important to use the nylon-bristle brushes to coax the finish from the pores and recesses, as this is the whole point behind using the chemical remover in the first place. If you feel you need some means of scraping away accumulated dregs before you begin the scrubbing process, avoid metal putty knives, which can gouge the wet wood, in favor of hardwood scrapers (available at fine woodworking shops). Above all, avoid hard-bristle brushes, especially the wire variety, and when scrubbing with the nylon brushes, be gentle. A heavy hand doesn't result in a cleaner wood surface, it only causes a more severely opened grain.

I have just described the process of chemi-cally stripping a piece that has been removed from the boat —perhaps a helm or the dreaded louvered door, or some other intricately carved piece of the portable variety. But what about a piece that cannot be so easily removed? At the risk of sounding as though I'm on 3M's payroll, have I got a tape for you! It's called Scotch Solvent Resistant Masking Tape #226 and is a crepe-paper backed polyethylene tape impervious to almost any solvent you can throw at it. To use it for a stripping project adjacent to a painted surface you don't want to ruin, follow the taping trick I described in the heat gun section (laying down first a strip of 3M Safe Release tape, then the solvent-resistant tape over that). If you are taping off gelcoat or some other surface where there is no risk of pulling up paint, the black tape alone is sufficient. When you've masked as closely as possible to the piece you want to strip, tape an apron of 4-mil plastic around the masking, tightly and closely enough to the first boundary to be sure the solvent and stripper can't leak underneath. Then proceed as above, being as controlled as possible about the runoff of lacquer thinner and chemical dregs while you work. If the piece is positioned vertically, substitute Saran Wrap for waxed paper, and press it flat against the stripper to ensure that it stays in place.

Naturally, this tedious masking process is one I'd resort to only if the piece couldn't be stripped to satisfaction some other way. If it's at all possible, strip most of the piece with a heat gun—wherever flat, open surfaces permit—and then do the rest with a chemical stripper, minimizing the mess.

One final word on chemical stripping —disposal. If you don't have a conscience to direct you on this issue, let the law be your guide. It is illegal to dump chemical waste of any kind into the waterways, down sewer drains, or into the abandoned pasture behind the toolshed. Call

Mahogany and Port Orford cedar, a striking combination.

your local dump and ask what they recommend as a means of proper disposal in your area. It's a small thing to do for the good of your one and only Earth, and we can afford little patience for people who violate this law of simple ethics on the feeble premise that "it's too much trouble."

Dry Scraping

If you have long rails or some other expansive area you feel warrants stripping to *beneath the surface of the wood* (the reason for choosing this method), dry-scraping can be the speedier way to strip under such circumstances. I hasten to say, however, that this method takes practice to perfect and is not something I would recommend to the occasional refinisher. Until you've spent quite a number of hours dry-scraping boats, your level of efficiency, combined with the ever-present danger of doing great damage to the wood, negates any perceived benefit in time or money. But for the person who wants to cultivate a full range of stripping talents, I think it's important to explore this mode of shaving off a finish. Just try to get a little time in at the "body shop" first.

You'll need a good, steel-bladed "hook"-style scraper, one made with high-quality steel that holds a sharp edge. It should have a handle designed so your secondary hand can be used for additional pressure and control. You'll also need a fine-mill file for resharpening. Unfortunately, some of the best steel scrapers I have ever seen were handmade and came from Sweden as treasured possessions of my sister. Short of a trip to some Scandinavian's toolshed, these magnificent examples of Swedish scraper technology cannot be acquired. We less fortunate types have to settle for whatever comes close at the local hardware store. Better still, this a good excuse to visit a shop that specializes in boatbuilding tools —if you need an excuse to visit such a wonderful place. See Chapter 16 for more specific recommendations.

Once you've managed to collect the perfect scrapers, doing the work is fairly uncomplicated. Holding the scraper at a correct angle to the wood, bearing down a bit, and pulling toward you is the standard operating procedure. When dry-scraping, it actually helps to pull at an angle slightly off the straight of the grain, as long as you're judicious about keeping the blade perfectly level. Leaning on the blade to one side or the other cuts a slash mark into the grain, which will require planing or extensive sanding later on. This defeats the purpose of dry-scraping, which is to cut a layer of wood off the surface along with the old varnish, thereby eliminating some of the heavy-duty sanding after the strip.

I would shy away from dry-scraping areas with design detail that might suffer. It's difficult to retrieve the symmetry of certain curved rails after they've been compromised by a scraper, and in these instances I would be more inclined to use a heat gun or even chemical stripping. It may seem a time-saver to rip down through to clean wood, but ultimately the time saved is reinvested in the more time-consuming reshaping process, and in occasional cases there is a loss of dignity to areas of special detail.

Dry-scraping is a project that proceeds more comfortably with a particle mask and gloves, and is best cleaned up with a vacuum, preferably the wet/dry variety.

A slight variation on this method of stripping is something I call "wet-scraping." I use this approach when the finish is extremely thin on a flat surface, and I don't need to scrape off a layer of the wood, such as a cedar deck that has weathered to the point of losing half its varnish. I wet down the wood until it is thoroughly soaked and then simply scrape off the remnants of the varnish. The wet wood releases the varnish more quickly than it does dry, and the scraping is easier. In fact, wood scraped this way needs a lighter scraping touch, or your scraper will begin ripping the grain. Follow the scraping with a bleaching, and you won't have to spend hours sanding off the weathered portion of the wood.

STRIPPING OIL FINISHES

As I've mentioned in Chapter 3, in our first year in the business, my sister and I contracted by telephone with a Kansas farmer to do the brightwork on his new Ingrid 38, *Kingsblood*. The hull had been trucked to the Midwest, where it was finished out, then trucked back to Seattle for launching and rigging. We were to do the brightwork while it was being rigged. The plan was to varnish everything except the decks, so we commenced sanding that first day to prepare the wood —which was filthy from its long haul on the interstate —for the new finish. After about an hour of arduous 80 grit scratching, we were shocked to discover that what we thought was dark ironbark was actually light chestnut teak! When the owner arrived on the scene later that day, we asked him what on earth he'd done to such relatively new teak to turn it so black. "Wahll," he started in his shy little Kansas drawl, "the people who built the boat said to put oh'l on the wood, so by golly that's what we did. We put ever kind of oh'l we could find on it: Crisco oh'l, dicscl oh'l, lemon oh'l —we even used lard." We stood there, mouths agape, until a merciful bystander stepped forward and informed us that, unless we wanted to spend the rest of our careers trying to remove the Kansas oil treatment, we should become acquainted with the Te-Ka A&B bleaching system.

The Te-Ka A&B bleaching system was designed for use on teak, but I have used it on everything from teak to mahogany to cedar to the real ironbark, and the result has been the same: in one easy treatment, it removes the oil finish, along with the mildew and other problems caused by simple exposure to Mother Nature. It will also remove a tired Deks Olje #2 coating, if what remains of that finish is not very thick. This is the only way to remove an oil finish

without sentencing yourself to a life's term of sanding, but you need to learn about the system's inherent dangers before you begin.

The company prints a warning on the label which reads "Te-Ka should be used only on teak and must not be applied on any other type of surface." This is their way of escaping liability for the havoc the bleach can wreak on things like paint, gelcoat, and metal surfaces, among others (including your skin). You can protect painted topsides, the boat's name, or any other vulnerable area by using what I call a bleaching skirt. This is an apron of 4-mil plastic (available at most hardware stores by the roll) attached at the base of the toerail below the scuppers (or just below the wood being bleached) with duct tape, encircling the entire boat or at-risk area. If there is a danger of pulling up paint, run a strip of 3M's Safe Release tape along the top edge where the duct tape would otherwise adhere directly to the hull, then attach the skirt as described. Before you commence bleaching, make sure you have a leakproof seal by spraying water along the top edge of the skirt.

If you're faced with bleaching oiled trims atop a painted house, things get a little dicier. Pieces that can be removed can be bleached on the dock with great ease, but handrails and other stationary trims are relegated to a more delicate treatment, specifically a careful "painting on" of the bleach with foam brushes. If you're neat enough about this (wiping the piece off after each step with a water-soaked terrycloth towel instead of rinsing wholesale), the piece should wind up sufficiently stripped of the oil finish and within an easy sanding of being ready for refinishing.

Burning the wood with the caustic solution can be avoided by remembering one little rule: Neutralize the hell out of everything and then, before you abandon the piece for the day, inspect for "bleed back": redarkening of a previously neutralized area. If you skip the inspection, it's almost a given that you will return the next day to little darkened spots where the "A" formula leached back out of some void and burned the wood. I always pick up an extra quantity of the "B" formula, which is the neutralizer, and apply it liberally.

If you're concerned about protecting nicely polished (or even nicely greened) bronze appointments, either remove them — if possible — or tape a watertight piece of plastic over them. If that can't be done, the worst thing you face is a polishing project. Anodizing, on the other hand, is a horse of a more vulnerable color, since the chemicals will score an anodized or aluminum finish. If it's not possible to cover the piece or remove it from the boat, give it a thick coat of carnauba wax before you bleach. Otherwise, you are doomed to permanent scoring — not a pretty sight.

You will need the following tools and materials for bleaching with Te-Ka A&B:

    Sufficient quantities of Te-Ka A&B, plus extra "B" (neutralizer)
    3M Soft (white) nylon tile scrubbers
    Large plastic funnel
    Soft-bristle toothbrushes, varying sizes
    Eye shields
    Construction rainsuit
    Nitrile gloves
    Deck boots (with no holes!)
    Kneepads
    Water hose long enough to reach farthest end of boat
    Spray nozzle for hose
    A source of fresh water
    Clean baby diapers

To prepare the whole boat for the bleaching process, make sure all ports are closed and locked, close and lock all hatches, cover all vents, pull as many lines as possible off the decks (pile them on top of the mainsail or anywhere above deck where they will not soak up the bleach runoff), and make sure all canvas covers are removed from their resident locations. Anything that can be removed from the boat, especially if it is not part of the bleaching project, should be taken off and set on the dock. Before you begin the actual bleaching, give the entire boat a good dousing and then check to make sure all drains and scuppers are clear for proper runoff during the project. If your boat leaks like the proverbial sieve, forget the whole thing. The damage that can be caused below by the bleach is not worth it. Better to solve the leaking problems first.

Personal protection from these chemicals is of utmost importance, since even a small amount of bleach can cause nasty burns on your skin. This is not meant to scare you off; the problems are easily avoided with a little common sense. For best protection, the get-up is as follows: nitrile gloves (anything else falls apart); eye shields of some sort if you are not already bespectacled (an absolute must, as a single splatter of this stuff can send you to the emergency room with serious eye damage); a lightweight pair of plastic overalls (construction rainsuits are ideal, and far cheaper than ruining your nice foulies); and deck boots. If you plan to spend much time at all on your knees, put your kneepads on under the rainsuit.

As with any new product, before you jump wallet-first into a large inventory of Te-Ka A&B, buy the pint set and test it on a small spot to make sure this approach is effective on your particular finish. When you've determined that it is, buy a quart set for each crewmember, then the balance of the quantity you estimate you'll need in the gallon sets, as they are less expensive by volume. It's important to work with the quart bottles, as the gallons are unwieldy. Be sure to take a funnel to the boat for refilling the work bottles.

In addition to reading the labels thoroughly and acquainting yourself with the basic application procedure, here are some little pointers that can help the job move along expeditiously:

It almost goes without saying, but logic and the cost of extra neutralizer dictate starting at

the highest point on the boat and working down. Otherwise you will find yourself constantly re-neutralizing areas you've already done as the runoff of the bleaching formula darkens completed areas.

If you are using Te-Ka for the first time, start with small, manageable areas while you learn the idiosyncrasies of the product. Nothing is more demoralizing than watching a large section burn away with the "A" formula because it took more scrubbing than you'd anticipated. Start small and work your way up to more expansive attacks.

Apply the "A" solution first, spreading it evenly with the nylon pad or your gloved hand (don't scrub, just spread), leaving no voids or

Gleaming bronze hardware sets off the well-varnished deck .

the finish will come off in a streaky, uneven fashion. If you are bleaching on a grand scale, have your helper minimize the runoff of un-neutralized formula by wiping down the runoff with a large cellulose sponge saturated with neutralizer (the "B" formula). Let the "A" solution sit until it has saturated the wood (rendering it alarmingly black), and then apply a second coating before you begin to scrub. When you've finished scrubbing, scrape aside most of the slimy goo, as it can hinder your neutralizing by not allowing the "B" formula to reach the wood quickly. As you apply the neutralizer, scrub lightly —especially around detail work where residue might be preventing the "B" formula from soaking through. As the neutralizer begins taking effect, the wood changes, almost miraculously, from the alarmingly black color to its natural golden tones. Any spots that are not sufficiently neutralized will remain dark; these should be given repeated squirts of "B" until they come up light. Give the neutralizer about ten minutes to do its job before you start rinsing it off. As you rinse, scrub the recesses gently to dislodge the stubborn scum.

Use soft white nylon tile scrubbers for flat expansive surfaces and long rails, and keep a range of small, soft nylon brushes —including soft-bristle toothbrushes —handy for getting into the less accessible areas. Don't scrub with a vengeance. This system's efficiency ratio is 75 percent chemical prowess to 25 percent elbow grease. Anything beyond a modicum of scrubbing is overkill and will result in added sanding time later in the project to plane down the ridgey grain. If anyone hands you a wire brush for use in bleaching or stripping wood, give it back and never accept refinishing advice from such a person again. Wood needs a gentle touch, not a brutal scrubbing, to come clean. Using a wire brush on even the hardest of woods is like washing your child's face with a Brillo pad!

To get your 75 percent rate of chemical efficiency, don't be a miser in your application of the "A" formula, which is the bleach, or the "B," which is the neutralizer. It's important to spread both evenly and generously. The system is only truly effective when it reaches the wood full strength, and will betray streaky application in a final presentation of a sketchily divested oil finish.

Water is your greatest ally in your battle against the dangers of bleach. If you are working alone, keep the hose running in a pattern that dilutes the runoff at all times. A jet spray nozzle on your hose is invaluable when it comes to purging the bleached dregs from the surface of the wood. Ideally, you should have a helper working with you whose sole function is to go around with the hose and keep things sprayed down (especially the hull). If this project encompasses a significant portion of the boat, "many hands make light work." If you're working solo, it's all too easy to leave the bleach sitting on the wood too long.

When you've completed the entire boat, or are finished for the day, spend about twenty minutes hosing down the wood with the jet spray nozzle to guarantee it is absolutely free of residual bleach or neutralizer. Then give the wood time to dry thoroughly (six to twelve hours, depending on the type of wood and the overall temperature) before commencing any further steps in your refinishing. If you've used this treatment on a teak deck and there are surrounding stretches of healthy, varnished brightwork, be sure to wipe the brightwork dry before leaving the boat for the day. This prevents water spotting of the finish.

Bleaching is best done on a calm, overcast day. If it rains, so much the better, though a full-on downpour can make things pretty uncomfortable for you personally, and can dilute the formula too much. If there is a strong wind, the project gets very difficult to control and ends up in the futile category. If the day is a sunny one, make sure you keep a fine spray of mist handy for remoistening the bleach if it tends to dry out as you're working.

A large bleaching job takes a tremendous amount of energy, so don't laugh when I stress the importance of preparing yourself physically for this project. Get a good night's sleep (don't attempt this job the day after the big office party), eat a good breakfast, and then get started early while you're full of energy. And make sure you pamper yourself with good repast and plenty of liquid refreshment (no social lubricants!) throughout the day. Also, if you're planning to bleach an entire boat, line up enough helpers to accomplish the task within one day. You will get your fill of this exercise within that amount of time, I assure you. If your bleaching is to include teak decks, I can't urge you too strongly to beg, borrow, or buy a pair of good kneepads to wear under your plastic overalls. Your knees will thank you.

Sanding Off A Finish

If you have, indeed, committed some despicable crime against humanity and repeated trips to the confessional have not cleared your conscience, I have a penance that will absolve you of your sins better than all the Hail Mary's in life: hand block sand the finish off your whole boat.

I hope that the only parts of the boat you'll be brazen enough to strip by this method are the ones not accessible by heat gun or scraper and that cannot, for whatever reason, be stripped chemically. For such undertakings, let me ease the pain with a few suggestions:

Refer to Part Three for information on the right sandpaper, masking tapes, and other items mentioned below. Bring your vacuum and a counter brush; you're going to need them to see where all your labors have gotten you. Be sure you have a sandpaper cutter on the job, wear nitrile gloves (unless you need to grind off your fingerprints, perhaps because your infraction has caught the attention of the FBI), and wear a good dust mask (unless you feel this would diminish the impact of the punishment).

Start with 60 grit and stay with it until you expose the wood. If the wood itself needs shaping (not for removal of weathering, but for recapturing a flat plane or intended curve), do that work with this same grit, then graduate to 120 grit to remove the scratches caused by the coarser abrasive. If the finish is very thick, sand through some of the buildup with 50-grit production paper first, then switch immediately to 60 grit once bare wood starts peeking through.

Sand with the direction of the grain unless absolutely impossible. Try to follow any cross-grain sanding with some grain-directional sanding as soon as you hit bare wood to remove the cross-grain scratches. If the area will be out of sight, don't be compulsive; cross-grain scratches are only a sin if they are visible.

To sand the finish from straight crevices or recessed areas, wrap the sandpaper around a four-sided steel cabinet scraper or any other thin, hard tool with a straight edge. To sand up to a vertical surface evenly without sanding against the grain, wrap the paper over the blade end of a wide putty knife and push the abrasive firmly toward the vertical border. Refold the paper often to maintain a sharp grit at the edge.

Keep recessed areas vacuumed while you sand—kind of the way the hygienist suctions out your mouth while the dentist is jackhammering away at your rotten molars. This keeps you from pushing debris back and forth instead of removing the finish.

Double-tape (thickness-wise) to mask all adjacent areas that could suffer permanent scratches from the heavy-grit paper. Even 120 grit will betray a wild thrashing, so spare the painted or gelcoated surfaces and get out the appropriate roll of masking tape.

And with that, you have the fundamentals of four sensible and one less-than-noble method of removing brightwork finishes. With luck, you won't have too much trouble determining which attack is most appropriate for your predicament and how you might combine techniques for optimum results.

Regardless of which stripping course you follow, remember that this phase of the project, while seemingly transient, is as vital to the outcome of the refinishing project as any of those to follow. Fudge on your stripping and you will pay later. Pay your stripping dues in the beginning, before they have a chance to start compounding interest.

8

INTERMEDIATE PREP WORK

*Art begins with resistance — at the point where
resistance is overcome. No human masterpiece
has ever been created without great labor.*
— Andre Gide

*B*rightwork refinishing is a three-act opera. In the first act, the evil villain is dispatched with hopes that he is never heard from again (the stripping); in the second act, the town is restored to order and made ready for a great celebration (the wood preparation work); and in the third act, the hero returns and the merry-making begins (the application of the new finish). Without the second act, the story would likely see the return of the villain sooner than hoped, and all that singing would have been for naught.

In the pursuit of truly fine brightwork, the one inescapable and most often verbalized fact is the importance of a good prep job. If you cut corners or hurry through any one stage of this middle act, you run the risk of shortening the life of the finish, not to mention compromising its appearance. While sanding stands out as the primary component of this phase, there are myriad "little things" that contribute to the total

picture, each simple and fairly straightforward, but nonetheless vital. These little things are like the singers in the opera chorus—without them, the tenor would eventually get pretty hoarse.

Intermediate prep work essentially entails working with the bare wood, and can be divided into three basic functions: shaping, repairing, and clarifying. "Shaping" refers to recapturing the original character or design of the piece you're refinishing. "Repairing" means restoring the surface integrity of the piece (this is from a cosmetic standpoint; structural repairs are a separate issue and should be addressed before you begin to consider the finish). And "clarifying" is the step that brings out the maximum potential beauty of the wood itself before a finish is ever applied.

In addition to this focus on bare wood, the intermediate prep phase involves some pre-varnish detailing steps that address problems attendant to the old brightwork finish. These are problems that have the potential to compromise the new finish, and they should be dealt

A cold-molded rowboat, finished bright.

with while you are still in "troubleshooting mode."

Sanding

Summertime in the marina would not be the same without the disquieting whine of orbital sanders filling the air. Like a swarm of locusts, Makitas and Porter Cables descend upon the sweet, fragrant stretches of hardwood and eat away at the fruited vessels until they've had their fill for another season. Unfortunately, many of these machines are being operated by people who do not realize what damage the sanders can do to areas surrounding their work.

The most ubiquitous bad note is the sound of a finishing sander pummelling away at an abutting surface. It's a banging that carries from one end of the marina to the other, and I cannot help but cringe whenever I hear it. I can just see in my mind's eye the brutal pockmarks the beating is leaving in its wake, and I know how bummed that person is going to be when he discovers, after he starts clearing away the sawdust, what damage he's done. The aftermath is a pathetic and demoralizing sight, especially when that surface is gelcoated fiberglass.

Before you ever start sanding, whether it's by hand or with a power sander, protect the vulnerable parts of the boat by masking them off. This takes little time and prevents the pointless havoc that can result from even careful working with abrasives. One swish of 60-grit paper is all it takes to leave deep, permanent scratches in paint and gelcoat. And that's by hand! I tape a double thickness —one strip stacked on top of another —of at least 1 1/2-inch masking tape where there is the danger of pockmarking an adjacent area with my Speedbloc; this provides an adequate cushion for the accidental blows from the sander. A single layer will usually suffice for protection from hand-sanding. I do this on cabin sides, topsides, even around stanchions that stand next to a caprail being refin-

ished. Learn, though, that the best protection is a firm hand on the sander; don't put this protective barrier to the test any more than you must. Tape only the area you think you will be sanding in about two hours, and then pull the tape off as you complete the sanding in that area, or before you leave for the day. You could tape each new little section as you go along, but this is more time-consuming in the end, and after a while, the tape starts refusing to stick to dusty surfaces.

The type of masking tape you use for sanding work should never be left on overnight, and I don't believe in wasting expensive long-term tapes on heavy- or medium-grit sanding projects that can shred the tape edges in a day's time. If you are masking a surface that is vulnerable to strong masking tape glue, lay a strip of 3M Safe Release tape on that surface first, under a second strip of regular masking tape.

Before you begin sanding, complete all your stripping. This discloses more accurate wood conditions, and in many instances you'll find you need to sand less than you'd first thought. When the stripping is finished, test one sheet each of the range of grits from 60 through 150. Take these to your boat and sand one small area (choosing the worst-looking spot) through the grits. You should get an immediate reading of which of the heavy-grit papers (60, 80, 100) best planes the wood to a flat, smooth surface and which of the finishing grits best clarifies the grain or removes the scratches left behind by the heavy paper. When you have a fix on the grit ranges germane to your needs, stock up on those papers.

Buy at least one of each type of sandpaper: a heavy paper for shaping and whittling down a wide open grain, and a finishing paper for the definition of the grain. This is a buddy system, and high-quality brightwork doesn't materialize when you skip either of these phases of sanding. Granted, many times a piece of wood can look just beautiful after a thorough 60-grit sanding; the grain markings are once again visible, the wood feels great. But the first coat of sealer makes a mockery of this seemingly perfect surface when it highlights all the scratches left behind by the heavy-grit paper. For that reason, sanding must always be looked upon as a two-part exercise, with but one exception. That notable exception is when you're working with a veneer, where you should work only with a finishing grit. Be very careful when testing on these areas, especially if you aren't sure how much hardwood depth you have to work with. I work backward when testing to find my veneer-sanding grits; I start at 220 grit and work through the coarser numbers.

When I'm working with solid pieces of wood, the standard rule of thumb is that if I shape and plane the wood with 60 grit, I finish-sand with 120; if I use 80 grit for shaping work, I finish-sand with 150 grit. Then, if I'm planning a wet-sanded sealer (as when I'm finishing teak), I choose 360-grit wet-or-dry paper to close up the pores and finally clarify the grain. If I'm planning to seal with a penetrating sealer (as on a piece of mahogany), I preface the application of that sealer with a 220 grit fine-sanding of the bare wood to clarify the wood's surface and close the pores. There are those who advocate sanding progressively through every single grit —say, 60, 80, 100, 120, 150, 180, 220 —to fair wood for a varnished surface. In the grand scheme, this is not only a waste of time and paper, but one of the great sanding myths of all time. If you put two pieces of wood side by side that have been sanded in these two different ways, you will be extremely hard pressed to discern a difference. Conserve valuable labor for use in the rest of the project, and don't fritter away your energies on such nonsense.

If you can't tell the difference between solid wood and veneers, put your sandpaper down right now. I will forever be reminded, when I think of veneers, of the rude awakening one poor woman had the first day she commenced refinishing her boyfriend's Cheoy Lee. I'm pretty sure the relationship ended that night. This sweet lady had probably never refinished anything more ambitious than the coffee-table top in her living room. After a couple of hours of work with her boyfriend's sander, she came over to where I was working in another boat, and with a very confounded expression on her face asked if I could help her with a little problem. She explained that she'd been sanding with 80-grit paper for all this time, by machine even, and yet the wood just seemed to be getting uglier—it had lost all its color. My heart sank. Sure enough, what had been a solid bulkhead of teak veneer was now a halo of teak veneer around a ten-inch gaping void, shining clear down through several layers of the plywood. I didn't know whether to laugh or cry; I wanted to help her sink the boat.

I wish I could tell you which parts of your boat are always veneer, and which are always solid, but it's not that simple. Probably the best way to ascertain whether the wood you're refinishing is a veneer, if you are in doubt at all, is to find a spot of end-grain on that piece and look for the plywood striations. This can take some real sleuthing sometimes, and on occasion you may not be able to find such an indicator. Don't gamble. Call the dealer or have someone more knowledgeable help you out.

If you are, indeed, working on a veneer, refrain from using an orbital sander. Even 220-grit paper on these high-speed sanders can blast through to plywood before you can say, "I didn't mean to do it." If you are building up many varnish coats, you can use a lightweight orbital (such as a Ryobi palm sander) to help plane down the varnish buildup after the fourth coat, but even then you must be cautious. Occasionally, especially on a brand-new boat where the veneer hasn't been touched before, you can get away with wet-sanding oil into the veneer, but only with papers of 400 grit or finer.

On solid wood, do all your machine-sanding

first, if possible, before you go back and start the handwork. When you're sanding "through the grits," (which means starting with a shaping grit, such as 60, and then moving to 120 for finish work), follow each area of machine-sanding with a hand-sanding with the same grit. This eliminates two-thirds of the sander swirls and leaves less work for the finer grits. Try to avoid detail-oriented areas with the orbital sander, as these lose their character with one unruly swipe, especially with the coarser grits of paper.

Your goal in sanding with the shaping grit should be twofold: to flatten the ridges of grain down so completely that a fingernail will not ripple when drawn crossgrain over the wood, and to "sculpt" the piece to recapture its original design. If it feels as though you can dip a nail even slightly into the woodgrain, it needs more fairing, but with the shaping issue direct-

ing your efforts as you work. Often, especially on boats that have suffered repeated bouts of neglect, areas such as grabrails reach such a whittled-down state as to be mere shadows of their former selves. At such points you must be conscious of the structural integrity of the piece, and ask yourself whether you might not be better served by replacing it.

Repeated sanding on a boat's smaller trims eventually compromises their intended shape. I liken this to the process of erosion along many of our shorelines, and in either case often wonder what things must have looked like fresh out of the factory. You don't always have to sand a piece to remove some types of surface problems. For instance, before you attack a piece of wood that, once stripped, is a collage of gray weathered spots on fairly decent-looking wood, consider bleaching, instead of sanding, the weathered spots out. This eliminates unnecessary loss of wood and leaves less actual sanding to be done in the prep phase of the project.

When working on flat surfaces or on long, straight rails of any appreciable width, it is important to maintain a perfectly flat, "fair" plane; otherwise, you can end up with a wobbly-looking surface that mocks even the best varnish job. To stay on this track from the beginning, after each machine-sanding use a hard sanding block wrapped with the current grit of paper to check for "wows." In other words, if you mow down the first expendable layer of wood with 60-grit paper on a half-sheet finishing sander, then follow that with a with-the-grain hard block sanding with 60 grit, inspecting for low spots and knocking down high spots until the piece is perfectly flat. Then, repeat the process in the same order (orbital machine/hard sanding block) with 120 grit for the finish-sanding work. It's a good idea on such surfaces to follow this course of action through all sanding that takes place, even between varnish coats, as this prevents the "wows" from creeping in and becoming "oh-no's" by the time you're through.

One area that tends to dip or wow more than most is any area surrounding a bung. These little darlings are typically harder than the chunk of wood into which they are set, and they respond more slowly to sandpaper. To guarantee that you don't create little recesses around your bungs, always sand a plugged area with the aid of a hard block, and then check your work afterward to confirm that the whole plane is flush.

In all your refinishing, but especially in the sanding phase of your work, it is essential to have good light. If you're working in a shop or shed or even under covered moorage; it's too easy to miss deep sanding scratches and surface blemishes that stick out like a sore thumb when the boat is finished and out in the sunshine. Supplement your lighting with inexpensive fixtures that can be moved around. The aluminum clamp-on variety is best, especially for setting up low-angle light.

To be sure your wood does not still harbor those deep sanding swirls or the scratches left behind by the heavy-grit paper, give it a good wiping with a clean rag lightly moistened with a slow-drying solvent such as mineral spirits before you apply the stain or first coat of sealer to the wood. The "wet wood" that results will mimic the look of the wood's surface when the finish is applied, and any flaws will present themselves prominently until the solvent dries. This is a particularly important thing to do when refinishing a softer wood such as cedar or mahogany, as the deep scratches are invisible on dry wood but blatantly visible under the final finish. (Such scratches look even worse when exaggerated by the application of a stain.) But it is important to be equally vigilant with such hardwoods as teak and oak. Incidentally, do not substitute water for the solvent in this test or you will raise the grain of the wood and have to sand the swollen cells back down before you can apply the finish.

You may notice that perfectly sharp corners or door edges are the first to break down or start peeling back after you've varnished. This is because realistically there is nothing for the varnish to hold onto at that corner. A quick "knockdown" with 150-grit paper is hardly noticeable and makes a huge difference in the longevity of the finish. Go around and do this all at one time, as a final sanding step, to ensure uniformity on all such edges.

If you must sand across the grain, make absolutely sure you follow with finish grits, even down to as fine as 220, otherwise the deep cross-grain scratches are an eyesore. Sometimes wrapping sandpaper around the end of a putty knife is a means to sanding recesses with the direction of the grain. Consider a trick like this before resorting to the uglier cross-grain technique.

Non-sanding Prep Steps

If you are refinishing wood that's waterstained, you should make a sincere effort to get those stains out. These discolorations are different from the harmless, bleachable weathered surfaces typical of such woods as teak in that they are a slightly pale shade of black and always go some distance beneath the surface of the wood. Black moisture stains are almost standard when dealing with non-oily woods (such as mahogany, oak, cedar, and spruce) that have been left too long at the mercy of Mother Nature. You rarely encounter them in teak unless the piece has harbored a puddle of water for so long that it is actually rotting.

The time to remove these stains is after the initial shaping work, at which point you'll have a better idea of the final wood surface you'll be refinishing, save that minute top layer you'll lose in finish sanding. The first step in removing what remains of the water stains is the application of an oxalic acid solution. For spot bleaching (if you just have a couple of little places that are troubling you), mix the necessary quantity of crystals with just enough boiling water to create a runny paste. This is tricky unless you have some means of heating the water right at the boat; otherwise, by the time you get your paste from the kitchen to the shop, it has cooled off and begun to recrystallize. For more wholesale removal of stains, mix enough bleach to do the whole piece, following this recipe: Mix 16 ounces oxalic acid crystals with 1 gallon very hot (almost boiling) water. Stir until all the crystals have dissolved, and then with a foam brush or small sponge immediately start painting the mixture on the wood, applying repeated coats until the solution is used up or until it cools off to the point where it begins to recrystallize. (Do not reheat the crystallized solution once it has begun to turn, especially in a microwave — which I made the mistake of doing once—as this will produce some very toxic fumes.) Allow this to sit on the wood overnight; the next day, if you are satisfied with the bleaching job, wash the bleach off with a neutralizing solution of 3 ounces borax to 1 gallon hot water, and then rinse thoroughly with fresh water. Actually, you can neutralize with borax, vinegar, or soda ash; they are all "basic," which is the key to neutralizing the oxalic acid. (Do not attempt to neutralize oxalic acid with solvents; this is not a proper neutralizing, and the acid left in the wood can later ruin the finish.)

If you want to make another bleaching pass at the wood, do not neutralize the day after the initial oxalic acid application, but instead apply another treatment of the hot solution and allow it to dry for yet another day, then do the neutralizing the following day. You can repeat this any number of times until you're satisfied with the condition of the stains, but if after the second treatment things aren't showing a significant degree of change, you are wasting your time with many more applications.

Certain waterstains are a fact of the brightwork, especially around end-grain at joints or surrounding bungs. These stains reach clear into the meat of the wood, having resulted from prolonged wicking of water at those sponge-like ends. If you hate the way these spots look, you have three options: Cut them out and scarf in a new piece; try to camouflage them with stain —lots of stain; or paint over them.

Anytime you are refinishing a piece that seems to exhibit a dramatic finish problem, try to determine the reason for the decline. Usually you'll find that the reason is simple neglect, but many times there is a specific culprit responsible for the ruined finish, and if you neglect to solve the problem — creating a way for the water to drain, for instance — the problem will reappear soon after you've gone to all the effort to clean it up.

If you have the luxury of finishing the brightwork on a new boat and that brightwork includes any doors or items that fit snugly into a frame, plane the edges of the doors slightly to accommodate the eight coats of varnish you will be applying. If you don't do this, you'll have a dickens of a time opening and closing those doors later. Check for drainage. I learned this lesson the hard way on a favorite client's Ocean 50. Louvered exterior locker doors sat in frames that were not set up for proper drainage, and when water seeped in it sat on the top of and underneath each door and quickly destroyed the varnish all around. The solution (once we'd identified the problem) was to plane the tops of the doors so that they sloped slightly outward, and to do the same with the lower edge of the frame, allowing water to drain back out rather than sit until it could create problems.

When you've completed the heavy-grit sanding on a piece (ideally on the whole boat), before you move on to the finer grits, there are some other things that should be tended to in order to ensure a beautiful and lasting finish. These have to do with restoring the surface integrity of the wood, and include filling voids in joinerwork, repairing or replacing chipped bungs, and cleaning up the surfaces where the brightwork meets the rest of the boat. If you skip these little details, not only will they be unsightly, but they will hasten the breakdown of your new finish. Take my advice and invest a little time fussing with these areas once the sanding is completed.

Filling voids and gaps that are too small to warrant scarfing in a new piece is easily done and gives you a smooth, uninterrupted surface to which varnish is more likely to adhere without premature "peeling back." Varnish doesn't stick well to all wood putty products. I have had the most success over the years using a concoction of two-part epoxy (Cold Cure—made by Industrial Formulators of Canada, Ltd.—is good, as well as a five-minute brand that comes in packets and is made by Hardman's) and some fine wood dust from the surface I'm filling. To be neat and efficient at this, collect your dust in a clean pa-

per cup (sand it off the wood with 220 paper — anything coarser nets too much sandpaper grit in the mixture); vacuum out the crack, and bathe it with lacquer thinner. Make sure the crack is absolutely free of loose grit and old varnish. Wipe down the surrounding area with lacquer thinner, and then tape a boundary along the edge of the crack with 1-inch masking tape, taking care not to overlap the inside edges of the crack. Mix up a small amount of the epoxy, add about a half teaspoon of dust to a tablespoon of the epoxy, stir well, and eat. No! Stir well and then with the aid of a popsicle stick or similar item, drizzle or press (depending on the way the piece lies or stands) the mixture into the crack until it fills up. It should take about thirty seconds for the epoxy to level out in the crack. If necessary, add more to top it off before the epoxy has too many seconds to set up. When the crack appears to be full, and before the epoxy begins to set at all, pull up your masking tape, taking care not to smear the excess over surrounding areas. If you don't get the tape up before the mixture has kicked (it takes on a stringy, rubbery appearance), let the whole thing sit until the epoxy is hard. If you try to pull the tape during that rubbery stage, you'll pull the whole shebang out—everything inside the crack—and you'll have to start over.

The important thing to remember when mixing your magic epoxy potion is that the wood dust is not just there to help the glue blend in with the rest of the wood—it's what gives the cement-like material the ability to flex. If you skimp on the dust, the filling may crack and break the first time the boat moves at all, and your efforts will have been in vain. If you add too much dust, the glue is too rubbery and doesn't stick well, so shoot for something akin to Goldilocks' favorite porridge, a mixture that's just right.

I save all my epoxy spots for one work session; it wastes time and epoxy to do them one at a time as you come to them. Mark the spots that need filling when you discover them during your sanding. Do this with a small piece of extended-use masking tape; then you won't miss a slew of them by trying to recall where they were later on.

Epoxies can provoke allergic reactions; take care that your skin is protected.

Other surface defects such as chipped or missing bungs should be tended to at this stage, and if you're recaulking something that will eventually be varnished or forms a seal next to a varnished edge, do that work now as well. Leaving these things for post-brightwork consideration often mars your new finish.

Replacing Bungs

When replacing bungs, pay attention to one oft-neglected detail: the direction of the grain in the bung. Be sure the grain runs parallel, not perpendicular, to the grain surrounding it, and if you are cutting your own, try to cut them from a piece of stock that is similar in type and color to the area receiving the new bungs. If there is a variety of hues to deal with, cut an assortment of bungs to cover that variety and arrange them accordingly. If you can't tell what color the bung will be when it's varnished, dip it in some mineral spirits, wipe a little solvent over the piece it's slated to match, and compare the two.

Here's a technique for removing damaged bungs: Drill a pilot hole in the bung, then drive a screw. Once the screw tip fetches up on the fastener head, additional turning will force the bung upward.

The classic way to get a good seal on a new bung is to make it fit so tightly that it seals itself at the first whiff of marine air. The real masters can do this in their sleep. Some people resort to dipping the bung in varnish before they tap it into place; others like to glue them in with Resorcinal. That's okay. What isn't kosher is setting bungs in epoxy —not unless you know you're never, ever going to need to get to that fastener again.

Preparatory Detailing

If the last person who did the brightwork on the boat left a bank of encrusted varnish scum, clean it up. This not only prepares your adjacent surface for a good varnish bond, but eliminates later detailing that could disturb that bond once it is in place. Razor blades are man's greatest invention when it comes to cleaning up most of these areas —try them first.

When you have carefully scraped away everything that will respond to the razor blades, wipe those areas clean with mineral spirits. If they are still a mess, and the surface is fiberglass, consider a treatment with Pintoff 299, a chemical stripper formulated by Interlux for use on fiberglass. A moderate application, allowed to sit for a couple of minutes, and a gentle scrubbing with a medium Pepsodent toothbrush should dislodge any embedded varnish scum. Clean off the residue with a rag moistened with mineral spirits, and then rinse the area with water before you resume the fine-sanding that remains to be done on the brightwork.

If your boat has old oil drips on the fiberglass,

detail them off with a very controlled application of Te-Ka A&B followed by a thorough rinsing. If you are not familiar with this product, see Chapter 7 on removing finishes. Here again, a medium toothbrush aids the cause, especially if the drips reside in nonskid areas. Pay close attention to all the caveats that go along with the use of this product; it is very caustic and is not appropriate for use around certain surfaces.

Clean Up the Dismantled Fittings

If you have the opportunity, take home all the fittings that are tucked into those Ziploc bags and begin the cleanup, so that by the time the boat is varnished they are ready to go back on. This is the perfect rainy Saturday or evening project, down in your basement with a toothbrush and some stripper for varnish-encrusted items, or some Te-Ka A&B for oil-slopped pieces. Putter away at these, and then when they're cleaned up, give them a good polishing with some Liberty Polish and return them to their plastic bags until it's time to reassemble the boat. If they need new fasteners, make a run to the hardware store with your collection of little bags and buy what you need, immediately placing the appropriate screws in the bag with their respective fittings.

This labor-intensive intermediate prep phase can be the most daunting of the three "acts of the opera." It is where people often give up and turn the project over to someone else, usually a professional. Don't do it! I know it's hard work, but it does not go on forever, and right around the corner lies the tangible proof of your efforts. Just keep reminding yourself how heart-stoppingly beautiful the wood will look after that first coat of finish is on. Such thoughts are the perfect carrot. Keep plugging away.

TOOLS AND MATERIALS FOR INTERMEDIATE PREP

Orbital finishing sander
Shop vacuum with brush nozzle and crevice attachments
Sandpaper cutter
Counter brush
Razorblade scraper with fresh blades
Hard sanding block
Clamp-on light fixtures
3M Fre-Cut sandpaper in appropriate range of grits
Masking tapes (inside Ziploc bags)
Nitrile gloves
Firm sanding sponges
Dust masks
Safety glasses
Large paper grocery bags
Oxalic acid
Borax
Foam brushes (2-inch to 3-inch)
Mineral spirits
Baby diapers
Five-minute epoxy and stir sticks

WEATHER

Nice and dry. If it's raining or even misting, go see a matinee or visit some long-forgotten friends.

ATTIRE

Shoes are good; a matching pair of britches and a shirt will keep the neighbors from talking.

CREW

Rope anybody you can into the sanding, unless of course that "anybody" is your totally inept brother-in-law, in which case you have someone for the all-important job of fetching snacks.

9

THE VARNISHING PRELUDE

Tis a lifelong toil till our lump be leaven—
The better! What comes to perfection perishes.
Things learned on earth, we shall practice in heaven:
Works done least rapidly, Art most cherishes.
                                    —Robert Browning

As we take each deliberate step through the refinishing experience, we must be mindful of that pentimento factor touched upon at the beginning of this book. From here on through the final coat of varnish, we create the concentric skins of the proverbial onion, those layers that when peeled back will tattle on us. This is not a time to be concerned with the consumption of time. It is the time to linger, to indulge immodestly in those passions that have as yet seemed unrequited.

Once you have disrobed the wood completely and sanded it to a finish stage, there are a number of treatments that can prepare the bare wood for the new varnish. Many people think they have to do them all, but only one is really necessary.

Fillers

Many people use a pastewood filler to top up the grain of the wood before the sealer or first coat of varnish is applied. The use of this filler may eliminate the need for a couple of coats of varnish, but the tradeoff is often ugly, opaque grain markings, even when the filler comes in a stain formulation. Take my advice, and don't do this to your wood. Bite the bullet, and plan to put on the necessary number of varnish coats. If you're going to seal your wood with a wet-sanded oil-type sealer, you'll be filling the wood pores anyway with the wood's own sawdust, and you'll get a much better surface without the offensive-looking grain. I dislike this pastewood filling step so much, I won't even tell you how to do it. You'll have to buy someone else's book if you want to go that route.

Staining

Another pre-varnish treatment is staining. If you feel evenness of color is vital to a piece of brightwork, staining the piece is the means to that end. And as long as I am holding forth here,

I will say that I don't understand some people's preoccupation with "monochromatic brightwork," which is usually at the heart of the decision to stain all the wood on a boat to match. Woods as they exist in nature, even planks cut from the same tree, are not identical in color. If they were I think we'd all be a little bored, as this variation in hue is one of the fascinating elements of working with woods. When I see a boat that has been subjected to the "one color fits all" refinishing scheme I am reminded of the gorgeous cherrywood rocker my paternal grandmother handed down to my mother when she married my dad, and which in the mode of the day my dear mother quickly painted pea green to match the room in which it sat (much to my grandmother's horror then and to my mother's regret not long thereafter, when it was no longer the stylish look.)

If staining is not something that actually solves some problem with your brightwork, maybe you should consider how beautiful the wood will look sporting its natural shades, and emphasize those variations in color with the application of varnish.

There are, however, occasions where staining is the traditional treatment or indeed the solution to some unsightly problem. For example, if a section of Philippine mahogany has had structural repairs, and the new pieces that have been scarfed in give the boat a patchwork-quilt look, staining is a way of tying things together. From the standpoint of tradition, some classic runabouts were built with an artistic eye to combinations of stain colors, from one section to the next. Restoring one of these beauties dictates that the original stain specifications be followed, if one is attempting to do the right thing by the boat. In these circumstances, I have seen boats that wear their makeup quite splendidly, and I can't imagine them going out "sans rouge."

To apply a pigmented stain, prepare the wood to a fine-sanded surface (180 to 220 grit), making sure that your last sanding was by hand. Sanding by hand to this fine a grit eliminates deeper sanding scratches and swirls left behind by heavier grits, and clarifies the pattern in the grain, which will then be more distinctive beneath the stain. Make sure the wood is smooth and dry before you begin the staining. If the project is outside and not under some sort of cover and you sanded the night before, the dew has probably raised the grain. If this is the case, sand again with the last grit, by hand, to knock the grain down before you commence staining.

Before you open the can of stain, shake it vigorously to disperse the settled pigment. Then, when you open it, check with a stir stick to see that none of the pigment is still stuck to the bottom of the can. If the stain has been sitting in your shop long enough, even if it has never been opened, the settled pigment can harden in the bottom of the can. If this is the case, treat yourself to a new can of stain, or you will end up applying a lot of oil and solvent and not very much color. (It's not a bad idea from the standpoint of time management to check this before the day you plan to do the work, in case a new can needs to be bought.) If, after shaking, the bottom of the can seems fairly devoid of pigment, the stain is good; continue stirring the stain every few minutes during application to guarantee evenness of color, as the pigment will continue to settle during the operation. It isn't necessary to transfer the stain to another container for the work, as you can't really hurt it by dipping the brush into the can. If you want to, though, pour the whole can of stain into a wide-mouth pint Mason jar, and instead of stirring you can then easily screw the lid on and give it a shake from time to time. Either way, write yourself a big note that says STIR ME UP! and attach it to the container, otherwise it's easy to forget to do it.

You can apply the stain with anything that will transport it from the can to the brightwork surface without leaving a trail of drips. I prefer foam brushes; some people use rags. I think using foam brushes results in a deeper, more uniform application of color, and I encourage you to follow suit. Once you've brushed the stain on, allow it to penetrate for anywhere from two minutes to a maximum one-half hour, depending on the climate. Do not allow it to dry out. When it has been absorbed to the desired extent, buff the excess off with a clean baby diaper until the surface sports a uniform shade and all residual stain is wiped up. If you wish a deeper effect, repeat the above as many times as necessary. I must warn you, though, that repeated applications of stain only serve to muddy the natural look of the grain, and eventually a lot of stain pigment begins to look like a paint job. Be conservative, unless you are trying to hide something, in which case you *should* consider painting.

As you work, clean any spills immediately with a diaper and mineral spirits. When you are finished, inspect all hardware and adjacent areas for stain smears, and clean those off the same way. Allow the stain to dry no fewer than 12 to 18 hours before applying a first coat of sealer or varnish. If you rush a sealer or new finish onto newly stained wood, it is likely the undried stain will contaminate the finish and prevent it from drying, or bleed into the first coat of finish.

If you are staining for the first time, it's always wise to start on a small, inconspicuous piece. If you end up applying the stain too heavily, you can quickly, before it dries, bathe it with some lacquer thinner and wipe it clean with a diaper. It will still show a bit of a tint, but it gives you a starting point from which you can try again in about half an hour. The key to second chances in staining is not allowing the stain to dry out appreciably.

When the job is completed, do not discard stain-soaked rags, but take them to your shop and hang them up to dry. Then throw them away. Otherwise, they are a potential fire hazard, as the oil content in the undried stain makes them combustible.

TOOLS AND MATERIALS FOR STAINING
Appropriate stain
Foam brushes in various sizes
Mineral spirits
Clean baby diapers
Stir sticks
Proper waste receptacle (for foam brushes only)
Eye shields
Respirator or charcoal mask (if indoors)
Nitrile gloves
Good ventilation (fan to draw fumes)

WEATHER
It need only be dry; can be cool or warm; windy is bad.

ATTIRE
Something in a tasteful plaid flannel is always nice, especially during cooler months.

CREW
Staining is easy to do alone, but it goes faster with helpers who know what they are doing. Sloppy helpers should be assigned to clean-up duty.

Sealing

"Why can't I simply apply the varnish now?" you may ask. Because varnish needs an anchor to the wood, and a sealer, which penetrates the surface of the wood more readily than full-strength varnish, provides that anchor. So, be prepared to seal your wood, whether pastefilled or stained or not, before you apply the first true coat of varnish. Sealing is the only nonoptional pre-varnish treatment.

FOUR APPROACHES TO SEALING WOOD
1) *Apply a commercial "wood sealer" formula.*

A sealer is not itself a finish, and no amount of Madison Avenue wizardry should convince you otherwise. A typical commercially packaged sealer is a very dilute version of varnish: oil, resin, and solvent. It's heavy on the solvent, which means when the solvent has dried all that remains on the wood is a minimal coating of solids from the oxidized oil and resin. The only time I would recommend using such a sealer is when it is recommended specifically by the manufacturer as the "must-use" sealer to precede its brand of varnish. None of the varnishes I use requires the use of such a sealer, and I prefer the following sealing options.

2) *If you are concerned about filling the grain before you varnish, wet-sand with a light Tung oil formula.* This is a richer-looking, far more flattering alternative to pastewood filling. It accomplishes the desired early leveling of the grain, since it fills the grain with a paste consisting of oil and the wood's own sawdust, and it helps speed you along to a level varnish finish that much sooner. This is my favorite way to seal teak.

To seal wood this way, turn to Chapter 10 for instructions on applying an oil finish, and follow the guidelines at the end of that chapter that deal specifically with applying the oil as a wet-sanded sealer for varnish.

3) *If you don't care about filling the grain prior to varnishing, seal with a dilute coating of the varnish you plan to use.*

This is the standard approach I take with most woods other than teak (with the exception of some mahogany projects), and is one used most universally by refinishers around the world. This is a foolproof sealer in terms of compatibility with the varnish that is to follow it, because the varnish is virtually identical to the ingredients you just used for sealing.

To seal with this mixture, first fine-sand wood that has already been prepped (to a 150-grit stage) with 220-grit paper, to remove the last of the 150-grit scratches and to clarify the pattern of woodgrain. Prep the boat as if for varnishing (remove every speck of sanding dust), and then mask everywhere appropriate. Thin your varnish 35 to 50 percent with the manufacturer's recommended fast-drying companion solvent. Make sure the varnish and solvent are well mixed (rock the bucket; don't shake or stir) and apply at once. Make sure you keep a supply of clean rags and thinner handy when you apply this sealer, because the mixture has a tendency to run at this viscosity. Allow the sealer to dry at least 12 hours, and then apply your first coat of varnish without sanding.

Before you proceed with this sealing option, I would recommend reading Chapter 11 as well as the general information on varnish in Chapter 17. This added information can help get you on the right track for the varnishing job that ultimately follows the sealing of the wood.

4) *The boiled linseed oil saturation technique, a special way to seal mahogany.*

This is one of the most beautiful finishes you could ever apply. African and Honduras mahoganies have grain markings that, when saturated with oxidized oils and finished with varnish, will look so three-dimensional they fairly dance in the sunlight. This finish is not for everybody; it involves some tedium and requires great patience to apply the sealer, and on woods that are just a little too dense, it will sometimes not absorb or dry sufficiently. But on boats where it works, it's well worth the price of admission.

Finish-sand to a 220-grit finish and prep the wood as specified for the dilute-varnish sealer above, but don't bother with masking until you get to the first actual varnish coat.

To seal wood this way, you need a warm environment or a sunny day, or the oil takes too long to dry and runs the risk of not drying at all. You need boiled linseed oil, mixed two parts to one with a good, light Tung oil finish (Daly's SeaFin is what I normally use). If you want a faster drying oil, add a small quantity of japan drier. Experiment with the japan drier to get a feel for the drying time it eliminates from the oil mixture; a tablespoon or two per pint is the general range. When you have your formula settled on and the weather is beckoning, apply the oil to the wood. Each coat, painted on with a polyfoam brush, is allowed to dry to the touch (requiring from 15 minutes to 2 hours, depending on the temperature, the number of coats that have already been applied, and the ratio of japan drier and SeaFin to linseed oil), then another coat is applied without doing anything to the earlier coat. This is continued until at least six coats have soaked in. Ideally, the project should begin early in the day so that the entire soaking can be accomplished by the end of that day. At the worst, it should take no more than two days; if it goes more slowly, the mixture is not formulated well enough to dry properly or in a timely manner, or the temperature is too low, or you are simply doing too much dockside visiting and not paying close enough attention to your project.

If you do get all your oil coats on and they seem to have dried sufficiently, proceed with the final coat; as soon as you've applied it, wet-sand it with 400-grit wet-or-dry paper, then buff the surface smooth with a clean, coarse rag (a commercial shop rag is perfect), rubbing delicately in a circular fashion. If enough time remains in the sun's day, repeat this last procedure (oil and buff) to ensure a well-saturated grain. Allow the sealed wood at least a day for the final oil coat to cure, and then very lightly, with 220-grit paper, sand the built-up oil surface to prepare for varnish. The dried oil will be very soft, so be gentle with it. Don't sand vigorously or sand so much that you break through to the wood, or you will end up with a blotchy look under the varnish. If the sanding residue seems to roll up like tiny worms, don't be alarmed; this is normal. Vacuum well, wipe down the oil

lightly with a mineral spirits-moistened (not soaked) baby diaper, and allow the sanded surface a couple of hours to rest while you tape and prepare for the first coat of varnish.

SEALING TO OUTSMART MOTHER NATURE
If you have prepped the boat to the point of just being ready to seal the bare wood and the weatherman predicts rain the next day, give yourself a little labor insurance by forcing yourself to quickly apply a coat of the oil or sealer to all areas that are exposed to the potential rain. Don't bother wet-sanding the oil or masking for the sealer; this is considered emergency sealing, and your first concern is getting something on the wood to keep it from absorbing unwelcome precipitation before you can get around to doing a proper job. When you get back to work, you can pick up where you left off. Those areas that got the coat of protective oil will just be that much better protected for having the preliminary coating.

OILING

Everything is soothed by oil because it smooths every part which is rough.
—Pliny the Elder

Are you one of those hopeless romantics who thinks an oil finish is just about the most sensual thing there is to touch in life? The only thing I have found that approximates that smooth feeling is my baby boy's bottom, after he's all bathed and powdered up. Unfortunately, an oil finish is not one I can recommend for the average exterior stretch of brightwork, since it is as temporary as the size of my son's breeches.

Many people lust after an oil finish not for its touchability, but for the perception that it is easier to apply and maintain. For those misguided souls, I would recommend turning back to Yacht Refinishing Commandment No. 3: "Understand thy chosen finish." A proper oil finish (proper being the operative word here) requires all the same labor-intensive surface prep as varnish. And any oil finish, beautiful or otherwise, does not last beyond a month or two without at least monthly refresher coats. The only exceptions to this rule are boats that live underneath canvas covers and boats that rarely leave their enclosed moorages.

I have given this speech in every class I've

Herreshoff 12 1/2s in a Maine harbor.

taught, and to every client who's asked for such a finish, and I have always been amazed at how many people prefer to see for themselves—as though I would be kidding about something so sacred! But see for themselves they do, and invariably they return to varnish, always a little bitter for the experience.

If you are one of those lucky exceptions to the rule, you might get away with an exterior oiling if your brightwork is teak or ironbark. Any other woods, regardless of moorage conditions, should really have a varnish finish to keep water from wicking into joints and causing irretrievable water stains.

An interior oil finish, however, is a horse of a different color. I can't think of a wood that is not a candidate for an interior oil finish, though certain woods such as Philippine mahogany are easier to maintain when varnished. But if you are trying to decide between a satin varnish and a rubbed-oil finish, I would say that having an oil finish inside your boat is a wonderful choice, and when done properly can feel positively magnetic. The big advantage in applying oil to woods that are not exposed to the elements is that once finished, they stay that way, with an easy annual refresher to restore the luster.

Most people think that oil is simply brushed on and left to soak in, or worse, wiped on with a rag and called good enough. These are people who will never know the thrill of a true rubbed oil finish. To apply an oil finish, first prepare your wood as instructed in previous chapters to a finish stage of sanding. That includes all the other prep phases as well, which should have you staring at perfectly smooth, healthy wood surfaces throughout the boat, as well as clean adjacent surfaces.

Mask around all brightwork areas with regular 1-inch masking tape, unless the adjacent surface is painted, in which case you should use low-tack safe-release masking tape. This masking will not prevent the oil from seeping underneath, so you must be vigilant with a wipe-up rag as you work. The purpose of masking is to protect the adjacent surface from sandpaper scratches as you wet-sand the oil. You may think you can be careful enough as you work, but it is very easy to leave hundreds of very obvious scratches in your wake during this type of sanding, scratches that only become obvious at cleanup time. Masking at the start is much less work than repairing the damage later.

To set up for the project, cut up a supply of 400-grit wet-or-dry sandpaper into quarters; fold some of these into tri-folds and save the rest for wrapping around the foam sanding sponge. If you plan to do any of the wet-sanding with the aid of the Ryobi, cut some sheets into sixths.

Have a quart of mineral spirits and a clean baby diaper handy for accident patrol; any drips that are allowed to sit until they dry will have to be removed later by more drastic means. Transfer your oil from the quart can it comes in to a plastic squirt bottle with a reclosable tip; this makes handling the oil a much neater proposition. And set up a double-thickness grocery bag near your work for disposal of spent sandpaper.

Wear nitrile gloves—rubber gloves will fall apart from exposure to the solvents in the oil formula—and make sure you have proper ventilation. The 3M charcoal filter mask #9913 is very effective, but if you're working outside, masks aren't usually necessary.

With a foam brush, paint the first coat of oil on the wood, being conservative in your application—a little bit of oil goes a long way. If you oversaturate the foam brush, you'll have a flood of oil running all over the place the first time you set it down on the wood. Allow this first coat to soak completely into the wood and dry to the touch. Unless it's freezing cold, this should take about twenty minutes. When the wood seems to have lost its greasy feel, repeat the first application entirely. When the oil is again dry to the touch apply a third coat to a manageable section, an area that can be sanded and rubbed within the amount of time that the paste stays workable. Start out small if you aren't sure of your speed, and work up from there. Allow this coat to soak in for a couple of minutes and then wet-sand the oil into the wood, sanding with the grain, until the mixture of oil and sawdust becomes a difficult paste. Be sure to turn or change sandpaper often, or you are not working with the benefit of good sanding grit.

Allow the paste to sit until it just begins to feel tacky; this will vary with the temperature, but will be around three to five minutes at the most, usually. Then, with a clean rag, buff off the surface paste in a circular fashion, taking care not to rub the paste out of the woodgrain. If you are working next to fittings or into cor-

ners, be certain to clean the thick residue off those areas and out of the crevices where it has a tendency to accumulate, otherwise these areas will show up later as muddy encrustments. A trick here is to wrap a single thickness of the shop rag or diaper around a putty knife and run it into and along crevices and corners where the paste may build up.

When you've wet-sanded the third coat of oil and rubbed it down, give it about an hour to dry. When the surface feels relatively oil-free, brush on another penetrating coat and allow this to dry for about 30 minutes. After this fourth coat, apply a fifth and repeat the wet-sanding process used before, except (very important) substitute 600-grit wet-or-dry paper for the 400 grit used earlier. Wet-sand with this paper (turning often to maintain a sharp grit) until the paste becomes almost tacky and difficult to work with. Allow this to sit about a minute or until it is very tacky (but not dry) and then buff off the residue, again in a circular fashion wherever possible. If you get distracted and the oily paste has dried so much that it is impossible to buff, simply add a little oil to the surface, which will return the paste to a workable state.

When I'm giving an unfinished piece of wood this oil treatment, I generally apply a minimum of four wet-sanded coats of oil, and after the second wet-sanding I allow at least a couple of hours cure time between coats. If the finish is being applied to exteriors, saturate the wood with an extra penetrating coat of oil and let it dry after the third and fourth wet-sanded coats are each rubbed down. This forces more oil into the wood, gives it more protection, and adds longevity to the finish. If you're looking for that absolutely magnetic smooth finish in your interior, you can always sand the last coat or two with 1,000-grit wet-or-dry paper (available usually only at auto body supply stores), but I think this is a step more appropriate for a hand-made cribbage board than for an entire cabin interior.

If you're working on a flat surface (a table or bulkhead, for instance), it sometimes speeds things to use a Ryobi orbital palm sander (with the 400-grit paper) for the first wet-sanded coat. This sander is ideal because it has a flat, hard rubber pad that keeps its shape. When loaded in multiple sheets, it eliminates a great deal of paper-handling time, not to mention expenditure of energy (the human variety). Just be cautious about using it on veneers, since oversanding can cut through the top layer in a hurry. When moving up to the finer grit, eliminate the Ryobi on flat surfaces but wrap the paper around a foam or cork sanding block for uniform and speedy wet-sanding.

Allow yourself about an hour at the end of the day to linger for what I call "bleed back patrol." As the buffed surface dries, little shiny dots of oil will bleed back out of the pores, and if they are not buffed out while they are still wet, they dry to a permanent shine. These sparkling freckles are very unsightly, and if they survive after your final coat they will need to be wet-sanded out with another final coat. Working in a warm environment keeps these spots to a minimum, as the oil dries more quickly and the majority of oversaturated pores will easily present themselves within an hour after you've stopped buffing.

Applying maintenance coats is the easiest part of the deal. Use extra-fine bronze wool (never steel wool) to rub oil into the wood, working with the direction of the grain, allowing the oil to penetrate for a few minutes. Before it gets too tacky, buff the wood clean and dry. If it's been a while since the wood was last oiled, it may require a couple of coats to restore the original color and sheen. But the pores of the wood, by this time, are well filled and sealed, and there should be little or no incidence of bleed back. So even if you're doing multiple coats, refreshers are a quicker process all round.

So, there you have one of the sweetest treatments there is for a wood surface —an oil finish.

Enjoy the very rewarding process of applying it to woods on the less vulnerable interior of your boat. And enjoy its sensual beauty without becoming a slave to such passions.

A note of caution: When you've wrapped up for the day, never leave oil-saturated rags in a pile, whether on the boat or in your shop. The term "spontaneous combustion" comes into play rather quickly in these circumstances. I have witnessed more than one boat fire as a result of such carelessness, though never through my carelessness, I'm relieved to say.

A Wet-sanded Oil Sealer for Application Before Varnish

A great way to seal wood before you apply the first coat of varnish is to wet-sand oil into the bare wood, much the same way described above. On oilier woods like teak, instead of using 400 grit on the first wet-sanding, use 360-grit wet-or-dry paper. After the first wet-sanded coat, you stop with the oil and move on to varnish. It is especially important to make sure all the paste buildup in crevices and around fittings is cleaned off, because it will look terrible lurking under the new varnish finish.

TOOLS AND MATERIALS FOR OILING BARE WOOD
1-inch 3M #2040 masking tape
Single-edged razor blades in a razor blade
    scraper
360-, 400-, 600-grit 3M wet-or-dry sandpaper
Mineral spirits or lacquer thinner
Clean baby diapers or commercial shop rags
A quality Tung-oil formula (transferred to a
    plastic squirt bottle with a closable tip)
Nitrile gloves
Safety glasses
Disposable 3M charcoal masks (#9913)
Polyfoam brushes in an assortment of sizes
Fine bronze wool
Sanding sponges

Leak-proof trash receptacle (for spent
    sandpaper only)
Sandpaper cutter
Ryobi palm sander
Narrow putty knives

WEATHER

If the project takes place inside the cabin, the
only condition that could complicate things
would be a hurricane, in which case I recommend postponing to another day. It helps, in
colder seasons, to work in a nicely warmed
environment, so stoke up the safe, out-of-the-
way electric heater for those occasions. And
then make sure you made provisions for absolutely proper ventilation. Otherwise, you could

Cedar planking, ash stem, and a gunwale of cedar or
cherry sealed with varnish.

be working inside a floating bomb.

ATTIRE

Anything that isn't too ripe, since you'll likely
be working in pretty enclosed quarters and be
subjecting those around you to the benefits —
or lack thereof —of your laundering program.

CREW

Easy to do alone; assistants provide a good
audience for old war stories. Inept helpers
should be put in charge of car washing up at the
parking lot.

VARNISHING

Genius is nothing but a greater aptitude for patience.
— George Louis Leclerc de Buffon

*I*n his 1903 volume on paint and varnish technology, A.H. Sabin remarks rather poignantly at the tenacity of varnishes in antiquity, especially those still in uncorroded condition on the Egyptian mummy cases, and he wonders at the dilemma responsible for modern dissatisfaction with varnish. Do we recognize our own culpability in his lamentations? "The most likely criticism of the evolution of varnish is that, as varnishes made now do not last but a few years, it appears that we have lost the art known to the ancients. I reply, we have not lost the knowledge, but we have lost the patience necessary to the use of the most permanent and durable preparations."

And in her wonderful book, *The Art of the Painted Finish*, Isabel O'Neil sums up one of the beginner's great downfalls in a bluntly honest assessment. "I plead that those who share my admiration, who find beauty in painted surfaces, and who desire the pleasure of rendering them for creative satisfaction, will give themselves a 'time for learning.' Adults have so little patience with themselves and dogmatically demand an immediate expertise. This is the epitome of arrogance."

Patience, indeed, is the key ingredient in the varnisher's pot. Learn to apply your varnish with tender, loving patience, and it will reward you with years of faithful service.

If you have patiently and thoroughly removed all traces of the old finish and sanded and prepared your wood as instructed in the preceding chapters, you should be ready for what I see as the zenith of this humble art—applying the new finish. Regardless of whether your wood is now stained and sealed, or sealed with a wet-sanded Tung-oil application, or just sealed with a dilute coat of the varnish you have chosen to use, the application of the varnish finish from here on is the same for all circumstances. The diverse families of wood and presentations thereof converge at this point to follow a single, simple path of varnish application. You are about to build the varnish foundation that will serve you for many years, as long as you keep the top coats refreshed.

Preparing to Varnish

If I'm working on a project that encompasses a good deal of brightwork and the boat still seems a bit dusty from all the initial sanding and prepwork, after the wood is sealed I take the opportunity to give the whole boat a good spraying down. This eliminates 75 percent of the battle with dust while I'm varnishing, and is most effective in providing clean surfaces for precision masking. Give the boat—brightwork and all—this big bath no sooner than twelve hours after the sealer has been applied, and wipe the brightwork surfaces dry (with a lintfree rag such as a baby diaper) instead of allowing water to sit on the oiled or sealed wood. If your boat has a tendency to harbor puddles, chase them away so you're not slopping through water while you tape.

TAPING

Whether you are varnishing the whole boat or a section of the cockpit, masking is the best means to a clean varnish edge. I have been chided many times for this by other "professionals" who point out that masking is for amateurs and that wholesale cutting in is the mark of a true pro. But I get beautiful results with complete peace of mind by taping wherever the adjacent surface is likely to be sloshed with varnish, and I truly believe the time saved in the less tedious approach to varnishing a taped piece far outweighs the time it takes to lay that tape down. Make it a point to read about the characteristics of masking tapes before you start ripping strips off the roll. To eliminate as much needless taping time as possible, I use tape that can be left on at least two weeks, regardless of weather. See Chapter 17 for information on such extended-use masking tapes.

Once the boat is masked, move on with the varnishing process. But keep these two tape thoughts at the back of your mind:

1) No product is infallible, which means that even though a tape is designed to be left on long term, you should check it every day you can to make sure it isn't becoming part of the boat. I pull a new three- to six-inch section every day as a test, and if at any point the test strip of tape gives me problems, the whole boat gets unmasked right then and there. I do not kid myself into thinking I can postpone the pulling, even if I had planned to varnish instead that day, the consequences being what they are. The first time you violate this rule, the tape gods punish you with unforgettable vengeance.

2) You will never get a clean varnish edge if you leave that initial taping on through the entire buildup of varnish coats. This has nothing to do with the type of tape used, but results from of the amount of varnish that has accumulated at that edge. No tape, under such a buildup of varnish, will cut away cleanly enough to leave anything but a ragged edge of varnish with bits of tape permanently embedded in it. For a scheduled varnish project of eight or more coats, I usually plan three tapings: one at the beginning, one after the fourth coat has been sanded, and one before the final two coats. If you find even at these junctures that the varnish buildup is too thick for the tape to cut away cleanly, score the edge of the tape very lightly (do not cut clear through) with an X-Acto knife. This may seem time-consuming, but it far outweighs the hassle of rebuilding torn away varnish edges.

One more pre-varnish tip: If you are working in your shop, and it happens to have something other than a dirt floor, swab the floor of your "varnishing booth" with a soaking-wet string mop before you start varnishing. This keeps the dust in the air to a minimum, especially as you move around during your work. And whatever the weather, keep a couple of windows open while you varnish and throughout the drying of each coat. If you're worried about neighborhood cats entering without an invitation, rig a screen or some other impediment to their entry. Good cross ventilation is not only imperative to your physical well-being but is a necessity if you wish to see the varnish dry.

PREPARING THE VARNISH

See Chapter 17 for all the particulars on varnish handling. The following is a brief recap of some of the points you will find there, repeated to give you a sense of order.

Never varnish straight from the can. Pour about a cup of varnish at a time into a clean paper bucket through a clean strainer, and if you are adding thinner, introduce it to the pot the same way. To disperse the thinner into the varnish, just rock the boat; don't use a stirring stick or you run the risk of creating bubbles in the varnish.

Applying the Varnish

When the moon is in the seventh house and Jupiter aligns with Mars, the wood is prepped and sealed and clean and dry and taped, the weather is right, you're dressed for the job, and the varnish is ready, then you may don your latex gloves and begin to varnish!

I love varnishing with foam brushes, but the type of brush you use is not as crucial as how you use it. Speed and consistency of application are the keys to successful brushing.

Set yourself up for the varnishing process. Keep a range of sizes of foam brushes at your side (heads up, in a clean paper bucket), so you always have the correct size at your fingertips and are not tempted or forced to jam a 3-inch brush into a 1-inch crevice. Then, before you dip that first brush into the pot, tack about a 3-foot section.

A speech on tack cloths is in order. A tack cloth is not the means by which you clean heavy sanding grit and grime from a surface before varnishing; that should be done by vacuuming thoroughly and then wiping the whole boat down before you ever pull out the tack cloth and a can of varnish. Wiping down sanded brightwork with a slightly moistened rag picks up residual varnish sanding dust, which due to its magnetic, powder-like quality does not re-

spond even to the strong pull of a vacuum. The cleaner your entire boat or brightwork is before you begin varnishing, the longer your tack cloth will serve you. The tack cloth is your companion while you varnish. It is your last ticket to a clean, smooth finish. Use it religiously. Keep it in front of you, adjacent to the point at which you last stopped tacking, otherwise it's easy to forget to tack. Never leave the tack cloth on the varnishing surface itself, especially during very warm weather, as it will leave behind a sticky residue that will prevent the varnish from curing properly in that spot. In fact, it's best not to set it down directly on any surface, but to keep a piece of paper or cardboard under it when not in use. And don't scrub or rub the brightwork vigorously with a tack cloth; just wipe it gently over the surface, only enough to pick up the offending particles.

Of course, if you were doing things the way the old Oriental craftsmen did, you would be taking your sampan to sea to varnish in a dust-free setting. Even then, I think you'd want a tack cloth along, just in case.

For the first three coats, I varnish in what I call plaid, which means the varnish is laid on cross-grain, liberally, in parallel strokes for about three to five widths (depending on the size of the area I'm varnishing), then "tipped off" (which is stroking such that your brush is just barely touching the varnish) with the direction of the grain, to evenly blend those individual widths together. Do not reload your brush for the tipping off part of the process, but use it almost dry to even out the finish and help it level. Doing this encourages the application of the most generous coat possible without leaving behind an excessive thickness of wet varnish. To get a feel for tipping off, practice holding the handle of the brush with your thumb and forefinger only, so loosely that you think you may drop it, and then pull the brush across the varnish surface. That creates the lightness of pressure necessary for effective tipping.

Cedar planking with copper-clenched laps, ash frames, mahogany thwart, ash knee, and varnish over all.

Don't set down a freshly loaded brush at the end of a piece and start releasing the varnish from that edge or you will end up with runs off that end. Regardless of coat number, varnish parallel to a trim's end first (which is almost always a cross-grain stroke), and then stroke back into the inside edge of that stroke before continuing across the piece. If the end has a sharp edge, make sure it is coated well, as this is usually a spot that gets the least amount of varnish and subsequently breaks down first.

The key to a smooth varnish coat is the unflagging maintenance of a "wet edge." If you tarry too much through the course of your varnishing, within discernible sections anyway, the varnish has the opportunity to start setting before you are able to blend continued brushings into the previous ones. This is called "losing the wet edge" and results in little raised lap lines throughout the dried finish. Working steadily, quickly, and with a minimum of chitchat helps to prevent this unsightly effect. It also is minimized by judicious use of brushing solvent in your varnish under less-than-ideal varnishing conditions.

If you are working on long, wide expanses (such as a transom), or on long pieces that have multiple planes (handrails, grabrails), varnish comes out smoother if you apply it as a team, with one person doing the underside, just ahead of the other who does the top surfaces; or one person rolling—this is especially great for transoms—while the other tips off. It is only the most seasoned professional who can varnish a whole transom alone without losing the wet edge somewhere along the way. Rolling and tipping is also a way to get a generous vertical application of varnish without runs and sags. A good foam roller is best, as it metes out a perfectly clean (no fuzz!) and appropriately thin layer of varnish. Be sure you roll vertically (or against the grain) and then tip off horizontally for best results.

Develop the habit of inspecting your work as you complete a section. It is much easier to blend in a discovered "holiday" if the area surrounding it has not begun to set. Any runs or sags that develop will present themselves soon, and should be removed immediately by stroking them out with a dry brush. If this does not remove the sag, then scrape it off with a clean, fresh razor blade and patch in a stroke of varnish over the area as though it were a holiday. You can fair the patch when the coat has dried. Allowing a sag to dry and then trying to fair it later is folly, as the uncured varnish in the bulb of the sag will only break when sanded, causing a broken blister effect that shows up in subsequent coats.

If a pesky little gnat has found its way into your fresh varnish, leave him there. When the coat has dried, break his little legs, bury him at sea, and sand out the tiny impression he left in the finish. His embedded limbs will barely be visible. You would make a bigger mess trying to wrestle him out of the wet varnish than he himself could ever leave after his kamikaze ritual.

Whenever an angled piece you're varnishing can be detached or moved from its original position, do so and varnish it horizontally. This not only discourages sags but allows you to varnish more generously. You will find that the vertical surfaces require on average about two coats more than their horizontal counterparts to achieve the same buildup of varnish.

If you are varnishing on a day warmer than 75 degrees, you must take the warmth of the brightwork itself into consideration along with the ambient temperature around you. In many cases, a horizontal piece will become much hotter than the air temperature, and so your varnish can be less cooperative in these areas than you may have expected if you prepared it according to the climate.

You can minimize the hot brightwork problem by taking a number of simple steps. First, and most obvious, start varnishing as early in the day as the barometer will permit, and then when you start, begin at the warmest spot on the boat. If it's 6:30 in the morning, such an area won't really be very hot, so it will take the varnish quite nicely. As the sun and the air temperature rise, that area will only become hotter, and you'll want it varnished and well on its way to being set by the time heat is really a debilitating factor. (Saving it for last could mean having to wait until late into the afternoon before the sun is no longer beating down on that portion of the boat, by which time it could be too late to be varnishing.) Then, move accordingly around the boat, varnishing each new piece that could become the next hottest area before it gets a chance to really warm up. As you do this, outsmart the sun by keeping areas covered—preferably with something white, such as canvas—until you are able to get to them. Of course, your covers should be clean and free of grit, since any movement of them will send any debris right onto the areas you've just varnished. The other trick to keeping brightwork cool until you can get to it with the varnish is to move any portable pieces to a shady spot, or best of all, inside the boat. If it's at all possible, consider varnishing such pieces in those protected, cooler locations and then moving them back to their resident spots on the boat after they've dried. (If you varnish below, make sure there is adequate ventilation to aid drying.) If you varnish pieces in the "cool zone," remember that moving them immediately back out into the sun can cause the varnish to bubble up, since the sudden exposure to heat causes gas bubbles to develop. If you can't afford to leave the piece below until the next day, at least give it a couple of hours to set before bringing it back out into the oven.

While we're on the subject of nature's idiosyncrasies, it is also pointless to expect a good-looking varnish job in windy conditions. Even if you've cleaned your boat as if for surgery, any strong breeze will carry the grit and pollution from the surrounding environment onto your boat, as if it were guided by radar. In addition, you'll have so many brush marks and lap lines you'll think you've accidentally opened a can of mucilage instead of varnish. If you can afford to postpone varnishing for a day, it's usually worth doing, since the coat you manage to get down under gusty conditions is often so full of garbage it is wasted by the time you've sanded out all the messes.

As you varnish, use common sense in planning your varnishing route. Don't paint yourself into corners, and do not varnish the areas that are your only means to turning a piece until you've coated all the other planes. Set portable pieces up so they don't have to be moved until the varnish has dried: Instead of taking dorade boxes to the dock, raise them on wood strips over a drop cloth on the foredeck, where no one can kick them into the water while they dry. And if you're working in tight quarters, figure out what is likely to get bumped most often as you varnish surrounding areas, and do that spot last.

Apply only one coat of varnish per day, and allow at least twelve hours before you return to sand that coat to prepare for the next one. If when you do return you find that some sags developed and set up, scrape off the soft, un-cured portions with a good, sharp hook scraper and wipe away the sticky varnish inside with a thinner-soaked rag. Then moderately sand the area to fair the surface to an even plane before you proceed with overall prep for the next coat.

A GENERAL VARNISH APPLICATION TIME FRAME
In months with average to longer days (sun time), begin varnishing as soon as the morning dew level has dropped. Stop varnishing before the afternoon dew point begins to rise. Typical varnishing parameters are spring: 9-2; summer:

7-1; fall: 10-2; and winter: 11-1. Those are ideal, which means they will allow you the easiest flow of varnish, given average clear weather conditions, without subjecting the varnish to a level of air moisture that will cause it to bloom. My rule of thumb is to stop in time to allow a coat two hours' setting time before the sun begins to drop and the air begins to get drinkable. Of course, these are very conservative time frames, and they are qualifiable by the latitude at which you are varnishing and the actual humidity on a given day. They also refer only to the actual varnishing time, not preparations. If you want to be wielding brushes by 7:00 a.m., you'd best be at the boat by 6:00 a.m., because the brightwork will invariably have a heavy layer of dew needing to be wiped off and varnish prep to be tended to (not to mention the catching up on dock gossip before you begin work). The main idea is to learn that there is a time of day that's best for your varnishing efforts, given all the variables that can come into the picture. Certainly you can varnish as late as 3:00 p.m. in the summer, especially in Seattle, Washington, on a typical 75-degree day; but in some hotter climes, from noon on the sun makes the varnish surfaces so hot you'll have to add copious amounts of brushing liquid to get the varnish down before it turns to glue. Better to rise and shine early, and spend those hot afternoons snorkeling or writing the great American novel.

If you're varnishing into late fall or winter months, even the prettiest day can be the devil in disguise, as a heavy dew point can lurk in seemingly clear air, turning fresh varnish into a flat finish. On these days, there is no "window of opportunity" for varnishing —unless it's on an interior.

WHAT TO DO IF YOU GET RAINED OUT
If your Dutchman's pants lied to you, or if you wake up to rain the day after you've prepped the whole boat for a coat of varnish, don't panic. A little water never hurts between coats of varnish.

There are some things to do, though, before you pick up where the rainstorm left off. If the varnish had been sanded in preparation for the next coat and then doused by Mother Nature, wipe down everything first to remove all standing water and residual moisture. Then lightly moisten a clean cotton diaper with mineral spirits and wipe down all the sanded brightwork to remove any water spot "halos" that might have developed in the sanded finish surface. These are especially prevalent when the downpour is the first one in a long time, when the air is more polluted.

If you start getting rained out mid-workday and the sanded varnish has not been vacuumed, quickly run around with rags before you abandon ship and at least wipe the bulk of the varnish dust off the brightwork. This will make the mess easier to clean up when you return. When you do come back, follow the procedure above to clean any residue off the sanded varnish before you resume the balance of the prep sanding. Obviously, if the threat of rain hangs over you as you are sanding, it would behoove you to keep the vacuum handy and clean each section as you complete it, thus eliminating the mad dash around the boat once the sky opens up.

When sanding between varnish coats, be especially gentle at corners and along all edges. These areas hold only a thin coat and are easily cut through even with fine sandpaper. I generally skip sanding a squared edge altogether, and am careful to sand only up to within about 1/16 inch of such an edge to assure sufficient varnish buildup.

If the extended-use tape seems to be getting a little tattered at the edges from repeated sandings between coats, pull the ragged strips and replace them. Otherwise, they present run opportunities wherever the varnish collects around the fringe.

THE STANDARD COATING SCHEDULE

For an optimum buildup of varnish coats:

1) Do not sand after the sealer, but wipe the surface clean, just before you varnish, with a rag moistened (but not soaked) with water or mineral spirits.

2) Thin the first coat by 15-25 percent, depending on type of varnish (more for Epifanes, less for Schooner), and apply it in "plaid."

3) Sand lightly with 220 grit —just enough to scratch the surface to see where you're going when you are applying the second coat.

4) The second coat is thinned 10-15 percent and applied in plaid.

5) Sand lightly with 220 grit, knocking off any debris and leaving a moderate scratch in the finish.

6) Apply the third coat full strength in plaid, with a capful of brushing liquid added per eight ounces of varnish if weather dictates.

7) Sand moderately with 220-grit paper, leaving a solid scratch.

8) Apply the fourth coat full strength, with needed brushing liquid added as above. Varnish with the grain.

9) Sand heavily with 220 grit to plane down ridges that have built up with the pattern of the grain, taking extra care not to break through the seal of varnish and sand through to the wood. On expansive areas, it sometimes helps to use a Ryobi palm sander to speed things. This lightweight orbital sander maintains a flat plane because of its hard rubber pad. Be very conservative, though, as it takes the finish down very quickly; if you get careless or heavy handed, you can go through the entire varnish seal to the wood in a matter of seconds. If you do not own a Ryobi, or you simply are nervous about breaking through the finish, do use at least some type of hard, flat sanding block. For curvaceous spots, wrap your paper around a foam rubber sanding sponge. Wrapping the paper around the soft, ungritted sides of a sanding sponge provides the perfect plane for sanding rounded edges such as grabrails. Don't be afraid to sand away at least a couple of coats, particularly on flat areas, since

this is how you arrive at a mirror-like finish in the end. If you avoid this sanding, your varnish will have a lumpy, grainy surface. The varnish surfaces should be completely white with scratch and almost totally flat, with very few shiny spots where the "dimples" of the grain have not yet leveled out.

10) The fifth through eighth coats are applied the same way as the fourth, except you should sand after each with 320 grit, by hand only, and just enough to leave a moderate, but finer, scratch.

11) The ninth and tenth coats are optional, but if the finish is looking thin —perhaps due to the type of varnish you have used, how much you thinned it, or the extent you sanded between coats —it's easier to add coats now for extra protection and beauty while the boat is taped and set up, than it is to come back later and top up the finish.

The first three varnish coats can be applied on successive days and each be cured sufficiently to sand the day after application. Each coat thereafter, up to number seven, needs a full day of curing time between coats, so plan a day off after each of those coats. I give each of the last three coats at least two days to dry, and many times three, before prepping for and applying the next coat. The reason for the added drying time is that the more varnish you build up, the more solvent there is escaping, which dramatically slows down the curing process of topcoats. While each of these earlier coats may seem well set and dry, a residual drying is still taking place.

After the last coat is truly dry, begin the reassembling process with hardware and start detailing the boat. All hardware should be clean and shiny before it goes back on (see Chapter 8's discussion on intermediate prepwork for hardware reclamation). Fasteners that are not in excellent condition should be replaced. Remember to bed screws with an appropriate bedding compound such as Dolphinite (never use adhesives like Sikaflex or 3M 5200 to bed fasten-

ers; remember, someday you will probably want to remove those screws again!), and tightened only enough to stop turning. Overtightening squeezes so much of the bedding compound out that it compromises its intended sealing quality. It also can create stress cracks and distortion in the surface of the newly finished wood. If you are using a power driver, put it on the slowest speed and be very, very careful.

Go around the whole boat with fresh razor blades in hand and inspect for drips on deck or over the sides. Nothing compromises the beauty of a new finish like long varnish runs all over the place, and such eyesores —if left behind —make a powerful statement about the boat's owner.

When you have scraped the last drip off the boat and given your floating work of art a nice bath, a moment for festive contemplation of your achievement is in order. Pop the cork on a bottle of really good champagne to celebrate your triumph. It's a ritual I encourage every person who has come this far in their brightwork labors to observe, and even if you happen to be a teetotaller, I still urge you to find some means of toasting your artistic victory. Make sure you invite somebody to share the occasion so you don't have to do your own back-patting; you've earned the kudos.

Varnish Failures and Problems and Their Causes

The following are some classic problems encountered with varnish finishes, with possible explanations for their appearance. With the exception of checking, chipping, and peeling, these are all problems that arise as a result of faulty application conditions.

Blistering, also known as bubbling, is evidenced by the appearance of blisters or bubbles on or beneath the surface of a dried varnish finish. Causes: Excessive heat, exposure to hot sun, or both during or immediately after a coat is applied; varnishing a wood surface that is itself very

warm; moisture in the wood prior to application; application of finish over insufficiently dried wood filler or stain.

Blooming, also known as blushing, clouding, or fogging is a white or opaque cast or matte finish that appears upon drying of a gloss finish. Cause: The presence of extremely high humidity or a heavy dew as the film dries. This is especially common as a result of application near the end of the day as the dew point in the air rises. Vertical areas do not show blooming as promi-

nently as horizontal surfaces, especially when the problem occurs during winter application.

Alligatoring is the appearance of a crinkled or "alligator skin" type of surface. Causes: The application of too thick a coat over an existing hardened coat of varnish, or undried varnish beneath the surface that could not dry once the upper layer skinned over. Similar to wrinkling in appearance.

Brush marks are uneven ridges in the dried surface of the varnish where varnish did not level out before it began to set. Causes: Brushing or "working" the varnish after it has begun to set; application of varnish in hot weather without proper thinning with brushing solvents; the addition of excessive amounts of accelerating solvents; or a combination of above causes. Brush marks are siblings to lap lines.

Checking is the deterioration of the surface of a finish into a web-like network of moderately deep cracks. Crazing is a less severe form of this condition, but checking is the stage at which the finish begins to fail. Cause: The drying out of varnish resins due to age and prolonged exposure to sun and heat.

Chipping is the flaking off of varnish in small areas. Cause: Brittleness of the finish or insufficient adhesion to surface, often brought about as a result of a blow to an aged or poor-quality finish.

Crawling, or cissing, is the creeping away or retreating of a finish from the surface to which it has been applied, before it has begun to set, leaving areas uncoated. Causes: Overthinning; application in extremely low temperatures; grease, moisture, silicone, or other foreign matter on the varnishing surface; varnishing over a high-gloss surface that has not been sanded enough to create a tooth into which the new varnish can grab hold.

Lap lines are periodic unleveled areas in a varnish finish, where a coating boundary has begun to set and then has been overlapped by a subsequent lap of varnish. Causes: Varnishing an area that, by virtue of its design, is too large to accommodate a continuous "wet-edge," thereby resulting in the development of lap lines; the failure to add a brushing solvent to the varnish, which aids in delaying the setting of the varnish; varnishing under windy conditions.

Lifting is the softening and raising into wrinkles of a previously dried coat by a subsequent coat of varnish that has been applied to that surface. Causes: Incompatibility of new varnish with old, usually as a result of "hotter" sol-vents in the new material, either because the brand is different or because you've added an inappropriate solvent.

Peeling is the separation of a finish from the wood surface. Cause: Loss of adhesion due to excessive heat exposure, or the presence of moisture in the wood, either from the time of application or as a result of water entering at a broken spot in the finish.

Sagging shows as thick "curtains" of varnish on a vertical or sloping surface, usually having bulbous reservoirs of uncured varnish at the lowest point. Cause: Application of an excessively thick coat of varnish, or the collection of quantities of varnish in cracks, etc., which continue to flow after the surrounding areas have been brushed out. The later is usually more responsible for "runs," which are skinnier, vertical-line versions of sags.

Slow drying or nondrying refers to the failure of an applied coat of varnish to reach a reasonable state of curing within a reasonable number of hours. Causes: Improper ventilation of the refinishing environment (shed, shop, boat interior, etc.); application of varnish to certain extremely oily woods (cocabola, e.g.) or to laminated surfaces containing strips of such woods; addition of excessive amounts of brushing liquid or slow-drying solvent to varnish; the application of varnish over a previously coated surface that has also not dried sufficiently. This last condition often occurs when the previous coat appeared to be dry but was in fact only skinned over, with wet varnish and unescaped solvents still beneath the first varnish skin.

Wrinkling, or rivelling, shows as puckered or raised wrinkles in the varnish. Cause: Application of an excessively thick coat or the pooling of varnish in an area such as a corner; insufficient brushing out of a coat; a sudden lowering of the ambient temperature during application; the addition of excessive amounts of drier to the varnish.

"Fish-eyes" show in the separation of a wet

varnish film in the form of many small crater-like voids. Cause: The presence of silicone or wax or other contaminants on the surface beneath the wet finish.

TOOLS AND MATERIALS FOR VARNISHING

Extended-use masking tape

Fresh razor blades

Your favorite varnish and its recommended thinners (one each: brushing thinner and fast drying thinner)

A couple dozen cone-style strainers

A couple dozen pint-size paper buckets

Slotted stir stick (only for rubbed-effect or satin varnishes)

Tack cloths (buy several)

Clean baby diapers

Polyfoam brushes, in an assortment of sizes

Ziploc bags

220- and 320-grit Fre-Cut sandpaper

Foam rubber sanding blocks

Ryobi palm sander (orbital)

Razor blade scraper (holder)

Rubber mallet

Ice pick

Sandpaper cutter

Hard sanding blocks

Vacuum

Disposable dust/mist masks (one for each day sanding)

Charcoal disposable masks (one for each day for interior varnishing)

Latex exam gloves (fresh pair per day)

Kneepads

Light-tint UV sunglasses

WEATHER

Cool and overcast is the ideal; if raining, you have the day off. Hot and sunny can make you and your varnish both unpleasant to work with, but since this is usually the case on summer varnishing days, such conditions should be met with optimism and a full can of brushing liquid (which is not another name for beer). In fall and winter months, check the barometer; the dew point that you can't see can mean disaster!

VARNISHING DAY SARTORIALS

When I am choosing an outfit for varnishing day, the legend of the Aleut hunter of yore comes to mind. These native Alaskan tribesmen believed in honoring the sea mammal spirits by wearing their finest costumes when hunting, in hopes that the spirits would then bless them with a bountiful hunt. To see these costumes (which I did at a traveling Smithsonian exhibit) is to marvel at the thought that garments of such exquisite detail and beauty, representing what must have been hundreds of painstaking hours of handwork, were worn to undertake such messy work. Honor the varnish gods similarly: Dress neatly and your show of faith will be rewarded with more beautiful brightwork. If I wear old, beat-up clothes, then I care less how sloppy I am at my work (and if I wear a bikini, I get severely sunburned, not to mention razzed). You'd be amazed how few varnish splatters end up on the boat when you're working in something other than tatters.

Don't wear a sweater, or if you must wear one due to cold temperatures, wear a painter's smock or a man's dress shirt over it.

Don't hold the cat before you venture off to varnish the boat.

If you have long hair, tame your wild tresses before you begin varnishing, or you'll end up using your head as a brush. And regardless of hair length, wear a painter's cap or even a simple scarf. It is not uncommon to bump heads against a wet surface during the course of your varnishing, and a protected head means it's only a one-trauma accident.

CREW

Many hands make light work, but all Oscar Madisons should be put in charge of refreshments.

MAINTAINING AND REPAIRING VARNISH

Nothing lasts. Even the continents drift.
—George Will

I would assume the conservative political columnist was referring to the problem of fleeting varnish when he made that proclamation. George should sell that line to a varnish manufacturer to use on its cans, so people can't come back later whining that the stuff came off.

You can, however, keep your new foundation of properly applied varnish in place for a number of years by refreshing it regularly and by taking care of it between refreshers. Here are a few pointers on the caretaking side of the coin.

Cleaning

When a ten-coat varnish foundation is completed, the boat should look ready for the prom. But that much fresh varnish will require about six months to "season" before the finish is really cured. Be gentle with the finish during this period. Don't subject it to great tests of abrasion; don't run mooring lines over it (avoid this anyway!); keep the grit and salt water hosed off, with

This nicely oiled teak swimstep requires dedicated maintenance. The transom is varnished mahogany.

a minimum of scrubbing; don't let your guests walk on the brightwork, ever (unless they are barefoot).

A cured varnish finish is best cared for with a regular freshwater hosing, wiped dry with soft, clean cloths such as baby diapers or a chamois. Avoid using harsh soaps, or even those "mild" boat soaps. If you feel the brightwork needs some kind of true cleaning, add a small amount of Murphy's Oil Soap to the water; but be sure even this is carefully rinsed off and the surface wiped dry before you leave the boat.

Never return from an outing with salt water on your brightwork and leave it there to dry. The salt crystallizes and then reflects damaging rays of sun onto the finish, hastening its demise. Think of saltwater crystals as millions of little magnifying glasses, and you'll begin to get the picture. Salt crystals also pose an abrasive threat to varnish if stepped on, even by bare feet.

Real chamois skins are your best friend when you are out sailing and want to keep the brightwork clean. Use a chamois first thing in the morning to wipe off the dew on all exterior varnished areas; this provides a natural source of fresh water and removes any salt crystals that may have formed from the previous day's sailing. A chamois should be cared for with as much TLC as befits its value; this includes soaking it in clean water until it is soft and pliable before you use it. Never start wiping with a dry chamois (unless you're adrift with no supply of fresh water at all, in which case I would suggest forgetting the chamois and licking the dew off the boat). Light, uniform pressure should be used in wiping the beads of dew from the varnished surfaces. Don't worry about wiping the surfaces absolutely dry, since it is nearly impossible, and any slight remaining moisture will evaporate quickly anyway. Wring the chamois out or you'll find yourself swabbing the finish with a soaking wet mass of hide. (See Chapter 17 for tips on chamois care.)

Covers

Of course, a canvas cover is the best plan of varnish care. Keeping Mother Nature completely at bay eliminates the most destructive culprits from a brightwork finish's life altogether. Let's suppose you've hired me to refinish your 40-foot brightwork bonanza and you've spent six grand for that luxury. It would then cost you about one-third that amount to go out and order a custom, full boat cover to protect your brightwork investment. While the boat would still need an annual refresher to restore gloss and repair dings and broken joints, the cost of those refreshers is easily cut in half, and you'll be saving two or three refreshers per year (and that's for a boat that doesn't live in the tropics). If you don't have the refreshers done, you'll waste the entire initial investment in less than eighteen months —because the varnish will all start peeling off by then. Unless the boat sits all covered up, which will probably keep the varnish in excellent condition. Even if you don't care about the aesthetic side of the issue and consider this purely from an economic stand-

point, it can only make sense to spend the money one time on a full boat cover rather than chase your financial tail repairing the damage that is normal wear when brightwork sits exposed between cruises. This applies to full boats as well as single trims.

I have some clients —my favorite of all time, in fact —who have but three brightwork areas on the exterior of their boat: two sets of louvered companionway doors, and a stern rail. The minute we finished varnishing those pieces, they had individual covers made and have kept the covers in place at all times when the boat was not in use. That was eight years ago. In that time, I have refreshed the original finish only once a year —to pep up the gloss, more than anything —and stripped and revarnished from bare wood once —two years ago, and that only because the owner just wanted to see what a new foundation of varnish would look like. The old varnish was still completely intact and looked quite respectable. The bottom line here is that, with the exception of annual light 320-grit scratchings, followed by single coats of varnish, this brightwork was a piece of cake once the covers went on.

It's money you'll spend anyway, so honor your brightwork and your labors by investing in a protective covering for your work of art.

Refresher Coats

Once a new varnish foundation has been applied, the refresher schedule should be set up immediately. Don't wait for the first signs of deterioration; don't even wait for signs of dulling. Schedule refreshers the way your dentist schedules check-ups: in advance of any decay. That way you defer such decline, with luck for years at a time. The Preventive Maintenance Commandment comes into play here; if you've forgotten how it goes, turn back to Chapter 5 and read it aloud.

To apply refreshers to a healthy-looking finish—one that has no dings or breaks at seams or signs of lifting anywhere; at worst, it may have lost a bit of its luster—follow this course of action:

Clean the brightwork. Give the whole boat a bath with fresh water and Murphy's Oil Soap and rinse well. Wipe down the brightwork with baby diapers and a mixture of one part water to three parts denatured alcohol. If you have reason to believe that wax or silicone polishes have been introduced to the finish since its original application, wash these off thoroughly with xylene- or a toluol-based solvent.

Remove the "easy fittings" and sand all the brightwork with 320-grit paper—not heavily, but enough to leave a moderate scratch. Vacuum, wipe down the whole boat with a diaper lightly moistened with mineral spirits, and mask wherever necessary. Apply varnish as you did for the last two foundation coats, keeping in mind that these applications are both presentation coats and should be executed with as much attention to detail and surface perfection as possible. Allow a day for the first coat to dry, then prep for the second. Do not apply fewer than two coats when refreshing your varnish. That is the rule and it should not be bent! Giving your brightwork a one-coat refresher is like feeding your hungry child naught but a Ritz cracker. It doesn't promote long life.

When applying refresher coats, always (unless there is a very good reason otherwise) use the same varnish you used to build the foundation. Too many times people get excited about some new and wonderful product and decide to try it out the next time they varnish. Unfortunately, the new and improved finish isn't always compatible with what it's refreshing, and problems, such as wholesale delamination of the new coats, can result. If you are refreshing a finish and don't know which brand of varnish is on the boat (you just bought it, for example) try to get the service records on that finish before you commit to a particular varnish for refresher coats, or your refinishing efforts may be wasted. If you simply cannot ascertain what is already on the wood, varnish one small but representative piece and watch for early clues of incompatibility. Such indicators might include a reluctance to dry in an appropriate amount of time, a tendency to remain inordinately soft after drying, or peeling away at the scrape of a fingernail. If these things happen on your test piece, you're wise to wood down the entire expanse of brightwork and start from the beginning with your own finish program.

Repairs

"Scratch and Patch" is a term that refers to repairing brightwork where it has begun to break down. My sister and I came up with the phrase one day years ago when we found ourselves sanding and building up spots on an otherwise healthy stretch of brightwork that was splitting at the seams. It's a convenient little term that sums up the process of fixing dings and broken joints that come along during the life of a finish before it begins to crumble at the foundation. It is not a process that takes the place of a complete re-do, but it can help postpone the inevitable and is the only means to a long-term return on your initial refinishing investment.

Scratch-and-Patch work is usually done as a preliminary step to your refresher work. Remember that your goal is to save whatever part of the original finish is still healthy. If the finish has simply "broken," say at a scarf joint, but has not begun to lift, it is often possible to lightly sand the surface of the varnish at the broken seam and "squish" varnish into it (mask on either side first) to reestablish the seal. Doing this several times before the full refresher coats are applied can be the ticket to a completely mended finish. Catching things at this early stage is the reward for planning your maintenance, as after very many months such problems turn quickly into lifted expanses of varnish.

If the finish around that seam has begun to lift (obvious by what appears to be a yellow "blister" along the seam), you must remove the lifted varnish. There is no "gluing" it back in place by forcing varnish underneath, so accept the reality of the situation and strip off the lifted parts of the finish. To keep from ruining the surrounding varnish, strip lifted or broken areas carefully, using a very sharp hook scraper whenever possible for the cleanest finish removal and the least damage to the wood. If the area beneath the broken finish has darkened, bleach carefully, using Teak Wonder and a soft nylon tile scrubber; if it's an area too small for the nylon scrubber, use a soft toothbrush, but resist the temptation to scrub. Allow the area to dry completely before you do any sanding. Often such areas of wood have darkened because of water in a joint or crack in the wood. If this is a possibility, put a wet-dry vacuum to work extracting the moisture (with the crevice tool attachment) and give it a day to dry completely, or you'll end up with the same problem very soon after the finish has been restored. Never seal a blackened area with new varnish (or with Sikaflex or any other type of sealant) without opening up the finish (removing it) and giving the area a chance to dry out. You risk locking in moisture and encouraging rot.

When the offending spot is stripped, bleached, and dry, sand lightly with paper no heavier than 120 to 150 grit (you're trying to maintain the original plane on the piece, remember), then follow up with 220 grit. If the area requires staining (on finishes that were stained originally), apply the stain and allow it to dry thoroughly and then seal as you did for the original finish. If you originally wet-sanded SeaFin Teak oil or another Tung oil sealer into the wood prior to varnishing, repeat that process. When the sealer has dried, make a "jet-speed" version of your regular varnish, diluting it 25 percent with its companion fast-drying solvent. Apply it to the patch, then apply another less diluted coat four hours later (without sanding). Build up the patch the rest of the way with the full-strength varnish, applying only one coat per day and sanding between coats with 220 grit. Don't be tempted to use commercially packaged jet-speed or quick-dry varnishes to build up the whole patch in one weekend, because this type of varnish rarely has the ultraviolet protection that the good varnish has, and areas where it is used will break down more quickly. Some of these varnishes are so diluted that they give you only a partial coat per application by the time the finish has dried and the solvents have dissipated.

When the patched area has leveled with the surrounding good finish, lightly sand all the brightwork to prep for the first complete refresher coat, and then varnish as instructed above for refreshing healthy finishes.

Scratch-and-Patch work on a piece that has been stained can be tricky because it will involve blending in a new application of the stain before you patch the varnish. Because the effects of sunlight and aging give the original stain foundation a distinctive patina, the color of stain on the wood is no longer identical to the color of stain in the can, especially after long periods. The newly repaired areas, while maybe only subtly different in color, will tend to stick out visually. This calico effect is inescapable unless you are willing to mix a new stain to match the current hue of the boat every time you do any Scratch-and-Patch work, something most people find highly impractical. The best advice I can give under these circumstances is to refinish an entire piece up to a natural breaking point or boundary—an entire grabrail, for example, or the whole coaming. The result will still be a slight variation in shade from panel to panel or rail to rail, but it will not be as conspicuous as a patch job.

Some refinishing how-to's suggest that to

provide an evenness of color from the patched areas on teak to the original surrounding brightwork, the patched areas should first be stained before applying varnish. This is folly. Once the offending layers of varnish are removed and the exposed wood is sanded or bleached, the area being patched is automatically darker, not lighter, because the oil intrinsic to teak is once again visible at the surface. There is no way to stain or bleach teak so that it becomes lighter than its natural self and apes its sun-lightened surroundings. In time the darker patched spots, too, will take on the honey-blond quality of the more aged varnish foundation around them. But at that, they will usually remain a shade lighter than the greater expanse because it, too, has continued to bleach in the sun. This is a function of the wood, not the type

Right: *A proper buildup of varnish nets a mirror finish. Mahogany planking, engine-access hatches with bird's eye maple veneer, and gleaming fittings on a classic runabout.*
Below: *Mahogany planking, seams paid with white seam compound or polysulfide.*

of finish. It is for this same reason that Honduras mahogany looks like a blond-and-russet patchwork quilt after years of little varnish repairs.

Discerning the Level of Deterioration

How do you really know if your finish is intact enough to simply refresh, or whether it's broken down enough to warrant a complete stripping? Actually, the signs are pretty basic and simple to read. As I stated earlier, the best question to ask yourself, if you are in doubt about the quality of the current brightwork finish, is this: "Will the refresher coat have more integrity than the finish beneath it?" If the answer is "Yes," take the original finish off and start from bare wood. If the answer is "No," great; the refreshers will be

worth the time they take to apply.

Here are symptoms of troubled finishes, in ascending order of deterioration, along with their cures.

1) Slightly dulled gloss, but generally healthy-looking varnish. Refresh the whole boat with two new coats.

2) Moderately dull surface, but no breaks. Refresh whole boat with two coats.

3) Dull surface, separation of finish at joints, but no apparent lifting at broken areas. "Mend" joints and refresh the whole boat with two coats.

4) Dull surface, separation of finish at joints, some lifting at joints and along edges adjacent to other surfaces. Scratch and Patch all joints and lifted areas, and refresh the whole boat with two to three coats.

5) Some checking or eroding of varnish surfaces and broken and lifting finish at joints with discoloration of wood beneath. Scratch and Patch all lifted varnish and discolored wood (bleaching where necessary), giving the wood plenty of time to air out before sealing. Find and fix causes of major problems. Refresh the whole boat with at least three new varnish coats.

6) Wholesale erosion of finish, broken at all joints, wood discolored beneath all lifted varnish areas, weathered bare wood wherever varnish has completely worn away. This condition is usually a result of complete "varnish starvation" for eighteen months or more; such decline can happen in even less time on a boat that resides in the tropics. If done properly, patching and refreshing such a finish will easily take as much time as a total re-do, and usually looks marginal by comparison. If this is the scenario on as much as one-half of the brightwork, it's a better investment of your time to cut your losses and refinish everything.

7) Original finish foundation is old (six years or more), hasn't resided under cover, and while faithfully refreshed and repaired through the years, has started to look ratty from all the Scratch-and-Patch work, and looks lifeless after each new refresher. Face the fact that your finish foundation has served its time and is now ready to go to the great varnish heaven in the sky. Take it all off and bring in the new guard. And drink a toast to the years of protection and elegance that original finish lent your boat, and to yourself for being an intelligent caretaker of the brightwork.

The Brightwork First-Aid Kit

Assemble the following varnishing ingredients for an emergency brightwork repair kit. That way, while you're cruising you'll be able to repair dings as they happen and can minimize any decline of the finish until you have time for more extensive repair when the cruise is over.

1 pint can of varnish

6 each 1-inch and 2-inch foam brushes in a Ziploc storage bag

1 tack rag in Ziploc sandwich bag

2 sheets each 80-, 120-, 220-grit Fre-cut sandpaper cut into quarters and stored in a Ziploc sandwich bag

4 clean, pre-folded baby diapers, rolled up

1 pint steam-distilled mineral spirits

1 roll 3M #2040 1-inch masking tape (in a Ziploc sandwich bag)

1 five-pack box of single-edged razor blades and a 1-inch Red Devil pull-scraper, sharpened, packed together in a Ziploc bag.

Paint can opener

Pack the whole kit into a plastic "Multi-file" (like the one you keep your sandpaper in) to keep everything clean and dry. Stow in a dry place inside the boat.

When you are repairing a varnish "owie," bandage it immediately (that day, if possible) in the following manner:

Make sure everything, including the surrounding area, is completely dry; clean the wound (with mineral spirits); lightly sand to fair the gouge; clean again with mineral spirits; tape, if necessary; tack; and patch with a coat of full-strength varnish. If it's a really deep gash and you have time, repeat the process to ensure a good seal.

This is the one time when it's OK to varnish straight from the can without straining. The patch is only a temporary one, and it doesn't matter how pristine the coat is. Your goal is to keep moisture out of the cut and prevent further deterioration of the surrounding finish until you get back to the boat's moorage or have a chance to pull into port long enough to refinish the spot correctly. When you get to a place where you can do a more thorough patch job, remove the "bandage" and follow the instructions above for Scratch-and-Patch work, ending with at least one whole coat on the entire piece to blend in and camouflage the patch.

Two Special Brightwork Projects: Spars and Soles

What though the mast be now blown overboard,
The cable broke, the holding anchor lost,
And half our sailors swallowed in the flood?
Yet lives our pilot still.
——Shakespeare, *King Henry the Sixth*

Varnishing Spars

A bright mast is a majestic floating obelisk, pointing toward the heavens in what seems to be reverent supplication of the gods. Is it petitioning for fair winds? Or is it simply praying, arms outstretched, that some one mortal soul will come along soon and tend to its varnish before it starts crumbling at the core?

There are two scenarios we can face in rescuing those bright spars: varnishing them from a bosun's chair, or refinishing them unstepped. As with a bright finish in any other area of the boat, the varnish on a mast demands regular refreshers —at least annually —to remain intact and looking good. And unless you and your entire circle of acquaintances are acrophobic, there is really no need to pull the stick for the purpose of refreshing a healthy finish. This can be accomplished with a minimum of expense and time from the "chair with a view." However, if the finish on your mast has disintegrated to the point of being even one-sixth decayed, your attempts to restore a protective finish to those broken-down areas will be convoluted and frustrating. You're well advised under these conditions to yank the mast and get it down to a level where your time can be more efficiently invested. Before you make a decision either way, get an expert to take an inspection ride all the way to the top. What might look healthy from the deck could in fact be a sick finish (especially from the spreaders up), or worse, a harbinger of impending rot, and is better scheduled for a total refinish reclining on a pair of sawhorses.

The following are some supplementary notes to the previous general guidelines for refinishing, specific to the task of dealing with spars.

COMPLETELY REFINISHING THE MAST —
OFF THE BOAT

Obviously, a mast that is being refinished on the ground can (and should, for the best job) have most or all of its hardware removed. Leaving the track in place can be a headache during the prep phase, and it should be removed during that time anyway to properly seal the wood underneath it. This also provides an opportunity to purge the track of varnish encrustations that have built up during years of refreshers from the chair. However, once the second coat of new varnish is on the wood, I recommend rebedding and installing the clean track at that point and then masking it for the balance of the varnishing. A track can serve as an ally during that process, as you will see later. If the wood underneath the track is badly weathered or is turning black from moisture penetration at the fastenings, the track absolutely must come off so the wood can be properly rescued and any possible deterioration of the wood stopped.

Set a big mast (40 feet or longer) up on at least four strong, well-engineered sawhorses for proper support, and plan to rotate the mast for efficient stripping, bleaching, and sanding. Once the varnishing begins, leave the mast in one position and see to it that you have clean supports, free of old bedding compound, paint, etc., under the mast at all times. If necessary, cover them with a thin strip of formica (glued to the top edge of the supporting beam). I like to keep clean, thick (toddler-size), cotton baby diapers —dry, of course —on all sawhorses during the stripping and sanding phases, to prevent "bruising" of the mast in those spots during the early operations.

On round spars, the fastest method of stripping can be a one-coat chemical stripper/scrape off approach. Apply stripper to no more than about eight feet at a time, allow the solvent material to sit for about five minutes, then scrape the softened varnish off with a sharp hook scraper. This is not one of those "if one coat is good, two coats is better" situations. Apply one coat only, just sufficient to soften the varnish; it doesn't need to bubble up, though this will undoubtedly happen wherever overlaps of stripper occur. This method of stripping is messy, and requires clean-up afterward to ensure that stripping dregs are not left on the dock or work area, to be trampled and tracked onto other surfaces (such as boats. . .). If the spar is

square, a heat gun is faster and much less messy, not to mention less toxic. Heat gun stripping of a long mast is best done as a team project: one person heats, the other person comes behind immediately and scrapes. Once the rhythm of this buddy system is established, heat-stripping literally flies.

Most spars will have a certain amount of black moisture staining in the wood where old varnish has broken down. Do the heavy-grit sanding first (60 or 80 grit, depending on condition), then bleach with an oxalic acid treatment, allowing it to stand overnight, and neutralizing the next day with borax. If weathering does not seem to have penetrated the flesh of the wood dramatically, bleaching with Te-Ka A&B might be sufficient and is quicker, since it can be accomplished, including neutralizing, within one day.

The heavy-grit sanding determines the whole look of a spar, and it's very important to ensure even sanding along the entire length of the stick. On round masts, a good approach to initial power-sanding is to sand with a Speedbloc across the grain, "round the mast" lathe-fashion. While this may sound shocking (with its guaranteed by-product of cross-grain scratches), it is the best means to an evenly sanded, "no-wow" mast. When the bleaching is finished and the mast is completely dry, the earlier sanding scratches are easily dispatched with a "with-the-grain" power-sanding with 120-grit paper, followed by a dedicated 120-grit hand-sanding, without compromising the shape of the mast. On square sticks, initial heavy-grit power-sanding can move along the flat sides of the mast with the direction of the grain (I prefer to use the half-sheet Porter Cable sander on long, flat stretches of a mast), but a second heavy-grit hand block-sanding with a long wood block (your longer homemade 2X4 sanding block) will help knock down any highs and bring the lows flush. Don't be tempted to sand out specific dark spots —leave those at the mercy of the bleaching, and accept that any such spots that persist after that process will have to remain as part of the mast's visual legacy. Better beauty marks than dimples, I always say (except when it comes to my men...). Of course, if those beauty marks are actually malignant spots, you may be faced with replacing, rather than refinishing, that mast. Don't shrug this off as a possibility, and don't hesitate to get out your penknife if you're not sure.

Once the shaping, bleaching, and scratch-removal work is completed, hand-sand with 220 grit before the first application of varnish. Choose a varnish that is rated for high abrasion and has a maximum level of added ultraviolet protection. A high-solids varnish is great for build-up; for even greater protection, use a polyurethane resin-based varnish such as Interlux Clipper Clear for the top two or three coats.

Seal the bare wood with a first coat of varnish that is thinned two to one with its companion fast-drying solvent. Allow this to dry at least four hours (but not overnight) and then, without sanding, apply a second coat thinned four to one with the same solvent. Apply all subsequent coats full strength (adding brushing liquid only to facilitate better leveling), at the rate of no more than one coat per day. After coat number seven, it's good to give each application a full drying day between coats. Apply no fewer than ten coats total —reminding yourself whenever you feel a pout coming on that these seemingly redundant applications are a far cry easier than they will be later from a chair.

A method of varnishing application that speeds things up and helps give the most generous coat possible (without being too thick) is the team "rolling and tipping" method. Using foam rollers, the first person rolls the varnish on around the stick, in successive laps, while the second person works immediately behind, lightly tipping the laps into one another. This eliminates the "where to leave off?" quandary in varnishing a mast, and prevents unsightly seams in the varnish finish. Obviously, the areas where the mast rests on its supports remain uncoated regardless of one's manner of varnishing. My way of compensating for this has always been to move the mast ahead or back by six inches halfway through the project; then I know those undernourished spots are at least getting a solid seal, if not the entire beauty treatment. Propping the mast up on the track after the second coat allows the person with the brush some access to these otherwise unreachable spots; totally masking the track at each support point keeps it from becoming completely glopped up as you varnish those areas by the braille method.

When the spreaders are built up to five coats, stop varnishing the tops, but continue varnishing the sides and bottoms. After the last varnish coat has cured for at least two days, mask with Safe Release tape and paint the spreader tops with white paint. Apply a second coat of the paint after the initial coat has dried for a day.

Allow a newly finished mast a minimum of two full drying days (a week is best) before re-stepping. Otherwise, soft varnish can take quite a beating in the rigging process.

VARNISHING SPARS IN PLACE

To reiterate a point made above, this is an arduous approach to varnishing a mast, and nothing is a greater waste of time (yours as well as that of the "support staff" on the deck) than gearing up for a mast job, only to get to the top and realize the finish is too far gone to be refreshed from a chair. Take that inspection ride well in advance of the perfect weekend you so patiently waited to have come along, and know as you are loading up for the actual task what conditions you will face once you get up there among the clouds. My overall attitude here is that, if the finish isn't in damned excellent shape —maybe two or three broken down spots (not the size of continents) —the mast should come down for the work.

Once you've confirmed that a chair job is in

order, there is a piece of business that must be attended to before you consider any part of the how-to. Line up a good, strong, trustworthy "winch ape." Varnishing from a chair is an exhausting enough job without worrying that the person below could at any moment turn you into a giant splat on the deck. Once you have found such a person (the good kind), begin the relationship with a meeting of the minds on the subject of communication. Here are some points to consider in that regard:

1) Once you're up the mast very far, whenever either of you speaks to the other, look in the direction of your audience and speak clearly and loudly enough to be heard (shouting is not usually necessary until you are about forty feet up). Do not expect the other person to hear you if you are facing another direction as you speak.

2) Always acknowledge understanding of requests, instructions, etc., especially as they relate to being raised and lowered. For example, if I'm finished with a section and want to be lowered, I give the person below about a minute's warning that I will be wanting to go down; this allows the deckhand to put down what he is doing and get prepared to lower me. Then, when I am ready, I say, "Down please," to which he responds, "OK; untying" (which gives me warning to clutch tightly to something —such as the mast, or nearby shrouds —in the event of any accidental line slippage while he unties); when he is ready to start letting out the line, he announces, "Going down," to which I immediately respond, "OK." To complete the transaction, I say, "Stop!" as soon as I reach my desired port, at which point (as I hang on tightly again), the person below quickly ties me off and then announces, "Secure." This good news allows me to relax and call back, "Thank you!" Work then resumes until I need the next dose of assistance. Obviously, this is all more dramatic as you get higher up the mast; the first couple of lifts are close enough to the deck so that the person in the chair can actually see for themselves what's going on. On an especially tall mast, things can get muddled easily as you near the top, and clear communication is vital if tempers are to be spared and energy is to be conserved for the task at hand.

3) If it is not possible to take all your work gear up with you on your first trip aloft, organize the extraneous items and discuss with your helper the fact that you will be asking for them at certain points (your lunch falls into this category). Assign "messenger line" status to one of the extra halyards, and rig a sturdy canvas bag or a basket at the end of that line for hauling these items up as you need them. If all these things are ready and understood before you get into the chair, a tremendous amount of time is saved once you get up the mast.

First trip —the prep ride. A few words on the bosun's chair itself: The one I use belongs to my sister, and was custom-made by the Schattauer boys, Frank and Axel, of Seattle sailmaking fame. The nice thing about this chair, aside from the extra round pocket at the side that holds anything from a soda pop can to a ketchup bottle (you will discover the need for this item later), is the wide piece of half-inch plywood that was used to form the seat. This firm, roomy seat provides for excellent support aloft, even for the steatopygic types among us, and never have we suffered from the sort of circulation cut-off that other people have complained about after spending seven straight hours in other chairs (like airplane seats, for example). If you don't already own a bosun's chair, or are currently in the market for one, consider having one custom-made by your favorite sailmaker or canvas company, tailored to your dimensions as well as needs (be sure to ask for a couple of extra D-rings at the sides for hanging things).

One other item while we're on the subject of chairs. Never attach the chair to the halyard by way of a snap shackle —unless you want the insurance company to think your suicide was an accident. Locking carabiners — the kind used for mountain climbing — guarantee a solid, safe union with the lifting halyard and should be used to attach a bosun's chair if you don't feel completely confident in the current connecter.

Items to take aloft on the first trip: If you plan to do any power sanding, a Ryobi palm sander is the best orbital to use because of its small size and light weight. Make sure your chair has at least one large D-ring at the side; tie the end of the power cord as well as the sander cord to it before you plug them into one another. Take clean baby diapers (about five), soaked with naphtha (cleans a little better than mineral spirits and evaporates more quickly for less latent residue) or mineral spirits, tucked into a thick plastic bag; a 1-inch Red Devil scraper; sandpaper in necessary grits, pre-cut to sizes needed for power-sanding and hand-sanding; foam rubber sanding blocks (at least two, since you invariably drop at least one); five dry diapers; a double-thickness paper grocery bag, cuffed six inches and taped to the back of the chair (using duct tape); nitrile gloves; a dust mask; a snack (granola bars) and light tint sunglasses and a visor, or both.

Even on a sunny day, the slightest breeze at the top of a mast can turn your body into an icicle. Wear long pants (old sweatpants are best, though make sure they are ones you don't mind ruining) with thick leggings for padding at the knees. Take up a jacket and a stocking cap that can be tossed down if not needed, and for the sake of the mast, never wear black rubber-soled shoes.

Wearing nitrile gloves, wipe the entire mast on the way up with thinner-soaked rags (to do this, have the deck person pull you up in stages). On the way back down, do the sanding (use the scraper to fair old drips or broken-down areas before sanding). If the varnish is in decent shape, 320 grit should provide an adequate tooth; if your last coat had many brush

marks, use the Ryobi or a 220-grit hand-sand to flatten it down a little faster. Anywhere you use the Ryobi, load it with 320 grit or finer, as the machine cuts through the varnish faster than hand-sanding. Bear in mind, too, that the coarser the grit — even one as seemingly fine as 220-grit Gold Fre-Cut — the more scratch there will be grinning through your varnish, and the result will be a compromised gloss. Unless absolutely necessary, I usually try to stay with 320 grit on a healthy mast. On thick drips or peeling areas that require fairing, use 120 grit after using the scraper, then minimize the scratches by going over the area with 320 grit. As you complete the sanding of each area, wipe dust off the mast with a dry diaper, then again with a clean, thinner-soaked diaper (lightly on this second thinner wiping, just enough to remove the magnetic particles of dust).

By the way, as you labor from your chair, the person below should be doing the same prep work on the mast at deck level, up to as high as he can reach. Nothing is quite so demoralizing after spending eight hours working under these less-than-ideal circumstances than finally reaching the deck and realizing that this area still demands attention. Your helper should be able to accomplish at least that much between hoistings.

The grocery bag that hangs behind your fanny is the receptacle for spent sandpaper, and it's a perfect place to stow the dry diapers and plastic bag holding the ones soaked with thinner. If you fold down a generous enough cuff at the top of the doubled bag prior to taping it to the seat, it should be shallow enough to reach into easily. If it's too deep, you'll likely give up trying to reclaim items from the bottom for fear of flipping over backwards.

Never keep thinner-soaked rags on or near your person while you are aloft; if the fumes don't get you, the solvent will when it soaks through to your skin and leaves a burn. Always keep a plastic bag in your kit for storing these rags while aloft. And try to resist the temptation to throw things down to the deck. They land, more often than not, in the water and fetching them gets to be a waste of your helper's time.

If you are refreshing a mast with a finish on the spreaders that is pretty well shot on the top side, scrape off as much of the dead varnish as possible and sand to fair the spreader tops evenly. Then, when you've completed the prep-sanding all the way down the rest of the mast, unless you just don't have the time or energy that day, make a point to go back up and seal the bare wood on those spreaders with varnish thinned two to one with its companion fast-drying solvent. Not only is this good protection for the bare wood (leaving it to sit overnight raises the grain), but it preps it for the full-strength coat slated to go on the whole mast the next day.

When you've finished the prep, give the boat (not including the mast) a quick spraying down to remove the light layer of dust that has settled from above. Do not leave this for the next day; it takes up valuable time you'll need then for other things, and working from wet decks isn't something you want your winch person do be doing.

Second trip — the varnishing ride. Take with you: Two mineral spirits-soaked rags in a plastic bag; eight quarter-sheets of 220-grit sandpaper; appropriately thinned varnish, poured into two clean ketchup squeeze containers with "tethers"; four each 1-inch, 2-inch and 3-inch foam brushes; two 1-inch chip brushes; two new, fully opened and crumpled tack cloths (the extra in case you drop one); 3/4-inch extended-use masking tape (a partial roll is best; since it takes up less space); a double-thickness paper grocery bag taped to back of the bosun's chair seat; a neat (as in not messy) snack; a large Ziploc bag attached to a D-ring on the side; two pairs latex exam gloves; and nitrile gloves.

Dress in the same breeches arrangement as for first ride, but add a scarf for hair (women and men) and a painter's cap, a lint-free jacket (a down vest with a nylon shell is my favorite body-warmer for masttop duty), and large wool socks pulled over your shoes to protect the prepped mast from sole marks.

Prepare the ketchup bottles by removing the lids, and checking to be sure they're clean. Then tie a 2-foot length of 1/8-inch shock cord around the body of each one, about two-thirds of the way up from the bottom of the bottles, and wrap tape over the cord to secure the lasso to the bottle at that location. Give it two or three wraps at least (half-inch electrical tape is best) to make the attachment solid. Prepare the varnish as you would for any other job, straining it into a clean paper bucket and adding one capful of brushing liquid per cup of varnish. Mix thoroughly, bend the edge of the bucket to form a pouring spout, and pour the thinned varnish into the ketchup bottles. One nearly full pint-sized bucket will fill one bottle. Screw the lids onto the bottles tightly, but don't overtighten as this causes the tops to pop back off; if they're too loosely screwed on they leak. When you get yourself situated in the bosun's chair, tie the first varnish bottle to a D-ring attached to the halyard, and stick the bottle into a side pocket on the chair (this is when that round pocket really comes in handy). Stow the second bottle in your "fanny bag." The nice thing about using shock cord instead of string or line is that it can be tied into a very secure single knot which will later untie very easily; shock cord also stretches, which sometimes comes in handy here. By the time your original 2-foot length of cord has been looped around the ketchup bottle and knotted to the D-ring, the final tether from chair to bottle should be no longer than about 15 inches. This is a perfect, unobtrusive length that still allows for that occasional moment when you want the bottle to reach at least as far as you do.

Before you have your helper hoist you up, spread drop cloths over the entire boat (including boom and mainsail) to protect everything on

deck from the inevitable sprinkling of varnish drops. Make provisions to either cover your neighbors' boats (one on either side) or warn those skippers that you'll be varnishing the mast and that this might be a good time for a day's cruising. If you don't have enough drop cloths to protect your neighbors' boats, instruct your winch person to be ready with mineral spirits and diapers, and try to notice where those spatters land, so you can direct your helper. As a goodwill gesture, plan to inspect neighboring boats thoroughly at the end of the day for any drops you may have missed.

As you go up, wear nitrile gloves and quickly wipe the mast along the way with the mineral spirits diaper (no need to stop in increments to do this; just have the winch person lift you slowly). When you reach the spreaders, stop and very lightly sand the sealed tops and then wipe them down lightly; next, varnish both spreader tops and bottoms. (Doing each set of spreaders on the way up makes it possible to varnish without interruption on the way down, which is vital if the finish on the mast is to come out unmarred at the end.) When varnishing spreaders, start with the tops, varnishing from the tips inward to the mast, then do the same with the bottoms. As you descend while varnishing the mast be careful not to step on the sticky spreaders. If you feel it might be impossible to resist, wait to varnish the tops as you descend, but do the bottoms first. You'll be glad later, when you're beginning to tire and all you want to do is get down that mast as quickly as you can.

When you get to the top, mask fittings where they're likely to get slopped with varnish. Then, tack down to about waist level and begin varnishing from the top, using the chip brushes for those really tight areas beneath the masthead. If possible to do without messing things up, pull the tape as you complete this area and stuff it into your Ziploc "holster" on the side of your chair. Keep a stocking-covered shoe (never omit the shoe, or your foot will feel like mincemeat by the end of the day) between your lifting halyard and the mast, and make sure you don't take it out until you get to the bottom of the mast. This prevents the halyard from slapping against the wet varnish, leaving a cable-patterned scar in the new finish (another very good reason to do spreaders on the way up).

Figure on spending about twenty minutes on the first couple of feet of varnishing. This area at the top of the mast is so tedious I always find myself wondering if I'm ever going to be done with it; the time chewed up working around all the masttop impediments seems interminable. By comparison, everything else from there on will seem to fly.

If you couldn't safely unmask things at the top, make sure you masked with extended-use tape or you'll return to a masking-tape nightmare. It's likely you'll be making a third trip up anyway, for completion of the spreader tops, so you can leave the tape in place until then if it's the right kind.

If you are planning two refresher coats, let the first coat dry for five days and then go at it again the next weekend, prepping lightly the second time and skipping the initial thinner wipe-down.

When you do go back up for that third trip (if this is a one-coat refresher), plan to take a few quarters of 320-grit sandpaper, a mineral spirits-moistened rag, a ketchup bottle filled about one-quarter of the way with white high-gloss marine enamel (do not thin the paint), a roll of masking tape, and a couple of 2-inch foam brushes. Attach the ever-important grocery bag to the back of the seat for stowing and discarding items as you use them. Take the express elevator directly to the top and then after the tape has been pulled at the masthead, on your way back down, mask the spreaders around the outermost top edge, lightly sand them, wipe them down, and then paint the tops with a generous but not overly thick coat of the white enamel. Remove the tape as you complete each side. This is the only finish that belongs on spreader tops, since varnish at that level, with no regular means of refreshing, will only peel right back off. The white paint reflects the sun's rays and provides long-term protection for the wood. You should never skip the initial coatings of varnish prior to the painting, though, as the wood demands a decent seal to keep the paint from doing a premature disappearing act.

Some miscellaneous notes on this project:

The reason I suggest putting varnish and paint into ketchup bottles is that I detest the feeling of panic that haunts me whenever I take an open can of anything aloft. Dropping a foam brush is bad enough; knocking a can of varnish over from that height would signal the end of my career —professionally and psychologically. A squeeze bottle with a generous opening allows me to mete out an adequate, controlled amount of varnish onto the foam brush, and since it is attached to me with its shock cord tether (you can buy 1/8-inch shock cord by the foot at any good marine chandlery), dropping it only means nonchalantly leaning over, retrieving it, and continuing on —boat and nerves relatively unscathed.

If there is even a moderate wind (which might feel non-existent at dock level), the job will be twice as difficult, take three times as long, and be four times as ugly when you're finished. You will also be frozen to the bone by the time you reach the deck, and the winch person will have to peel you out of the bosun's chair. If at all possible, wait for the forecast of an ideal weekend before attempting this project; the prep day doesn't have to be perfect, though calm conditions beget nerves in kind. Varnishing day is more critical; you should offer up great treasures to the gods in exchange for mercy; if they turn you down, just remember to dress warmly and add your brushing liquid to that ketchup bottle.

One unfortunate predicament that attends weekend mast refinishing, especially during the summer, is the amount of boating traffic in and out of the marina. The slightest wake can make you feel like that tiny man living in The World of Giants, clinging to the top of a metronome. If this project is on your master "boat cosmetics list," try to coordinate a couple of days off during the middle of the week. Tell your boss you're attending to a sick family member; in its own way, this is a truism.

Above all (so to speak!), if you've already resigned yourself to the fact that going up and working 60 or 70 feet above deck is no big threat, you have no reason not to relax and enjoy this project. Once you've ascertained the security of your chair and its linkage to the halyard, and you have complete faith in the integrity (and strength) of your winch ape, you should sit back, drink in the awesome view, and mentally spend all that money you're saving by not paying premium rates to someone like me.

P.S. Don't forget to take your camera up with you; this is a trip you'll want to remember with pictures! (Just send it back down on the messenger line.)

Varnishing Cabin Soles

In the good old days, cabin soles were made of teak planking separated by holly strips that stuck up proud. They were constructed this way to provide sure footing below during adverse sailing conditions. Most cabin soles on today's pro-duction boats are fashioned of plywood boards that sport a thin membrane of hardwood at the surface, and while these floors simulate the look of a teak and holly sole, they can in no way, shape, or form function as heartily as did their forebears. These veneers, while charming to look at, lose their countenance in a hurry if they are not well protected from the start.

Here are some tips for finishing new cabin soles, as well as refinishing ones that have seen better days. If you're starting out with a new boat with a bare sole, the job is half done. Make sure you take advantage of that fact by keeping it covered until you have time to apply the finish. Cardboard sheets make a lovely interim floor covering; tape them in place and do all your commissioning first. Then uncover the sole and give it the finish it demands.

My favorite soles to refinish were Swan cabin soles, because every single board popped out at the turn of a few screws. Many a winter found a sea of teak-and-holly plywood boards from somebody's Swan filling our shop. If it is possible to take your sole out like this, do so. The final finish will not only be nicer looking, but you will have a back left when you're through with the project. If, however, only a few boards from your sole are removable, I recommend leaving the entire thing in place. It's easier to work on those stationary boards if you're not trying to keep from falling into the bilge where removable ones are missing. Additionally, the finish buildup will be more consistent if everything is done together.

If you are refinishing an older sole, figure out what sort of finish it has on it before you start attempting to strip. Many boats from the Orient are now being finished on the interior with epoxy-type materials. Stripping these with a heat gun is next to impossible, and a chemical stripper is almost always your only recourse. Do some stripping tests before you commit to any one program.

It's possible that the old finish is a heavy,

resin-based oil finish. These can be bleached off with Te-Ka A&B (though very, very delicately, as scrubbing can wipe out the skin of veneer instantly). However, if the oiled cabin sole is not completely removable, a wholesale acid-type bleaching may be too great a threat to surrounding furniture. Under these circumstances, the two-part hydrogen-peroxide bleach made by Daly's (you mix the two parts together to create the strength of bleach appropriate to your situation) is a wonderful treatment, because you lightly scrub with it on a first pass, wipe off the residue, and then "paint" on a coat to dry overnight. This treatment returns a muddled, dirty cabin sole to its original vibrantly contrasting teak-and-holly self, and makes you wonder if the boat fairies came in the night and left you a completely new floor. The next day, you simply wipe off the crystallized bleach with water and alcohol, and allow the pristine wood to dry overnight again.

Once you are looking at bare, bleached, and clean wood the varnishing is pretty straightforward. The following tips supplement the general refinishing chapters, for cabin-sole projects on or off the boat:

When removing a sole from the boat, always make a map of the board shapes and their original locations, and label the back of each board with a corresponding number. Also, put an "N" on the north edge—that edge that faces the bow—of each board. I do this with a black fine-tip indelible laundry marker, so it doesn't disappear during bleaching operations. This will save labeling headaches later, when you're trying to put the sole back into place.

All power-sanding should be done with paper no coarser than 220 grit; if you're working on a veneer that has been around for a while, consider hand-sanding only. Above all, test sanding grits first on the least conspicuous board on the boat, and work backwards grit-wise to find the one that works best.

If you have the sole boards in your shop for the project, go ahead and pull all the hatch-pull fittings out of the boards. Believe or not, it's a good idea to label them as to board number, since they're sometimes inconsistent in size. If you are refinishing the sole in place, leave the pull-hardware in place, but mask over it precisely, with the rings in the up position in case you need to lift the boards during the project.

Pull up all the hatches at the beginning, if you're varnishing the sole in place, sand the outside edges, and run some masking tape around not only those edges on the hatch boards, but along the abutting perimeters where they go back into place. Replace the tape every three coats, and then when the last coat has dried, varnish the edges (with the boards out, of course, until they've dried), giving them no more than two coats total, just to seal them. Any more than that makes the hatches fit too tightly, and they will stick when you're attempting to remove them later.

If you're doing the sole in place, a couple of things will make your coats come out looking like something other than nonskid. First, after you finish each sanding (even between coats), completely vacuum the entire boat—not just the sole—and then with lightly moistened diapers, wipe everything down. To minimize the amount of stirred-up dust during vacuuming, have an extra-long hose made for your wet-dry canister vacuum (go to your local hose-supply company for this), and leave the canister itself out in the cockpit during vacuuming. While you wipe down, have a big fan going in the companionway, sucking the dusty air *out* of the cabin, and then, when everything looks very clean, go home. Allow the boat to sit undisturbed overnight; and the next day, return, wipe down what settled out of the air, and then tack and varnish.

To keep yourself from feeling pickled at the end of each onboard varnishing day, set up your companionway fan again, make sure you have a hatch open at the bow, and during varnishing run the fan, set on low, to draw fumes out of the boat. Interlux #60 Rubbed Effect varnish, which is my favorite type for a cabin sole, is extremely potent to breathe, and I never apply it without wearing a 3M disposable charcoal-filter mask. I highly recommend following suit, on the boat or even in your shop.

If you are working on boards propped daintily atop sawhorses at waist level in your comfortable, well-lit, controlled-environment shop, spoil yourself even further by rolling and tipping all the coats. Mask around the edges of each board at the beginning, and remask halfway through, leaving the tape off for the final two coats. There is absolutely no reason on God's green earth to apply varnish by brush to these flat expanses, and the rolled finish builds up quickly enough so that a fair deep finish (with proper sanding between coats) is attainable in record time, possibly with fewer coats (the average best number of coats is eight when rolling).

If you are planning a rubbed-looking finish for the sole, varnish the first six coats with a high-solids gloss varnish (one that is rated for high abrasion) and then use a rubbed-effect varnish for two or three coats. This not only gives you a more tenacious finish on the sole, but keeps the wood from losing its clarity from excessive buildup of pigmented varnish. I don't think the extra time and labor it takes to actually rub out a finish (for an authentic, rubbed look) is worth the effort as long as there are products on the market such as Interlux #60. This is not only a very rich-looking finish, but it is a very forgiving material to use. What may look completely inundated with grit and dust when freshly applied usually dries to an even, satiny, rubbed-looking finish. And given the high resin content of this varnish, if a few flaws do remain after drying, or if you feel after it has dried that you'd like a little more sheen to the finish, you can always give it a buffing with extra-fine bronze wool and SeaFin (followed by a diaper rubdown) to polish in the desired look.

Give a newly varnished cabin sole at least one full week to cure before walking on it—two weeks is even better. Consider imposing a "stocking feet only" rule for the first month, and if anyone comes near it with sand on their shoes; sentence them to head-cleaning duty for the rest of the trip.

Refresh varnished cabin soles when they start looking scratched or battered (don't wait for them to start peeling, though). A proper eight-coat initial finish should last at least a couple of years before it needs refreshing, but that will vary depending on how much you use your boat. Repair any damaged or high-wear areas when you first notice them, or at the end of each cruising season. Late fall is the best time for annual sole maintenance—it gives the sole a winter to cure and brace itself for those sandy Timberlands.

OTHER CABIN SOLE FINISHES

If you are lucky enough to have a cabin sole that is constructed of solid planks of wood —and my bet is that those are teak planks —you might consider an oiled cabin sole finish (in which case, you should turn to the chapter on oiling for guidance down that path). Or you could even find that a bare, foot-worn patina is most befitting of the character of your boat. The luxury of solid planking underfoot is that you can choose your option "solely" on the basis of personal preference.

14

RESCUING TEAK DECKS

*I like work; it fascinates me. I can sit and look at
it for hours. I love to keep it by me: the idea of
getting rid of it nearly breaks my heart.*
—J.K. Jerome, *Three Men In A Boat*

Some boats come into this world intended to strut their exterior brightwork au naturel. The Swan, that belle of the Baltic Sea, is one of the best examples of a boat that would fall under this heading, and it has been my great pleasure over the years to look after a number of these magnificent vessels, whose hallmark is an acre of teak decking. A Swan owner's primary brightwork concern is the care of those decks; this can be as easy as mopping one's floor if a program is mapped out and adhered to from the start. But often those simple caretaking tasks escalate into a major retrieval program —all through misunderstanding the basics of teak care.

There are many, many boats besides the Swan that sport teak decks, and most of them boast a complement of varnished brightwork trims. For anyone with this double burden, the responsibility of wood care can seem overwhelming, and what usually goes first is the decks. I've lost track of the number of boats that have come to me in

a state of deck horror: black as the night from mildew, green with moss, grain so excavated into mountains and valleys, seam caulking missing. All the disasters were fixable, but they could have been prevented with some common sense and forethought.

Often decks get into this condition because the owner is trying so hard to keep them clean that he goes after the poor defenseless teak with stiff bristle brushes, Ajax, and a bucket of water heavily inundated with Spic and Span. (Does this crime sound familiar?) I can just hear the decks screaming in agony after every attack.

Another felonious assault is the promiscuous application of oil formulas. A preoccupation with "brown wood" leads most people to this often disastrous treatment, despite frequent warnings from those around them whose experiences have served as mentor. Even if such treatment doesn't destroy the seams (which is a standard side effect of oiling decks), the mildewing rate is increased dramatically (because the oil encourages the lingering of moisture on the wood), doubly so if the grain is not absolutely flat. The combination of mildew and deteriorat-

Weathered teak decks and varnished teak bulwarks and caprail add sturdy grace to a fiberglass hull.

ing oil creates a nasty clean-up job, one that usually cures the owner of "brown-wood-gotta-haves" once and for all.

The prettiest decks I've ever encountered were on a Swan in Southern California named *Pristine*. Talk about your appropriate monikers! This boat was lovingly kept by its owners, the Doug Prestine family, and the most awe-inspiring thing about her perfectly silvered decks was the fact that they got that way chiefly through sponge moppings and regular saltwater dousings. This boat won the hearts of all who saw her, and her decks were the envy of every boatowner who hadn't learned the secret of her beauty. That secret, in a nutshell, was the understated approach to maintenance.

Cleaning Teak Decks

To effect a simple plan of deck care, you must first begin with healthy decks. Starting at any other point would put you in a league with the farmer preoccupied with closing barn gates after the horses have already run off.

How to tell if your decks are basically healthy? First of all, do they look that way? A healthy teak deck is one that is completely flat of grain, naturally light brown as a result of either being brand new or having been freshly bleached and sanded, or silvered out from judicious weathering under watchful eyes, with seam compound flush and completely intact. You can check to see if the grain is in proper condition by running a fingernail across the grain. If it runs smoothly across the wood, it's in good shape; if it "ripples" as you scrape, the grain is too open and as such presents an opportunity for decline.

The program is embarrassingly modest to keep decks healthy. Give them a weekly washdown and flush them regularly with clean salt water whenever you're out at sea. If you happen to be cruising Mother Ocean, a nightly dousing is best, as it not only helps the decks absorb needed moisture, but it provides a store of that crystalline moisture for the next day's cruising. If you don't have regular access to the salt water, you'll still do fine with regular freshwater washdowns, but salt water is Mother Nature's bleach, and helps the whole program by preventing mildew from taking hold. If you initiate this program and are faithful to it from the day you take delivery of your healthy decks, they will stay healthy forever. But if you stray from this program, or if you start using bristles on the wood, you'll say goodbye to those healthy decks.

I have to applaud the guy who came up with the bristles campaign — he should be crowned King of Madison Avenue. The universal 20th century approach to cleaning any piece of bare wood seems to be the bristle brush. Even more frightening is the frequency with which those bristles are *wire!* Once you open the grain with a bristle scrubbing, that grain then collects more grit and fosters more mildew, and the only way to excavate those elements from then on is with more scrubbing in kind. And with each subsequent scrubbing, the grain opens more, to the point that it finally becomes impossible to get clean. The grain becomes so deep that it turns into a network of little valleys where water sits, ultimately turning the wood black.

Tear a page out of the Prestines' book and don't subject your decks to this torture anymore! Think of decks as living, breathing creatures with feelings and treat them with the respect that was obviously bestowed on the lovely *Pristine*. That deference translates to *proper* care and maintenance.

Of course, if your decks are already in a state of calamity, it's too late to just be thinking proper care and maintenance. However, fear not; there is hope. It can take some Herculean labor, but it's a good bet that those pathetic-looking decks can find their way back to their original glory — then you can take up the recommended maintenance program. Hope, for most people in this predicament, comes in a set of bottles aptly marked "Teak Wonder." However, the success of this product depends upon one very important condition: that the decks have not been treated with any type of oil or sealer (except the sealer made by that company, which can and should be removed by the Teak Wonder system). If your decks have been oiled or sealed with another product, your only hope is another bleaching-type product, called Te-Ka A&B. (For information on that product and its application, turn to Chapter 7.) If your untreated decks are utterly black with mildew, and that mildew sits in grain that looks like the Grand Canyon, you can choose from a couple of reclamation options. First, because you must eventually sacrifice that open grain to some heavy-grit sandpaper anyway, consider mowing it down before the bleaching, sanding enough to remove the bulk of the ridges. Then, test a small quantity of Teak Wonder on the worst remaining spot to see if it easily dispatches the mildew. If it doesn't, and you can use the Te-Ka system on your boat, then turn to that product for your bleaching. Te-Ka A&B is the bigger bully of the two systems, and will do a greater amount of work more quickly. Of course, this option would apply only if the boat has a fiberglass body, since a painted cabin and/or topsides would suffer from exposure to that product.

Why then, you may ask, not just use Te-Ka to bleach the decks whenever necessary on a fiberglass boat? Unless you really need the brute force of the Te-Ka system, your wood is better served by the less caustic Teak Wonder treatment. The latter is also infinitely more comfortable to work with, if only from the standpoint of peace of mind, as there isn't the constant danger of burning the wood by forgetting to neutralize something. It does, however, require the same personal safety protection. Cover up, cover up, cover up!

Teak Wonder is a heavy detergent with an added enzyme; it comes with a companion "brightener," which is essentially a citric acid that purges and stops the action of the residual detergent, bringing back the teak's natural lighter hue. Do not be confused by the instructions on the label, which lead the first-time user to believe that use of the brightener is optional. It's important to use the brightener to remove the detergent residue from the wood.

While Teak Wonder will not harm most paint and varnish finishes, it is murder on anodized aluminum. If your boat has any anodized trims on it, they must either be covered over tightly (duct tape and heavy plastic), removed from the boat (if this is convenient), or coated with carnauba wax before exposure to this system. Apply the wax generously, taking care not to get any on the surrounding wood (mask the adjacent wood before applying the wax). Leave it on until the boat is bleached and has dried, then buff it off for a return to shiny, unharmed anodizing.

One other item I would especially bring to your attention in Chapter 7 is the bleaching skirt, a method of protecting topsides during a wholesale bleaching operation. Consider carefully whether this might be applicable to your bleaching project, as it can save big headaches later. Please also refer to that chapter for instructions common to both the Te-Ka A&B and Teak Wonder systems, and heed all advice regarding personal safety. There are some critical differences, chemically, between these two systems and those differences dictate the following qualifiers for the Teak Wonder system.

In spite of what the label says, be sure to use the brightener. I don't recommend following the cleaning with an application of the Teak Wonder sealer, as suggested on the label. While easy to apply —you simply slosh it on—this sealer is a very unnatural color and its protection is short-lived. But do pay attention to the Teak Wonder first-aid instructions, and by all means shake the bottle during use, as the materials have a tendency to settle out.

Give the whole boat a hosing down before

A nicely silvered teak deck contrasts with the mahogany bulwarks and caprail.

you start and then begin the bleaching with the blue solution, labeled "Teak Cleaner." Apply the cleaner generously and evenly, but do not scrub until you've allowed it to sit and penetrate the moist wood for a couple of minutes. Then, with a soft nylon tile scrubber, scrub in a circular pattern until the solution becomes a veritable lather. Allow the froth to sit, and move on to another section, repeating the application of the cleaner in the above manner. While the unscrubbed second application is soaking in, go back to the lathered area, add a little more cleaner and whip that section back up into a froth. Allow that first section to sit, return to scrub the second section, and repeat the whole process progressively back and forth between previous and subsequent sections until each new area has been lathered up three times. Don't worry about rinsing anything off as you go. In fact, the longer the foam sits on the wood, the cleaner the wood becomes; conversely, wood that is rinsed too soon will come out looking a little under-bleached. If it's a warm or sunny day, take care to keep the foamed-up areas moist by giving them a fine spray of mist before each rescrubbing. When you finish an entire section, such as the port side of the deck or everything on the cabintop, then rinse off the cleaner from that whole section. As you rinse, if there are nooks and crannies or crevices where bleaching residue and dirt have collected, nudge the residue loose with a soft toothbrush, but don't scrub with a vengeance. To help rinse things off thoroughly, scrub very gently with the soft tile scrubber as you douse the wood. If you have a jet spray nozzle on the hose, use it on a light spray setting during your rinsing; powerful blasts from spray nozzles can excavate the soft wood from the grain. (This brings to mind a new service that is popping up in marinas around the country —"power washing" by companies who can blast your 40-foot deck clean in about 15 minutes. Unfortunately, they leave behind the worst imaginable cases of excavated grain, as the high pressure knocks the pith completely out of the wood.)

When all the teak has had "cleaner" treatment, give the whole boat one more thorough rinsing, bow to stern. Allow the water to drain off —but don't allow the wood to dry —and then apply the "brightener." The operative difference between this and the Te-Ka bleaching system is that with Te-Ka, the bleaching solution must be neutralized within about five minutes of the initial application; with Teak Wonder, the whole boat can be bleached before any neutralizing (using the brightener) takes place. And Teak Wonder's brightening solution only requires a short standing time before it can be rinsed off. You do not need great amounts of the brightener; I spread it over the cleaned teak with a large cellulose sponge and as soon as the teak is transformed to its natural golden color, I rinse it off. If I miss any spots, they will be obvious by their contrast in color —noticeably darker —and I need only go back and apply the brightener to bring them even with surrounding areas.

When all the cleaned teak is brightened, rinse everything again, this time with the spray nozzle, but on as gentle a setting as possible. Continue rinsing until you've made about three complete, thorough passes over the boat. When you've finished rinsing and have wrapped up for the day, inspect below for leaks and wipe up any water that has found its way inside the boat.

Because the focus of the Teak Wonder system is its enzyme cleaning factor, the key to its success is keeping it in a lather as it sits on the wood. This foamy state heightens the efficiency of the enzyme by shielding it from sunlight, which reduces the enzyme's effectiveness as a cleaner.

Allow the wood to dry completely before commencing the sanding phase.

MATERIALS USED FOR BLEACHING DECKS
Sufficient quantities of Teak Wonder (unless bleaching with Te-Ka A&B, in which case be sure to buy extra "B" —the neutralizer)
3M Soft (white) nylon tile scrubbers
Large plastic funnel
Soft-bristle toothbrushes, varying sizes
Eye shields
Construction rainsuit
Nitrile gloves
Decks boots (with no holes!)
Kneepads
Water hose long enough to reach farthest
  end of boat

Spray nozzle for hose
A source of fresh water
Clean baby diapers

WEATHER

The work is best done on a cloudy, cool day; it can be done when it's warm and sunny, however, but the job then requires more bleaching material and your undivided attention.

ATTIRE

If it's a warm enough day, you can wear shorts and a light t-shirt or even your bathing suit underneath the plastic overalls; just keep the bleaching solutions off your skin as you work. On cooler days, I suggest something in a tasteful college sweatshirt, or on a really cold day the cozy protection of a washable bunting sweater.

CREW

Teak Wonder bleaching is easy enough to do alone, though it's heartening to have some company; Te-Ka projects will send you over the edge if you are a novice working alone. Helpers who don't know how to work while they talk should be put in charge of lining up massages for the end of the day.

Sanding Teak Decks

When you've bleached your decks, especially decks whose grain was not in particularly good shape before the bleaching, it is vital to understand the importance of sanding the wood as a follow-up to that treatment.

Bleaching, regardless of the system used, raises the grain and often pulls at least a little of the soft wood out of the grain, despite efforts to scrub gently. If you walk away and leave the grain wide open, rain and dirt will sit in those little valleys and pores and accelerate the mildewing process that forced you to bleach in the first place. Sanding the grain flush again gives the wood a more efficient runoff surface and pre-

vents excessive moisture from lingering on the wood.

If you have selected the option that entailed sanding down the ridges prior to bleaching, you still must follow the bleaching with a second sanding step to remove the bleaching "fuzz" and the deep scratches left behind by the heavy-grit paper. Either way, if your boat has had "the big bath" it is now due for "the big grind."

Sand as soon as possible but no earlier than one day after the bleaching. Waiting longer, especially with very open-grained wood, can allow the return of mildew if much rain falls on the decks in the interim, necessitating a repeat of the bleaching routine. However, if you have brightwork trims that are slated for varnishing, it is wise to save the deck-sanding until the varnishing project is completed, so that you can clean up any "accidents." If possible though, to minimize the suffering, try and keep drop cloths and protective barriers between your decks and any truant varnish.

TRIM DECK SEAMS FIRST

Sometimes decks are built from teak that is so well cured that when the boat hits the water, that teak has a heap o'swellin' to do. And swell it does —so much, in fact, that the seam compound is squeezed until it protrudes well above the level of the wood. While this creates a remarkably effective non-skid deck, it eventually becomes a problem because the caulking, over time, starts to get kicked loose and then pulls out altogether. Even if it doesn't get to that stage, it can hinder your program of deck care by impeding the necessary sanding work after a bleach job. The first time I tried to run a power sander over some bloated seams, it took me about one hour to do two square feet of deck. On a 40-foot boat, that gets you from one end to the other in about 25 years!

Here's a little trick, born of some of my early Swan deck jobs, that cut the sanding time in half.

Take a single-edged razor blade and bend it

just slightly in the center to create a gently curved blade. Then, starting at one end of a seam, run the concave blade under the caulking —pulling it toward you, keeping it steady and flush with the level of the wood as you go. This actually requires two steady hands, as you hold each end of the blade between thumb and forefinger. Given the angle at which you hold the blade, you'll eventually start rubbing the small knuckle on each forefinger raw. Prevent this by wrapping a couple of layers of masking tape or a wide Band-Aid around the top halves of those digits. You could wear gloves, but it's harder to control the blade, so I recommend the wrapped approach.

Don't be cheap with the razor blades; a fresh, sharp edge is the means to a clean, even cut and smooth-looking seams. Buy a box of 100 if available, or at least ten 5-blade boxes. Before you begin, bend a good supply of blades and then at about ten- or fifteen-minute intervals, retire the one you're using and get a fresh blade.

If the boat is large and you have an entire deck to trim, the project can seem never-ending; enlist the aid of some friends and promise a six-pack to the one who can come up with the longest continuous strip. Or better yet, schedule the trimming for a nice sunny day, and have it coincide with the radio broadcast of a baseball game.

When the decks are all trimmed, be sure to vacuum up any little slivers of caulking, or they'll become ground into the wood as you walk around. Dispose of all the trimmings properly — do not bury them at sea.

NOW YOU MAY SAND

Once the seams are leveled, the sanding can begin and should move along nicely thanks to the trimming. Before you plan your sanding project, though, read the sanding section in Chapter 8, as well as the sections on sanders, sandpaper, and masking tapes in Part Three. These will give you the basic details you will need to get safely and fruitfully through a deck-sanding campaign. A word of caution, however, in choosing your weapons for this war: while disc and belt sanders may seem obvious candidates for their ability to plow through a job like this in record time, the price to be paid for the express treatment is dear. In the hands of all but the most seasoned professionals, these sanders cause more damage and create more work than they do good. Stick with the safer, albeit more deliberate, approach of an orbital sander. If time is a big consideration, increase the labor force.

If the grain is open wide enough to yodel into, consider using something as coarse as 60- or even 50-grit paper for the planing down of those teak Alps. Buy one sheet of each and test for the best sanding time, both by hand and by machine. Figure on going through at least a sleeve of this heavy grit for a 40-foot deck. And buy a sheet each of 80 and 120 to test for finish-sanding to follow up the heavier paper. In some cases, especially after 50-grit work, it takes two finishing grits—80 then 120—to clean up the scratches. If the decks are moderately open-grained, 60-grit paper should work well to flatten out the grain, followed by 120-grit to finish. Using anything finer than 60-grit for the flattening phase could mean investing unnecessary time in the project.

When you are ready to sand the decks, prepare the boat in the following manner: Set up all your materials, cords, tools, and equipment in an easily accessible order on the boat — above decks — where they won't have to be moved later. Cut up as much paper as you think you'll need for the day. Lock down all the hatches and ports, and stuff rags in the dorades. Double-mask (laying one strip over another) all vulnerable areas adjacent to the wood with the appropriate tape. Remove any spinnaker poles or other movable items that stand in your way and set them on the dock; pull up any fittings that are not bedded or that come away easily (placing them along with fasteners in a Ziploc bag), and

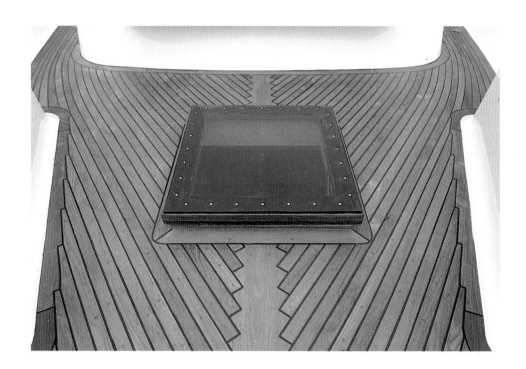

Above: *This oiled teak deck has a full-time professional caretaker.*
Below: *Bare teak decks, varnished teak cockpit staving.*

double tape around any that cannot be removed.

Start by machine at one end of the boat and work your way toward the other, keeping the storm of sawdust brushed aside as you proceed. When the buildup of dust keeps you from seeing ahead clearly, stop and vacuum up the bulk of it; if you are sanding off extremely deep ridges, this will probably need to be done frequently. Keep a brown paper grocery bag (with the top edge rolled down one turn) next to you as you go for discarding sandpaper. Leaving shards of spent paper in your wake just makes the job less manageable.

When you've sanded everywhere the machines will fit, go back and hand-sand the areas too tight for the sanders. Then, begin again from the start with the power sanders, switching from the heavy-grit paper to a finishing grit to remove the deep scratches and swirls. This second pass over the wood will fly, since the hard part —mowing down the ridges —is what takes the most time. Be sure to repeat the sanding by hand, with the finer grit, wherever the machines missed, since the earlier hand-sanding with the heavy grit also leaves deep scratches in the wood.

This job can be utterly and absolutely exhausting. I guarantee you will want a massage the night after you start it. Do yourself a few favors to alleviate some of the burden. If you have gotten this far in life having made not a single friend, make one now. Do not attempt this task alone; no man or woman's back is intended to bear the ache of such a chore without the company of an equally miserable comrade. Even if you have to buy that friend's assistance, do so. And don't be a fool while you work —it is never Miller time until the job is wrapped up for the day. Not unless you plan to put in a short day. A tall, cool one may sound good to you as you slave away in the sun, with the nasty taste of teak dust on your parched lips. But reach for a pint of juice. It will fuel your body, where beer will sabotage what little energy you may have left. Choosing juice instead will also help you stay alert while handling power tools.

If you stop for the day before the job is done, pull any tape and vacuum up as much of the accumulated sawdust as possible before you leave. If you've finished sanding the whole deck, vacuum carefully, pull all masking tape, and move everything —equipment, supplies, cords, trash, etc. —either below decks or to a spot on the dock where it will stay dry. Then, get out your hose, hook up your spray nozzle, and —starting at the bow or from the flying bridge —let there be water! Spray the entire boat, including spars, lines, and sailcovers, and chase as much of the filthy water out of the gunwales as you can. This is the only way to get rid of the dust that pervades every little corner of a boat after such a dusty experience. Flush the boat until you can't stand to hold the hose any longer.

Allow the decks to drain completely before setting resident paraphernalia back in place. If any fittings need to be bedded, wait until the boat has had a chance to completely dry before doing so, using your wet-dry vacuum to suck out any water that might still be sitting in the holes. If there is varnished brightwork on the boat, wipe it dry, after thorough rinsing, with a clean, cotton baby diaper or other soft, clean rag, or with a chamois.

Follow-Up Deck Care

It is inconceivable to me that anyone who has put forth the effort to complete this job would knowingly and purposely turn around and allow the decks to fall back into ruin. To prevent this from happening, consider one or both of the following deck-care measures: 1) Buy a full boat cover, and leave it on the boat whenever it is not in use; 2) Blackmail, beg, or hire someone — if you can't do it yourself —to give the boat a proper washdown at least twice a month.

Adapt these basic guidelines to your own boat in setting up a regular routine of deck and overall boat care:

Close and lock down all ports, hatches, and other openings to the boat. Remove all canvas covers from windows, hatches, winches, etc.

Spray the entire boat down at the start, including spars and sailcovers.

Clean plastic lifelines with Softscrub; if they don't respond to this treatment, try some mineral spirits or possibly lacquer thinner (though with the latter be conservative, since it can melt the plastic); clean all fenders and other plastic items in a similar manner.

For washing the decks, mix Lemon Joy dish detergent or a mild boat soap and a little bit of TSP (of the latter, no more than a couple of tablespoons per bucket) with fresh water and mop the decks. If you are out cruising and washing the decks with salt water, you can skip the TSP, but not the Lemon Joy. (Lemon Joy will lather in salt water, but many other soaps will not.) Use either a string mop or the cellulose sponge variety, or a soft nylon pad (the kind that comes on the 3M Doodlebug swivel-head system). When using the nylon pads, lightly scrub in a cross-grain or circular pattern; avoid scrubbing with the grain as much as possible, as this can pull the soft wood out of the grain. Then, rinse the decks clean with a gentle spraying from a jet spray nozzle. Never use bristle brushes on the decks.

If you're trying to remove potato chip oil or suntan lotion from the decks, make an oxalic acid solution and spot-clean these areas, but don't really scrub them out. The chemicals, and not your elbow grease, are the agents of dispatch for this occasion. Another product that can help remove such oil stains is a spot-cleaner similar to that used by dry-cleaners for clothes, called "K2R."

Scrub the waterline with a soft- to medium-bristle brush or the Doodlebug (using a different pad, not the one you used for the decks).

Spray any plexiglass surfaces with fresh water and squeegee them dry before replacing covers.

Remove black runs around winches (on fiberglass) with full-strength boat soap or by hand-rubbing with Seapower or Supercoat fiberglass cleaner/polish products.

Clean around stanchion bases with a soft-bristle toothbrush to dislodge grime. Polish all stainless stanchions with a good metal polish like "Brite Boy" or "Liberty" polish.

Squeegee all standing water out of corners, recesses, etc.

Rinse all brightwork with clear water (do not wash with soapy water), and wipe dry with cotton baby diapers or chamois.

Uncoil all lines and use a jet spray to rinse out any grit; squeeze out excess water and re-coil the lines.

Inspect the boat's interior for leaks, and wipe up any water that may have found its way inside.

If you don't have time for the whole list, make washing the teak deck your highest priority. The other things will live, but the decks need regular attention to keep mildew and grime at bay.

If you plan to wax the fiberglass on your boat, do so after a deck bleaching and sanding project, and then make sure you mask every bit of teak deck adjacent to areas that will get the wax. Once an errant swipe of wax or any boat polishing compound finds its way onto the teak, it's an appointment with Monsieur Sandpaper before you are rid of the mess in the grain of the wood.

If your boat resides in a dirty moorage, you may need to supplement the regular washdown routine with a yearly "light bleaching" with Teak Wonder. Even the most dedicated maintenance programs in polluted areas can find the decks slowly turning an ominous grey —not silver — from petroleum pollutants; the only way to turn them back around is to use something more intense than the normal deck-washing formula. If this is necessary, be very delicate in your scrubbing during the bleaching, and then any follow-up sanding will be slight, and necessary only to remove a layer of fuzz raised by the bleach. If the boat lives in a region inclined toward moderate to high levels of rainfall, especially during winter months, and those decks are not covered during that time, even boats in trouble-free moorages can demand the added attention. Schedule your annual bleaching for spring, as this is when the decks tend to need it the most.

Oiling Decks?

Want my opinion? I say don't do it. Remember what I told you in the chapter on choosing a finish: teak doesn't need this protection, especially the decks. They are designed to withstand life on a boat without a finish. Inundating them with oils, dressings, sealers, and the like is only something you do to satisfy your own whims, and in this case that satisfaction can exact a steep toll.

We've already touched on the fact that most oil formulas have the ability to demolish your seam compound; they do this by virtue of their solvent content, which systematically breaks down many types of caulkings. Sure, there are oil formulas on the market that promise they won't do this to most types of compounds, but there are other reasons for shunning the whole idea of treated decks.

The fact is, unless you have a full-time skipper hired to babysit those artificially bronzed decks, using the right cleaners to remove suntan lotion and potato chip grease without stripping the teak oil, re-oiling them religiously as the oil disappears under the sun, bleaching them religiously because the buildup of oil turned black during a wet spell, sanding them after each bleaching, and re-oiling them after the bleaching/sanding regimen, and possibly replacing the seam compound because the oil did in fact ruin the seams (all this between cruises on the boat), an oiled deck is just not a practical way to go. If you want to lie down on the ground and kick your feet and scream "but I want to oil them, I want to oil them, I want to oil them!" then fine. Go ahead and oil them. I'm not the boss of the world, nor certainly the captain of your ship. I am just a concerned advisor who has seen this treatment cause otherwise impassioned sailors to fall out of love with their boats.

TOOLS AND MATERIALS FOR DECK BLEACHING

Teak Wonder or Te-Ka A&B bleaching systems (buy in gallon quantities; plus one quart set per worker)
Plastic funnel
Hose and spray nozzle
Soft nylon tile scrubbers (one per worker)
Soft toothbrushes, varying sizes
Cellulose sponge
Baby diapers
Bleaching skirt: Duct tape, safe-release tape, and 4 mil plastic; Carnauba wax and masking tape (to protect anodizing)

PERSONAL PROTECTION

Construction rainsuit, nitrile gloves, knee pads, eye shields, deck boots

TOOLS AND MATERIALS FOR DECK SANDING

Half-sheet and quarter-sheet finishing sanders (plus Ryobi sixth- sheet palm sander if available)
Sandpaper cutter
Hard sanding blocks
Counter brush or whisk broom
Wet-dry vacuum with brush nozzle attachment
Power screwdriver or VSR drill and driver bits or set of screwdrivers
50-foot power cord (one per sander)
Shore power adapter (optional)
Sandpaper supply: one heavy grit, one finishing grit (buy by sleeve quantities)
3M 2040 masking tape —1-inch and 2-inch widths
Ziploc storage bags
Single-edged razor blades (if trimming seam compound buy several boxes)
Large paper grocery bags
Heavy-duty dust masks
Nitrile gloves

WEATHER

It must be dry, but the work can be done most comfortably in cool weather; wind makes it hard to keep your eyes open.

ATTIRE

Anything goes (though a bare back is a good way to get a bad sunburn on a sunny day).

CREW

Should not be attempted alone, especially by someone already poised near the brink; a good way to make enemies of your friends, unless you promise them lifetime sailing passes.

15

DOCKSIDE REFINISHING ETIQUETTE

Fine manners need the support of fine manners in others.
—Ralph Waldo Emerson

Working on a dock shared by others is something that requires a little extra in the way of consideration for our fellow man. Dockside etiquette. My mother would simply call it showing good manners.

Here, then, are some good manners to show when spending your days messing about with boats that are still tied up.

If you reposition the bow of the boat so that it protrudes out over the dock, hang something large and brightly colored off the end so that people passing by do not accidentally bean themselves.

When sanding, stripping with a heat gun, or otherwise creating large volumes of debris from your refinishing efforts, do *not* sweep the debris into the water for the tides to carry away. In some places — Marina del Rey for example — this is against the law (even if it is biodegradable sawdust), and you can be fined.

When working from the dock, don't leave materials in the pathway of passersby, and especially don't leave open cans of chemicals, solvents, or varnishes out for the curious explora-

tion of any animals or children that might wander along. You never know when that dog is a *lawyer's* best friend.

If you are using a hose that stretches across the dock, make provisions for easy passage, if the hose is dragged over the dock itself, ensure that all who approach realize it is there. It's a sure bet that the person whose arms are loaded with provisions will not see it, and will likely not appreciate the unplanned "trip."

If you must work to the beat of your favorite drummer, have the decency not to foist your musical tastes on the boating community around you. For these occasions, God invented the Sony Walkman. Crank it up til your eardrums shatter! No one will be the wiser, and you will be much loved for what *couldn't* be heard blasting from your boat.

If you think your brightwork is beautiful and your neighbor's is ugly, try to refrain from mentioning that fact to your neighbor or their neighbor or the guy on the next dock. There is nothing more irritating than a know-it-all brightwork expert. Give your neighbor this

This oak deck on an antique boat needs varnish for protection.

book as a Christmas present, and let it go at that.

If you think you will be sanding next Saturday, check with your neighbors on each side and across the dock to see whether they plan to be varnishing that day. A true horror from hell is having an inconsiderate dockmate ruin fresh varnish with clouds of sawdust, and I have witnessed some pretty tense moments between otherwise cordial folks under such circumstances. The same goes for wild spraying of water on the boat next door while varnishing is in progress.

Don't ask people if you can borrow their tools —unless it is an emergency and you only need it for a minute. People don't like to lend tools, but it's very difficult to say "no" when we're put on the spot. The tool mooch usually becomes a very unpopular person around any dock.

Don't ask to "borrow" materials either. How do you return a sheet of sandpaper after it's been used? Rarely does the borrower remember to come back the next time with replacements, and the nice guy who did the lending just has to go out and replenish his own supply. This is another way to become very unpopular around a dock. Plan ahead and buy your own stuff.

Before you launch into one of those "Did I ever tell you about the time . . ." stories, ask the person who is on his boat trying to varnish or sand or do anything else if he feels like visiting while he works. Time and time again I have actually had people ask me to turn off my sanders so they can gab—about trivial stuff!—or worse, so they can ask me to talk them through an entire varnishing project. The person whose ear you are bending may be on the clock and cannot in good business conscience talk to you at that time. Or he may have a difficult time talking and varnishing at the same time. Or he may be the average boatowner desperate to finish varnishing the boat in the limited amount of time available. Whatever. Ask his permission before you assume he wants to chat. And if he says "No," don't take it personally. He's just trying to get the job done.

Part Three

TOOLS AND MATERIALS

TOOLS

Here is the answer which I will give to President Roosevelt. . . .
Give us the tools, and we will finish the job.
—Winston Churchill

*T*homas Carlyle once wrote, "Man is a tool-using animal. . . .Without tools, he is nothing, with tools he is all." I would amend that sentiment by saying that without the *right* tools he is nothing, and with the right tools he can *do* all.

Whether it is an instrument modified to perform as a tool, like my pet dental picks (which are indispensable for all sorts of stripping applications), or an electrically powered machine engineered to cut otherwise daunting tasks down to manageable size, the fact is we have become dependent on and grateful for the modern-day variations on the cave dwellers' sticks and stones.

I give you here a list of some of my favorite brightwork toys, along with some tips for getting the most from these prized possessions.

Power Tools

On the wall at my favorite Porter Cable service center hangs a modestly framed set of guidelines for the power tool operator. Good advice bears passing on, so I share it with you as a preface to other tips on buying and using these sometimes dangerous instruments.

Use your power tools:
When it's light, not dark
When you're dressed for the job
When soil or surface is dry, not wet
When you've taken time to know a new tool
When your work area is clean, not cluttered
During "your" most productive hours
When you're vigorous, not vanquished
When you're smiling, not angry
When you're relaxed, not hurried
When you get the help you need
When tools are in good condition
And—know when to take a break!
Hand-print a version of this on a big poster and hang it in your shop; these are words to work happily and productively by.

THE HEAT GUN
Heat as a method of finish removal has its roots in a more dastardly instrument: the propane torch. Today, unless your goal is nuclear finish meltdown, a heat gun is the quickest, as well as the safest, way there is to take old varnish or paint off a piece of wood. For much less than the price of admission to the local burn ward you can own one of the best guns on the market, the Easy Gun

(see below), and unless you're a hopeless klutz, you can strip the majority of the brightwork on any boat with ease, without burning up wood, flesh, your bank account, or even much physical energy.

Heat gun prices range from $35 to $100, and their quality is directly proportionate to their price. Buy a cheap heat gun, and you may *hope* to finish the project before the gun burns out. My favorite gun, which lists for around $90.00 (but some stores sell it at a discount), is the Easy Gun, made by the Easy Time Refinishing Products Corp. in Glen Ellyn, Illinois. What makes this gun so special? First, it is so lightweight that working with it for hours on end does not become a test of biceps endurance. Second, the element, which resides in the nozzle rather than in the body of the gun (which is the case with most other heat guns), gives you 1,200 degrees Fahrenheit of heat to work with and is estimated to last a whopping 2,800 hours. Should it happen to burn out, however, it is easily replaced by exchanging the old nozzle for a new one (at the turn of one small set screw) for a paltry $16—effectively giving you a brand-new gun. I have used my Easy Gun, with its original element, on almost every project for the past seven years, and it still works like a charm. I wish I owned stock in the company.

The third and I think most valuable feature of this particular gun is the design of its heat flow. Most guns brag about their expansive pattern of airflow, with the claim that it heats a greater area of the surface at one time. This is fine if you only expect to be stripping transoms or bulkheads and never need to concern yourself with an adjacent surface that could be harmed. The Easy Gun has an airflow that can be trained precisely on a trim and barely warm the adjacent surface, much less melt or burn it. This business of having to worry about adjacent trims is the *typical* scenario in stripping around boats, and you're well advised to use a gun that won't pose a constant threat to sister finishes.

One overheard criticism of the Easy Gun is that it has only one heat setting. Trust me when I tell you, unless you decide to go into the shrink-wrapping business (which is a selling point used by companies that put a low heat setting on their guns), you will never need any but the hot level for stripping and the cool level for cool-down before turning the gun off. If you do decide you want a cooler setting than 1,200 degrees, you can buy from the Easy Time Company nozzles with 600- or 800-degree elements, which can be interchanged with the hottest nozzle for whatever application you may have in mind.

POWER SANDERS

Porter Cable Speedbloc. This orbital quarter-sheet sander, originally a product of the Rockwell Corporation, is the workhorse of the industry, and for the more-than-occasional refinisher the most important power tool to own. Heavier than other quarter-sheet sanders, its design aids your sanding work by providing a perfect weight for the ideal sanding pressure. It is also the most durable of the models on the market. Through an excellent service network, worn-out motors can be rebuilt to like-new condition for much less than the cost of a new sander.

New Speedbloc's come with a "key" that assists in loading the paper, but you have to *look* for the key in the bottom of the box. Tie that baby to the cord immediately with something more permanent than a piece of twine; I usually borrow a length of leather lacing from my Timberlands, and tie it on with about fourteen knots to keep the thing from falling off. If you happen to lose your key, or accidentally threw yours away before you had benefit of this sage advice, you can get another one for about seventy-five cents from your Porter Cable service center. Go buy one now! The longer you use that screwdriver to open the clamps, the sooner you'll ruin the slot intended for the key, and ultimately you will not be able to open the clamps as far as you should be able. It is also one heck of a lot more convenient to reload with a key that is always right there with you than it is to scramble around looking for where you might have left the screwdriver the last time you used it.

To get the most from your Speedbloc, and to appear to those around you to be the smartest person alive, I have a little secret to impart. If you cut your sandpaper sheets into perfect little quarters (see "Sandpaper Cutter" later in this chapter for the means), you can load multiple sheets onto the sander, and then as they wear out, you simply 1) turn off the sander, 2) rip the offending sheet off the sander, and 3) turn the sander back on and resume working. You will reload, instead of *every* time you need fresh paper, every fourth time (in the case of heavy grits). My sister, Kristine, and I used to have contests (we had to do *something* to keep ourselves entertained) to see who could load the most efficient sander. I think she holds the record at eighteen sheets of 320 grit on one load! Of course, that was after the pad had worn down a bit; this would never be possible on a brand-new pad. At any rate, pencil this into your profit margin when you start figuring what your time is worth and how much time you've been wasting reloading sanders.

By the way, a newer feature on the Speedbloc is the standard foam-rubber Stikit pad developed by 3M to facilitate use of its new line of stick-on papers. The standard pad used to be thick felt, which was neither better nor worse but would not allow use of adhesive-backed sandpapers. You can get some information on this line of sandpapers from Chapter 17, but I prefer the stack of pre-cut sandpaper quarters to this one-at-a-time stick-on routine. The argument 3M uses to promote the newer approach is that cutting a strip only as long as it takes to cover the pad (rather than the length required to clamp dry sheets in place) wastes less paper. While this is true, the greater cost of the Stikit paper negates the savings. Slippage of clamped-on paper, which reduces its cutting action, does not occur when the sander is loaded tightly.

There are times, however, when a piece of Stikit paper gives you a better cutting surface, especially when working on softer woods. I keep a roll of each basic grit (80, 120, 150, and 220) in my supplies box for such occasions. If you have a project that encompasses a great deal of sanding work (restoring a whole boat rather than two handrails), or you just like amassing every material available to the refinisher, you're probably a candidate for the supplementary rolls.

Porter Cable Half-Sheet Heavy-Duty Finishing Sander. The larger member of the Porter Cable orbital family, this is the tool that speeds up a deck-sanding job or heavy work on large, flat surfaces. Trying to sand a deck with the Speedbloc is like trying to bail water with a measuring cup. You need a more serious machine for this expansive, often seriously open-grained job. The half-sheet sander is expensive, but durable and worth every penny; I still have the one I bought nine years ago, and it's had one rebuild of the motor in all that time. This is a very good investment for the person seeking a good assortment of power sanders. If you're weighing the difference between having your decks sanded professionally and doing it yourself, you'll come out way ahead by purchasing two of these sanders and doing it yourself, with the aid of a friend. And when it's all done, you'll own the equipment!

To cut sheets that fit the sander tightly (if you aren't using Stikit papers), trim 1/2 inch off the end of a full sandpaper sheet, then cut the balance of the sheet in half the long way; load stacks, but take great care to clamp paper onto the machine tightly. Loosely loaded paper is obvious immediately by a loud, fluttering sound.

Ryobi Orbital Palm Sander. This little jewel is so named because it fits into the palm of your hand, as well as many nooks and crannies inaccessible with the quarter-sheet sanders. It takes a one-sixth sheet and has a rubber pad that facilitates wet-sanding with oil when applying oil finishes to large, flat surfaces. It makes an ideal second sander for the refinishing buff, for use not only in oiling projects, but on overhead work (very lightweight) and small trims. It is the only sander I recommend for power-fine sanding between varnish coats (after the fourth coat), because its light weight lessens the possibility of cutting too quickly through the varnish.

HANDLING ORBITAL SANDERS

When you turn your sander on, always allow it to rev up to full speed (when it reaches its highest-pitched whine you're usually there) before applying it to the surface you're sanding. Likewise, always pick it up and away from that surface before you turn the machine off. This helps keep the motor in good condition, but more importantly, it prevents the deeper sanding swirls that ensue when the orbit of the machine is too slow.

Sand as you would by hand, *with the grain* whenever possible.

Don't lean heavily or bear down while working with a power sander, as this not only wears out the motor but, in slowing down the orbit, reduces the cutting efficiency of the machine.

Change paper as soon as the piece you're using has lost its ability to really cut the wood. You accomplish nothing running a spent piece of sandpaper over the wood; you're just wasting time polishing an area you should be sanding.

Be sure to load sheets tightly, since flapping sheets (obvious from a distinctive fluttering noise) do not cut effectively.

When you finish sanding for the day —especially after all-day sanding —vacuum the motor housing of the sander to free it of caked-on sawdust. This keeps the motor clean and working longer between rebuilds.

When using an orbital sander, make sure it's the only thing running off that extension cord. Reduced power burns out the motor much sooner and lessens the efficiency of the sander.

Porter Cable service centers can rebuild the motors on their sanders when they finally start to go (the first sign being such extreme vibration that you feel you can barely hold onto the machine), at a cost about half that of a new sander. Tender loving care keeps the need for a total rebuild at a distance. I don't recommend any more than one rebuild during the life of a machine; by the time you've worn the re-built motor out, it's time to buy a new sander.

Handtools

To me, used tools are far more charming than something off the retailer's shelf, and on average far less expensive. Knowing a tool has come to me with a legacy of service makes using it an honor. An afternoon in the local antique hardware store is like a treasure hunt; you cannot imagine what wonderful scrapers and other handtools are out there waiting to be discovered in such a place. Treat yourself to the adventure of such a visit and welcome the ghosts of old woodworkers into your toolbox.

SCRAPERS

Here's the most important thing to know about scrapers: They must be properly sharpened and kept in that condition in order to serve you efficiently. Once the burr or lip has worn off the edge of a scraper, it's time to get out the file and resharpen the edge. A scraper's sharpness is easily monitored, if not obvious by its performance, by dragging a thumb against the inside of the blade's edge. If it feels smooth, or does not seem to resist or pull against the thumb, it is probably too dull to use.

Some people like to round off the sharp corners of their scrapers to prevent gouging. This is OK if the scraper is going to be used as a dry scraping tool, where muscle is the power source. For heat-gun stripping, leave the scraper corners intact and learn that proper heat stripping involves scraping with a minimum of force. In so doing, you will have more flexibility in using your scrapers, as the sharp edges provide a means of stripping detailed areas and areas right up next to perpendicular surfaces.

Keep scrapers and files in a dry place, or they rust in a hurry.

Red Devil makes excellent, inexpensive scrapers with hard plastic handles; some have replaceable blades. My favorite is the 1-inch hook scraper. Red Devil also makes a nice, fine mill file for sharpening, usually sold wherever the scrapers are available.

The Canadian-made Murphy scrapers have nicely shaped wooden handles and come in various sizes. Replacement blades are usually available where the scrapers are sold. Usually found at boatbuilding or woodworking specialty stores, this line of scrapers has a nice blade design flared at the sides for detail work.

SANDPAPER CUTTER

To get perfect quarters for your Speedbloc, perfect sixths for your Ryobi, or perfect halves for your big finishing sander, or just to cut up multiple sheets of paper in lickety-split fashion, add this wonderful homemade tool to your collection. To make one, cut a piece of wood (I use particle board because it doesn't warp) to measure about 8 x 14 inches; attach a medium-toothed hacksaw blade to the board—teeth facing right—1 inch from the right-hand long edge of the board, using stainless steel #6 3/8-inch panhead sheetmetal screws. Drive the screws through a #10 flat washer under the blade at each end. With an indelible black marker (medium-point laundry markers are perfect), draw three lines parallel and to the left of the blade at these distances from its toothed edge: 3 inches, 4 1/2 inches, and 5 1/2 inches.

When you use your sandpaper cutter, the most important habit to get into is to put pressure on the blade with two fingers while you tear the paper upward with your other hand. If you don't do this, the paper will slip and cut un-

evenly, and over time the blade will become so bowed upward that it will not cut straight edges.

Practice cutting more than one sheet at a time —for instance, cut a stack of four sheets of 220 grit at once. Becoming proficient at this, again, saves a lot of time on a big refinishing project.

To prolong the life of the blade, always cut paper with the grit facing down.

MISCELLANEOUS TOYS

Power screwdrivers. Whether you use a power screwdriver or a simple utility drill with driver bits, once you've removed fasteners with the aid of power you'll have a hard time going back to doing it the old-fashioned way, one hand twist at a time. Driver bits for your drill come in every imaginable size and configuration and cost virtually pennies. Here is one of the absolutes in having the right tool for the right job. You'll save a ton of time that is better invested in more contemplative refinishing of your brightwork.

If you are a consummate tool junkie and don't mind spending money on tools that have limited application, the Milwaukee Cordless Screwdriver is an excellent example of a tool designed specifically for this purpose. It is a heavy-duty reversing-power screwdriver good for only one thing —driving and removing screws. Pretty to look at (it's red! just like the Easy Gun), it also has one very handy feature: it bends, for easier access to screws in tighter spaces.

Aluminum clamp-on lamps with 75-watt bulbs. These lamps are vital when working in dimly lit interiors or under covered moorage. They are always inexpensive, and available at most hardware stores. Don't use bulbs higher than the recommended wattage; 75 watts gives ample light without overheating the aluminum hood.

Tekna Keyknife. This is a high-quality, small steel pocketknife on a keychain, made by a company that specializes in diving equipment. My Tekna knife is nine years old and as sharp as the day I bought it. It's great for excavating old bungs, and even handy for some stripping work. It's always there when you need it, for cutting the tips off Te-Ka bottles or digging encrusted varnish out of the slot on that screw.

X-Acto knives. Take a trip to your art supply store and buy a set of these precision cutting knives. You'll be amazed at how indispensable they become when working on any boat project, from brightwork to wiring to woodwork. Always keep a sharp blade in the knife, and store it in a protected box between uses. A supply of replacement blades is important to have on hand.

Interlux slotted metal stirring stick. Usually only about fifteen cents, these are a wise investment not only for stirring paints, but for stirring the one type of varnish that will allow such treatment —a satin or rubbed-effect varnish. This cleverly designed wand with its legion of holes does the job quickly and efficiently, without whipping up a froth of bubbles. It can be cleaned with any brush-cleaning solvent and then reused, though I would recommend owning separate ones for use in paint and varnish.

Dental picks. I have a collection of dental picks with plastic handles that I bought at Doc Freeman's years ago; since they're virtually impossible to find anymore, I guard them with my life, as they are invaluable for all manner of brightwork applications. I use them for stripping minutely detailed areas, cleaning out reefed deck seams, scarf joints, and on and on. If you run across a source of these disposable picks, buy them by the dozen. Otherwise, a call to your local dental supply company or even to your favorite dentist might net you access to other types that work just as well.

Wet-dry vacuum. These versatile vacuums are made by a wide variety of companies; a ten-gallon size is ideal for the average refinisher's needs. My favorite is the Sears Craftsman 16-gallon Wet-Vac, for its incredible power and wide hose for sucking up large volumes of shavings, varnish scrapings, and sawdust. This size is a little unwieldy and expensive, though, for the occasional refinisher to justify. The smaller ones in the Craftsman line are of equal quality and may be more appropriate for the do-it-yourselfer.

Change vacuum filters or clean accordion-type filters regularly, or the sucking power will be drastically reduced. With accordion filters, caked-on dust must occasionally be scraped out with a screwdriver or stiff nylon brush.

Unless you're sucking debris from narrow crevices, use a brush nozzle attachment. This prevents the hard plastic hose end from leaving scrape marks on brightwork surfaces, and it helps clean things up faster by brushing a wider swath into the airstream.

Counter brush. This is a nice alternative to the standard whisk broom, as the finer bristles help sweep debris away more cleanly and give you a clearer idea of the condition of the grain of your wood as you sand. A width of 3 inches is best; lengths usually run around 10 inches or so.

A good tool bag. This is a must. Nothing breaks my heart quite like the sight of a collection of tools rattling around in a plastic tub. Handtools should be organized so that you know where to find any certain one when you need it; they should also be protected from the possible damage that can result when they're all banging against each other in some fishing-tackle box. Most woodworking shops carry some variation on the canvas bag that is compartmentalized to hold a nice variety of tools. Amortize the cost by reminding yourself how much you would spend over time replacing banged up tools.

Sony Walkman. This piece of equipment (or any other variation on the "personal entertainment device" theme) will earn you more friends than any other. If you don't know why, turn to the chapter in this book entitled "Dockside Etiquette." Aside from the socially beneficial consequences, losing yourself in this private world of entertainment while you work can be a boon because it helps you get any refinishing job done in the minimum of time. Why? Because it absolutely precludes the possibility of talking while you work—the second biggest impediment to brightwork progress (after inclement weather).

Bungie cords. The ones that come with little hooks at each end are good for tying power cords to lifelines to keep from them dragging across varnished rails, or for pulling flapping halyards away from a mast while you varnish from a bosun's chair. I keep an assortment of short- to medium-length bungie cords in my tool bag, and they come in handy for all sorts of impromptu binding exercises.

Interlux can opener. Here's a little gadget that is far superior to and much handier than a screwdriver for properly "unlidding" a varnish or paint can. These are usually free (or sold for a nominal fee, depending on the chintziness of the vendor) and available wherever Interlux products are peddled. Pick up five or six, and put one everywhere you plan to be working.

Collapsible ice pick. Many chandleries carry ice picks that unscrew to become their own covers between uses. This is nice, as it prevents unplanned impalements when reaching into your tool bag. This is the perfect tool to use for piercing the inner rim of a varnish can to help keep varnish from building up in the lip.

Rubber mallet. Get that hammer out of your tool bag and replace it with the professional painter's recommended mode of lid closure. These are available at most commercial paint outlets, are not very expensive, and will save your lids and varnish cans from the cruel torture typically in-flicted by less sensitive instruments of poundage. This translates to more varnish for your dollar, since you get a better seal when closing cans with a rubber mallet, thereby preventing   unnecessary loss of varnish to skinning over.

On Loaning Tools

Bear in mind the wisdom of the nursery rhyme:
I had a little pony
His name was Dapple Gray
I lent him to a lady
To ride a mile away.
She whipped him, she slashed him,
She rode him through the mire;
I would not lend my pony now
For all the lady's hire.
                                    —Anonymous
I admit to being a soft touch when someone asks me nicely enough to let them use something. I have gotten less and less generous about loaning my tools, however, after too many unfortunate incidents involving well-meaning but careless borrowers. A brand-new Speedbloc, loaned to a muscular boyfriend, came back nearly burned out from the pressure he exerted on it over a weekend sanding his decks, and when he didn't offer to pick up the tab for the rebuild on the motor I had to bid him adieu for good. My treasured set of chisels, borrowed by a beloved friend who absentmindedly left them on the dock for several days in the rain, never were the same after I got them cleaned up, and I didn't have the heart to make that dear person buy me a new set. My gorgeous Bosch drill, borrowed by a coworker, also spent a few days in the rain and has never worked as well as it did before that torture. The only solution is to be selfish. My dad, Mr. Generosity himself, has even confessed in recent years that his tools are now off-limits to would-be borrowers. It isn't really selfishness; it's an investment in those relationships, which are easily strained over unfortunate, unintentional accidents.

MATERIALS

There are Six Essentials in painting. The first is called 'spirit'; the second, 'rhythm'; the third, 'thought'; the fourth, 'scenery'; the fifth, the 'brush'; and the last is the 'ink.'

—Ching Hao

I once heard a story about a violinist renowned not only for his talent but for the priceless Stradivarius he played. It was believed that the marriage of this instrument to his virtuosity was the key to his impeccable performances, and his concerts were preceded by as much hoopla over the violin as over violinist. He adored this prized possession and treated it like his child. One night, before a sellout crowd at Carnegie Hall, this man came out on stage, bowed, and proceeded to play to such perfection that by the end of the first piece the audience was in a state of delirium. They were on their feet the instant the piece was finished, crying "Bravo! Bravo!," and as he completed a series of bows he held up the legendary instrument as though offering it to the gods. The audience again went wild, cheering as mightily for the violin as they had for the virtuoso. Then, almost in slow motion as the cheering continued, he brought the violin downward and with a sudden vengeance threw it against the stage floor, where he crushed it underfoot like some oversized cigarette butt. The crowd was aghast; women shrieked, men booed. Everyone thought the man had lost his

mind. Almost obliviously, he turned and walked over to the edge of the stage where he retrieved the real Strad, and amid a deathly hush he then returned to center stage. Speaking barely above a whisper he shyly announced: "A true artist needs but the humblest of instruments to make his music sing." The concert went on, shards of the lowly fiddle at his feet. And never again did the Stradivarius enjoy equal billing to its great master.

Fact or fiction, I think this story makes an appropriate parable in the context of this book. So many times people have oohed and aahed over a boat I've just finished and, without even taking a breath, asked, "What varnish did you use?" I admit certain wonderful varnishes have made my life easier, but if I were faced with no choice but to use a "lesser" varnish, I guarantee the result would look the same. Conversely, couple a thirty dollar can of varnish with a lack of total commitment and you will no more get a professional-looking finish than Henny Youngman would get sweet music from the maestro's Stradivarius.

If I were to translate Ching Hao's list, it would

read as follows: There are six essentials in brightwork. The first is a sense of perfection; the second, a commitment to the finish; the third, an understanding of the function of the finish; the fourth, the potential beauty inherent in the wood; the fifth, the skill guiding the brush; and the last is the varnish. Learn these truths and only then will the differences in varnishes, brushes, or any other instruments of the art mean anything in the course of your endeavors.

Sandpaper

Abrasives have followed a curious path of evolution through the generations. In the 13th century, the Chinese used crushed seashells bonded to parchment with natural gum for polishing. In 16th century Switzerland, paper was coated with ground glass to provide abrasive materials for artisans and craftsmen, though it did not hold its sharpness for long. Not until the 19th century, in the United States, was sandpaper resembling the product we know today introduced. Flint quartz was used in the early decades, replaced later by garnet, which was superior in hardness and sharpness to flint. In 1891, silicon carbide was discovered by Edward Acheson while he was attempting to produce artificial diamonds. He called his new product Carborundum after the company he worked for at the time. This was followed ten years later by the discovery of aluminum oxide, and in 1934, in the quest for a material harder than any known, scientists discovered boron carbide, which is next to the diamond in hardness.

Today, 3M is considered the king of the abrasives industry (among other industries). For marine application, they focus primarily on silicon carbide and aluminum oxide for use in manufacturing abrasives. Silicon carbide sandpaper is marketed under the 3M trade name Tri-M-Ite and is noted for its refracturing characteristics, which means that under use, instead of wearing down, the mineral breaks down into new sharp slivers, essentially regenerating its scratching quality. Silicon carbide is used in the making of dry sandpapers as well as wet-or-dry papers. Aluminum oxide, while not as hard as silicon carbide, is inherently tougher and is equally favored as a finishing abrasive because its chunky grit has less tendency to fracture and dull during use. It is marketed under the names Three-M-Ite and Production papers.

When you buy a sheet of 3M paper, you choose your product on the basis of two features: grit and paper weight. Dry sandpapers come in five weights: A, C, D, E, and F. Wet-or-dry paper comes in two: A and C. The paper weight on this scale is in ascending order, which is to say that A weight is light, and F weight is very heavy.

Grits range from a coarse grade of 12 (we're talking rocks here!) to "micro-fine 1,500." A range of 50 to 600 is not unheard of in the restoration of a single boat, and it's wise to have the entire range on hand during the project to prevent a needless waste of time sanding with a less-than-ideal grit.

If you are buying sandpaper sheets in what I call the "shaping range" for brightwork application—that is, the coarse grits from 50 to 100—the paper should be C or D weight for maximum support of the heavy coating of minerals on the paper. If you are buying papers in the "finishing and clarifying grits" (120 to 400), then A-weight paper is best for optimum flexibility.

Sandpaper gets its grit number from a grading system using shaker screens and air chambers. To illustrate, imagine a 1-inch by 1-inch screen with 80 openings per lineal inch. A "grade 80" mineral will just fit through the openings in this screen, hence the designation "80 grit." And so on for all the coarse grits. The air-chamber system is used for the finer grades of mineral. The smaller the number, the coarser the grit; ergo weathered teak decks are planed down with 50- or 60-grit paper, and we sand between varnish coats with 220-grit paper.

When you go into a chandlery, hardware store, or wherever you buy refinishing supplies, you can identify the sandpaper that best suits your needs by looking on the back of the sheet for all the vital information. Besides the trade name depicting the type of mineral used (Tri-M-Ite or Production) and the paper weight and grit number, the one most important word you should look for on 3M sandpapers is the trade name Fre-Cut. This means that the grit, after it has been glued to the paper, has been coated with zinc stearate. This coating is of significant importance because it acts to retard clogging of the grit as you sand oily woods and finishes. Any paper that is not treated with this material is a poor substitute and will be about half as effective in use on brightwork projects.

The 3M Company has recently introduced a new twist in its Fre-Cut line. The silvery-white or gray papers made from silicon carbide are still widely available, but so too is a ceramic aluminum oxide resin-backed paper called the Fre-Cut Gold. This paper, which really is gold in color, is designed to withstand changes in humidity better than the original Fre-Cut line, because resin is substituted for glue in affixing the minerals to the paper. The Fre-Cut Gold still has the zinc stearate in its final coating, and this is what continues to make this the most appropriate line of abrasives for use on marine surfaces. One fact that is important to note when making the shift from the original silver to the new gold Fre-Cut is that the grits are not equivalent in cutting ability. The gold is almost exactly one grit sharper, which is to say that 220 Gold cuts about the same as 180 Silver. Take care not to forget this, especially in the finishing grits, because using 220 Gold between varnish coats, for example, can wipe out a lot more varnish buildup than you may have intended. It also leaves a more pronounced scratch in the varnish surface.

The standard presentation for sandpaper has been in 9-inch by 11-inch sheets. In recent years, 3M has come out with a line of self-adhesive abrasives called Stikit, which are discussed in Chapter 16. To that discussion I must add that a good deal of sanding is done by hand, and even with the attendant toys 3M puts out for using Stikit papers by hand, the simple trifold (see below) is faster and economically the winner. The biggest reason, though, for buying sheets instead of rolls is that you can buy sheets in any quantity you need, whereas a roll of one grit must be purchased in its entirety. This gets pretty expensive when all you want is the equivalent of 10 sheets of 80 grit paper. For really big projects, I think it wise to invest in three rolls of Stikit—80 grit, 120 grit, and 220 grit—for those frequent occasions when this paper is really useful. Beyond that, I think, sheets are still to be preferred.

Proper storage of sandpaper sheets is vitally important. Leave a stack of 120-grit paper in your dockbox for a few days in the hot summer weather and you'll find out why. You will return to curled sheets that are virtually useless. The same thing happens in humid air, with the exception that the curl goes the opposite direction. The smartest, neatest, and cheapest way to store sandpaper is in a plastic box called a Multi-File, available at most office supply stores. They are the exact dimension of a sheet of sandpaper, and a single box will hold approximately three full sleeves (a sleeve is the cardboard encasing a 50- or 100-sheet lot of sandpaper, with exact quantity determined by the coarseness of the grit). I keep a range of grits in each of two boxes: one for my shop, and one on the work site. I never find myself without the proper grit or with ruined sandpaper.

USING SANDPAPER

• For general use, cut sandpaper sheets into quarters (see "Tools" chapter for instructions on making and using a sandpaper cutter).

• For handsanding detail areas, fold sand-paper quarters into trifolds. This makes it possible to use every square inch of the paper, and the third (inner) fold keeps the paper from slipping around and wearing out the inner faces before they've had a chance to perform. When the outer sides are worn, open it up and refold so that the still-fresh inner side can be used.

• When handsanding long, flat expanses, get into the habit of wrapping your sandpaper quarters around a foam-rubber sanding sponge. These grit-coated sponges are designed to be abrasive in and of themselves, but the grit loses its effectiveness too quickly to justify buying and using them on that basis. They are excellent, though, as a shape around which to wrap sand-paper quarters, since the grit holds the paper in place better than a normal cellulose sponge would. Handsanding this way promotes an even plane, because your sanding is not at the mercy of the uneven pressure of your fingertips. This is best used as a method of sanding flat areas between varnish coats. Good brands include Gerson and Red Devil. Buy the ones coated with coarse grit; they hold up and keep their shape longer.

• Make a couple of hard sanding blocks for flattening uneven wood surfaces, especially as you sand over bungs. The longer one is a must when sanding transoms, as it is too easy to leave a wobbly plane when sanding such large expanses of wood without the aid of a hard block. These blocks are necessary only for the shaping-grit work—60 to 100 grit. Turn to the softer foam blocks for the finer finishing grits.

Make your blocks from two lengths of 2 x 4 (no knots!), one about 6 inches long and the other about 11 inches. Glue a thin layer of cork (no thicker than 3/16 inch) onto the bottom side of each to help keep the sandpaper from slipping. If you want to get fancy, carve a groove into each side for a better grip on the block.

Explore your favorite boatbuilding store for interesting variations on the handsanding block theme. Solid cork blocks, for example, are usually tucked into some little corner of the shop; these are lightweight and wonderful to have in your tool bag. A collection of various shapes and sizes of handsanding blocks encourages you to do a better job of sanding, and such items are inexpensive.

Chemical Strippers

When you apply varnish to wood, the varnish turns from liquid form into a hardened membrane by virtue of oxidation and the evaporation of its solvents. When you want to remove that same varnish, one way to do so is by reversing the process and turning the hardened membrane back into liquid form. You accomplish this by reintroducing the solvents to the varnish, and you do *that* by applying a chemical stripper. A semi-paste finish remover is a mixture of special solvents and methylcellulose, the latter acting as a thickening agent that facilitates application on vertical surfaces. Such strippers also typically contain paraffin or another type of wax to create a barrier, keeping the solvents from escaping into the air and literally forcing them back into the varnish below. As this occurs, the varnish wrinkles up and pulls away from the surface to which it had adhered.

The best chemical strippers are nonflammable and have a standard solvent base of methylene chloride. Such finish removers can be ignited, but have such high flash points that a flame will only flicker and then die out. Unfortunately, attendant to their superiority in removing finishes is the fact that methylene chloride strippers are very toxic, and they are gradually becoming the black sheep of the solvent world. Research and development labs around the country are seeking friendlier chemicals to substitute for methylene chloride, but the consensus is that the safer the chemical strippers become, the less effective they are.

For now, the products that contain methylene chloride should be used with circumspection. Be thankful for their efficiency (the job will be over sooner), look for stripping methods that obviate having to use chemicals (heat guns, for example), and above all adopt a survivalist mentality whenever working with a solvent stripping system. Excellent ventilation, a good respirator, and appropriate skin protection are always advised under such circumstances. Methylene chloride products have negligent warning properties, which means that the vapor can attack your system without your smelling or otherwise becoming aware of it. As a result, even when you wear the recommended respirator with organic vapor cartridges (which contain activated charcoal filters), you must guard carefully against the vapors from the solvent sneaking through the spent charcoal. The ideal protective gear for using methylene chloride strippers is an air-supplied respirator. If your budget simply cannot bear the expense of this type, then do use the standard respirator but make sure you change the cartridges often, and above all, do the work where the ventilation is unimpeachable. And for heaven's sake, read the labels on these products. The information there is provided for your personal safety and more informed use of the product.

Two excellent chemical strippers are Interlux Pintoff 199 and Dayco Marine Strip, both useful for any brightwork stripping project. For stripping next to fiberglass or for removing old varnish from gelcoated surfaces, Interlux makes a second stripping product called Pintoff 299, a gentler formula that will not melt fiberglass surfaces. It takes a little longer to do its intended job because of its weaker solvent base, but for detailing varnish-slopped gelcoat, especially in nonskid areas, this stuff is the cat's meow. Just get out your Pepsodent toothbrush, pour a tiny bit of stripper on the drip, let it bubble up for a couple of minutes, and scrub it away. Then wipe the area clean with some lacquer thinner, and you're looking at a clean stretch of nonskid.

A few tricks for optimum results in using chemical strippers:

• Lay down a thick coating and immediately cover the entire surface with a sheet of Saran Wrap or waxed paper (the latter is best, especially on wide, flat expanses.) This prevents early evaporation of the solvents and increases the wet time, and therefore the stripping power, of the application. Remove the protective sheet when the bubbled finish appears to be drying out and repeat the application *without* scraping off the first layer (usually within fifteen minutes of the first coating), covering with a fresh sheet of Saran or waxed paper. If the first coating does not appear to have dried but remains wet looking, and the varnish beneath seems completely dissolved, the stripped finish can then be removed from the wood.

• If the finish is relatively thin, allow the stripper to bubble up and dry out on the wood surface and then scrape it off dry for less toxic handling of the dregs. Vacuum the scrapings.

• Before sanding, always give a surface stripped with chemical removers a lacquer thinner bath to remove all traces of stripper (especially those containing paraffin), which could contaminate a subsequent varnish finish.

• Instead of scraping dregs of chemically loosened varnish and remover off the wood with a putty knife, scrub the melted finish gently, while adding lacquer thinner, with a flexible nylon scrub brush, a true natural bristle brush (soft bristles only), or for little nooks and crannies, a Pepsodent toothbrush (soft-medium). Then pour the liquid mess into a tub and wipe the stripped wood clean with lacquer thinner-soaked rags (shop rags or baby diapers). If you are working on a vertical surface, have a layer of heavy plastic topped with a thick layer of newspapers taped beneath to catch and absorb the solvent runoff.

• Check the label to see if the stripper can be neutralized with water, and if so, use water instead of lacquer thinner to clean stripped wood.

This can raise the grain slightly, but if sanding is in the schedule anyway, the point is moot. Neutralizing with water lessens the expense and threat to personal health attendant to solvent washing. This only applies to stripping solid pieces of wood. Veneers should be washed with solvents only, to prevent delamination of the wood or potentially disastrous additional sanding.

Bleaching Products

There is a multitude of different brands and formulas on the market designed to aid in purging the sins from the surface of your stripped wood. Many do what they claim to do; some do even *more* than they claim; and others claim to do things that only in their dreams could they do. Since there are no "bleach police" on duty to arrest the impostors, the next best thing is a posse of citizens —*you,* for example. If you find yourself being wooed by a certain bleaching product, buy the smallest quantity available and test it to see if it gives you the result you're after. If it doesn't, let the chandlery know that you were disappointed by this product; if you used it incorrectly, they might be able to help set you on a more productive course. But it could be they've had a number of complaints about that product; yours could be the one that gets it yanked from the shelf, and then you'd be a hero. As David Horowitz always says, *speak up!* If enough people do, then buying things like wood bleaching products becomes less a crapshoot and more an exercise in informed consumerism.

Following are the bleaching products I have always had success with:

Te-Ka A&B. This product is for bleaching badly mildewed or oiled woods (always buy an extra supply of neutralizer). It was formulated exclusively for teak, but I have had success using it on many other woods. Buy a pint set and test it on the least conspicuous spot on your boat before you jump wallet first into the whole program. Unless you need to remove an oil finish, a treatment with oxalic acid might be just as effective and easier and safer to work with than this potent system. Te-Ka eats right through paint, can score the wax job on your gelcoat, and burns unprotected skin —in short, it's a chemical bully. But when the job calls for something powerful, this is the right stuff.

Teak Wonder. This product was formulated for bleaching light to moderately weathered and mildewed woods (especially teak). An excellent annual cleanup treatment for teak decks that reside in troubled moorages (under airport landing patterns, for example), this is the kinder, gentler (than the Te-Ka) approach to serious deck bleaching projects where an oil finish is not involved.

The wisest way to buy either of the above bleaching systems is by the gallon set. However, these behemoth bottles are unwieldy to work with, and you end up wasting a lot of product. To solve this, buy also a quart set of the system for each worker; take a plastic funnel to the boat and refill the quarts from the gallon bottles.

Oxalic acid. This is an excellent, inexpensive means to removing mildew or water stains from bare wood. For spot bleaching make a paste; neutralize with borax, vinegar, or soda ash. If you are bleaching a large expanse, use the following recipe: 16 ounces oxalic acid to 1 gallon hot water for bleaching; 3 ounces borax to 1 gallon hot water to neutralize.

Trisodium phosphate. This salt is a utility bleaching substance that is best used as a maintenance material in caring for decks or other wood that is being left to silver out unfinished. Added in small quantities to soapy water, it helps arrest the growth of mildew in woods such as teak; too much can rob the wood of surface oils and pro-

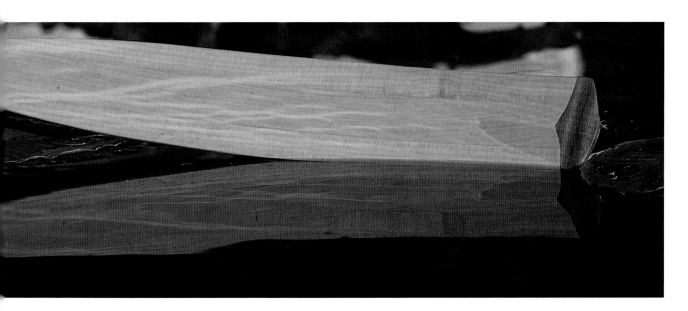

mote cracking. Copious rinsing is a necessary second step after using TSP for any cleaning or bleaching operation.

BLEACHING ACCOUTREMENTS

Aside from Pepsodent soft toothbrushes, you should never use anything with bristles to assist in your bleaching efforts. The ideal instrument for this job is the soft nylon Tile Scrubbing Pad, which comes affixed to a hard plastic handle and is made by the 3M Company. Use *only* the soft pad, which is white; the blue, or black, or brown pads are much more abrasive and will rip the surface of the wood as thoroughly as would a wire brush. One tile scrubber will see you through one 40-foot deck-bleaching job; after that, it's pretty shot and best reserved for light deck-cleaning jobs.

A larger version of the nylon pad comes with 3M's Doodlebug Pad Holder, which is the approach to deck swabbing for those who don't wish to get down on their knees with the hand scrubber. The Doodlebug has a swivel-head holder that attaches to a standard broom handle, and while this is not an instrument you would want to use for bleaching your decks, it is a nice way to keep them clean once they're in shape. The kit is expensive (around $35.00 for the holder and two pads—handle extra!) but a wise alternative to the traditional deck broom if you want your teak decks to stay healthy. When you purchase the kit, it comes with one brown (coarse) pad and one white. See if the chandlery will let you trade the brown one for another white one out of stock, if you don't have a barbecue grill to clean or barnacles to scrub off your boat's bottom. Stock up on some extra white pads, too; they wear out soon with regular use.

Masking Tapes

When it comes to masking tapes, the crown is worn by 3M. With Scotch Tape 3M established itself as the king of the tape world and never looked back. (Rumor has it that the "Scotch" in the name came from some early sentiment regarding a stingy coating of glue on the tape; what's ironic now is that their wildly successful Post-It-Notes, with a light coating of low-tack glue, seem to celebrate that sentiment.)

The following 3M masking tapes have application in the marine world, and are the most ideal for various taping needs on a brightwork project:

• #2040 Scotch Masking Tape—A painter's grade masking tape that boasts balanced construction (which translates to optimum combination of weight of crepe paper and distribution and tack of adhesive). This is the perfect everyday tape for use on one-coat varnishing tasks and general masking whenever you're sanding adjacent to a vulnerable surface. It must be removed before the day's end. It is available in five widths, but the most applicable for brightwork are 3/4 inch, 1 inch and 1 1/2 inches. Painted surfaces may require a strip of Safe Release tape beneath the 2040.

• #225 Silver Weather-Resistant Masking Tape—A tape designed to stay on exterior surfaces for up to thirty days, though I would cut that back to about half to ensure a clean varnish edge. This is basically 2040 with a silver coating that prevents deterioration from the elements. It is easy to apply, though edges must be firmly pressed down at the moment of application to get the longest seal. My only complaint about this tape is that it sometimes leaves behind a little black lip of glue when you've sanded between and applied multiple coats of varnish. To prevent this, the tape is best left on for only a couple of coats at a time. If you are shocked at the price of this tape, remind yourself that it is almost equal to the price you'd pay for two tapings with conventional masking tape, but without the additional time invested in laying them down. It is available in four widths, from 3/4 inch to 2 inch.

• #256 Scotchmark Green Masking Tape—If you have access to this brilliant lime-green tape, I recommend it as an extended-use tape over the 225, despite the fact that it was not designed nor is it marketed by the company to be used as such. Through the entire range of weather conditions, and after repeated sandings and of multiple varnish coats, this tape comes away cleanly and cooperatively after as many as 30 days, and that without the residual glue edge that is sometimes a byproduct of the silver tape. Because of its flatback quality, it keeps a smooth, sharp edge, which helps in producing a crisp, smooth

varnish edge when it is removed. (Limit the number of varnish coats to three per taping to achieve such an edge.) This tape is available in seven widths, but the 3/4-inch and 1-inch rolls are all I ever use. It is as expensive as the 225 and worth every penny for the same reasons. Note: Some people have mistaken this for a low-tack masking tape; it most definitely is not, and disastrous results will attend its application to any vulnerable surface.

• #226 Solvent-Resistant Masking Tape—This black, polyurethane-backed masking tape is *very* expensive (over $50 for a 3-inch roll!), but it is the only way to protect an adjacent surface when stripping with chemical removers. This is the tape to use when you simply must chemically strip a piece of brightwork that sits atop gelcoat and you need something stronger than Pintoff 299 to achieve that end. It has the same tack as regular masking tape, so if you need to protect an adjacent painted surface that could be pulled up by this tape, you can first lay a strip of Safe Release (low-tack) tape and then stack this on top to get the protection you need. It can be left in place for up to three months (but why would you want to?) and is available in four widths, from 3/4 inch to 3 inches.

• #2070 Safe Release Tape—This white flatback masking tape is the solution to any masking problem that involves a vulnerable surface, such as painted topsides on a wooden boat. It is not an extended-use tape, but you can leave it in place for a couple of days if it doesn't get rained on. Use it as a base tape on fragile surfaces, over which you then lay either a strip of 2040 for sanding work adjacent to such areas or a strip of solvent-resistant tape when chemical stripping is underway. Fine by itself as a masking tape for paint and varnish work, it comes away cleanly and leaves a smooth edge after single applications of varnish. This tape is available in 1-inch rolls that usually come individually wrapped in cellophane.

• The only other tape worth mentioning in

this context is one made not by 3M but by the Daubert company, and usually available at paint supply stores. It is called Easy Mask painting tape, and it is a lightweight brown paper tape usually about 3 inches wide with a 1/2-inch gummed edge. It comes in handy for varnishing areas that are so awkward that a wider tape is called for to protect surrounding areas from a wholesale mess. It does not have application as a masking tape for sanding projects, and when used on exteriors should be pulled at the end of the day.

TAPING TRIVIA

• The minute you get a roll of tape to the boat or shop, put it in a Ziploc sandwich bag to keep the edges clean. Nothing ruins tape quicker than tossing around in a dirty box of sanding and varnishing supplies, and once the edge is full of grit and dings you no longer stand a chance of masking a clean, true edge on the boat.

• *Never* leave regular painter's masking tape—the crepe paper variety designed for one-time use only —on the exterior of a boat overnight. Masking tape that experiences the difference in temperatures from day to night to day again exchanges vows with the surface beneath and enters into an unholy marriage. *If* you are fortunate enough to get it off the next day, it will not be for lack of resistance to your efforts. At the worst (which is what usually happens), it won't come off without scraping or without using an adhesive remover to soften the glue. If you are masking for several coats of varnish use a tape that is designed to stay on for the long term. If you are masking to protect adjacent areas during sanding, mask only about three hours' worth of work. As you complete the sanding of that portion of the boat, remove the tape, then mask the next three-hour segment or as much as you think you'll be able to get to within the remainder of that day. One of the great wastes of valuable refinishing time is having to pull tape beyond your work area at the end of the day. It is also a waste of materials.

• Though a tape may be made for "extended use," retain a healthy skepticism about its long-term wearability. You never know when weather conditions will pose the exception to that tape's rule of tenacity, especially once it has been in place for about a week. Test a different area each day after it goes on to ensure that the tape still comes up without a fight, and if a section seems determined to stay put, untape the whole boat then and there.

• If you think you may take the boat sailing even just for the afternoon, forestall taping brightwork—especially along toerails —until after the sailing trip. If these areas are already taped, either postpone the sailing or remove the tape. Dousing the tape not only messes up its glue edge, it can shorten the "extended life" it was designed to give you.

• When masking for sanding, lay down a double thickness of tape (one strip on top of another) for proper protection of the surface below. If you are sanding with a power sander this is especially important, two or even three thicknesses of tape (3M #2040, for example) prevents the pockmarks one often sees as a result of relentless sander-banging on an adjacent wood or fiberglass surface. If you think such preventive measures are too much trouble, consider the unsightliness of those permanent scars or the cost of fixing them.

• Lay masking tape no closer to the brightwork than 1/16 inch to encourage an adequate varnish seal at the brightwork edge. Much closer than that and the varnish will tend to peel back at the edge because there is no seal between the wood and the adjacent surface.

• When laying down tape, tear it by ripping it against a single-edged razor blade scraper anchored firmly on the strip. This nets you a perfectly clean tape end, with no waste and no obnoxious tape "tails" to curl up and create varnish runs as you apply the finish. It takes practice to learn to tape this way, but before long you will find that doing so speeds up the whole process of taping, as you become more and more adept at laying and ripping. Keep the razor blade holder in the same hand that holds the roll of tape. Don't ever "slice" the tape with the razor or any kind of knife, as the obvious result would be a cut in the surface beneath the tape.

• Always mask in the longest continuous strips possible; tearing off short pieces and laying them down one at a time not only triples the time it should take to mask but creates a messy, choppy edge that promotes varnish drips. It also adds unnecessary time to the tape-removal process.

• For greatest efficiency and economy, use the narrowest width possible when masking for varnishing. Crepe paper tapes, especially, have a much greater ability to take a curve when they are between 3/4 and 1 inch wide, and unless you are an incredibly careless varnisher, you should never need a wider mask for your work. For sanding work, a wider tape is recommended, although 1 1/2 inch should be the maximum width necessary even for power sanding.

• Here is a tip that has more bearing on painting jobs (such as bootstripes) than brightwork: Run a piece of 220-grit sandpaper along the edge of the tape that is to be painted, just enough to create a foolproof seal at the edge of the tape. This not only prevents bleed-through but gives you a near lipless paint edge. It works on any good masking tape and is something I do whenever I have to repaint nonskid areas after I've varnished adjacent trims.

• If you are oiling, don't expect your masking to protect the surface below from the oil; oil seeps underneath the tape, regardless of how carefully you've sealed the edge. This forces you to be very careful while you oil, applying conservative coats to minimize runoff and keeping a rag and lacquer thinner handy for immediate cleanup when a run does occur. Do be aware of the importance of taping for an oiling project,

however, when application of the oil involves wet-sanding. Failure to do so can net you sanding scratches that may not be apparent until you're finished with the project. Best to tape, not only for the protection but to speed things up by reducing the need for excessive care as you work.

• An invaluable taping tool is a 3/8-inch soft wooden dowel, sharpened to look like a fat pencil. I scratch off the sharp tip with a bit of fine sandpaper, then use my fake pencil to trace around taped edges that are susceptible to varnish leaking underneath. Such vulnerable edges include those around grabrail bases or along any nonskid surfaces, especially waffle-patterned gelcoat surfaces.

• To pull off reluctant tape in cold weather, train a hair dryer (on its warmest setting) over the tape as you pull it slowly from the surface. This may seem to proceed slowly, but it's a far cry faster than chiseling the tape off later with the aid of adhesive remover.

• If you are concerned that the tape you are using might be too sticky to come up later without pulling up the finish beneath it, and you don't have a roll of Safe Release or low-tack tape handy, "spoil" the tape by running the strips between your fingers — a couple of times should do it; just enough to reduce the stickiness of the glue — before you lay them down.

3M GENERAL-PURPOSE ADHESIVE REMOVER
A number of years ago an architect called wanting to hire my sister and me to work on his Cheoy Lee; he mentioned something in passing about a little tape that was stuck on the fiberglass, but overall he was concerned about having the brightwork done and having us get to it as soon as possible. When we met him the next day at the boat we were tickled at his sense of urgency, which had stemmed primarily from the tape problem. The problem, shall we say kindly, was moot. He had hired his teenage son and a friend the *previous summer* to work on the teak,

but their excitement over a summer job at suntan central flagged at precisely the point where they had finished masking off the last piece of trim (they had believed this to be the necessary first phase of the project). Apparently masking was as far as they had gotten in their brightwork pedagogy, and a year later it was obvious to Dad that they wouldn't be picking up where they left off.

I believe some liquidation of stock took place to finance the removal of that petrified tape.

When you make the mistake of leaving tape on for too long a time, or you try to get away with using a cheap masking tape and are caught with permanent crepe paper adornments all over your boat, General Purpose Adhesive Remover is the antidote. This specially blended solvent quickly and easily removes residual glue as well as grease, tars, certain oils, and waxes. It is slow drying, will not cloud or harm Plexiglas or Lexan surfaces, and is safe for use on painted, fiberglass, vinyl, varnished or even fabric surfaces. To remove strips of bonded tape, hold a rag soaked with adhesive remover over the tape long enough to allow the solvent to seep under the crepe paper, then slowly pull up the tape. If necessary, use a good putty knife—one with a beveled edge—to help scrape off the loosened tape, taking great care not to gouge the surface below.

Foam Brushes

Since I happen to be a foam brush adherent (or shall we admit fanatic?), the application of varnish is described in this book with reference to that instrument. I make no apology for this, because it springs from my utmost confidence in that modern variation on an old theme. I could, to be democratic, discuss varnish application in broader terms encompassing bristle as well as foam brushes, but then I would be defeating the whole purpose of this book, which is to impart *my* favorite varnishing tricks. I have nothing against fine bristle brushes; in fact, I used to own a nice collection of them. But cleaning and maintaining a stable of $20 brushes was a daily exercise I could never entirely abide, and I gave them away when I found that I could achieve the same and often superior results with their foam cousins *without having to clean them when I was finished!*

There are those who challenge the use of foam brushes on the same grounds as I myself have argued against the use of disposable diapers: the environmental impact of their disposal. But the discarding of foam rubber brush heads (the wooden handles, being biodegradable, are not at issue) is no less responsible than the disposal of spent brush-cleaning solvents. Either way, something gets into the environment, and I daresay that my spent foam brushes end up in more appropriate places than most people's brush-cleaning solvents. In addition, with foam brushes I am not facing the compounded dangers of physical exposure to the toxic solvents that are in the average brush cleaner.

In a way, the "foam vs. bristle" debate is a moot issue, at least from the standpoint of performance, because the majority of brushing techniques apply to both. The one possible difference is that, in the hands of a beginner, a foam brush may mete out a thinner coat. With practice, though, that ceases to be the case, as the seasoned varnisher learns to "unload" the foam brush. In the interim, the price to pay is an extra coat or two.

Granted, certain finishes cannot, by virtue of their content of hot solvents, be applied with a foam brush. Indeed, stamped on the handle of the Jen Poly-foam brush is the announcement, "not for use with shellac or lacquer." Such finishes cause the foam to bloat like a salted slug and then fall apart before your eyes. If you are using a finish that has a hot solvent base, do some checking to see whether it can be applied with a foam brush before you buy a case of them.

The trick to getting a good coat from a foam brush is, first, loading it sufficiently. Dip it, regardless of size, into the varnish about 1/2 inch above the bevel—a couple of times at the start. Don't soak the brush in the varnish the way you would a piece of bread in egg batter for French toast. A couple of five-second dips should give you what you need. Then "lay" the varnish down, applying a bit of pressure (not too much, though, or you end up creating a varnish froth) to dispense the majority of the load. Don't stroke madly away, back and forth, back and forth, as the more you continue to brush the coating, the less varnish you leave behind; the brush, because it *is* something of a miniature sponge, will sop up the finish in spongelike fashion. When a brush becomes overloaded (which often happens on long varnishing days or when working on overhead areas), I throw the saturated brush away and start with a fresh one of that size.

Twenty years ago a gentleman by the name of John Chisolm invented the Jen Poly-foam brush, and since that time his little company in Worcester, Massachusetts has sold over 500 million of the little things. The distinguishing feature of the Jen Brush Manufacturing Company's foam brush, apart from its brown-stained wooden handle and dense black foam head, is the construction of the brush itself. Unlike other foam brushes on the market, the heads on these brushes are firmly glued to the inner plastic form, keeping them from falling apart when saturated with the average oleoresinous finish. The grade of polyurethane foam is also the highest of any brush on the market. There simply is no other foam brush to buy for use in fine refinishing work. Most chandleries sell Jen Poly-foam brushes singly and in cases; the boxed or "case" quantities vary with brush size: 48 per box in the 1- and 2-inch sizes; 36 per box for 3- and 4-inch brushes. Buying them a case at a time is preferable if you are doing a job of any appreciable scope, as it not only saves you repeated visits to the store but keeps them stored in a clean, organized container. If you don't need that many brushes, buy the open stock but place them immediately in sealed Ziploc bags and store them somewhere *lying flat.*

Never buy foam brushes that come with plastic handles and "replaceable" foam heads, as they are, by design, ineffective and are usually of an inferior foam quality. They are also more expensive than Jen Poly-foam brushes.

FOAM ROLLERS

The best ones are once again made by the Jen Brush Mfg. Co. and are covered with a thin skin of the same dense black foam used to make the foam brushes. This is the only roller I would recommend for rolling varnish, as it does not shed, and it metes out a perfect thickness of varnish when properly loaded. An additional advantage of these disposable rollers is the fact that you can cut them with an X-Acto knife to widths suitable for specific applications, such as a long, flat caprail.

Varnish

There are as many wonderful varnishes on the market as there are opinions about how best to apply them. There are also some swine among the pearls. As tempting as it is to name the swine, I realize that such pronouncements could be subjective. So I will dwell on the pearls, but with a repeated admonition for those who think the brand of varnish is the key to nice brightwork: Without proper stripping of old finishes, proper prep of the bare wood, and proper application, "the best varnish" will be a disappointment and a waste of money. Brightwork magic is an aggregate effect. It does not emerge like some genie from a quart can.

Any varnish that has all the components listed under "Characteristics of a Good Spar Varnish" in Chapter 4 is a varnish I can recommend. I will say that I have gravitated to certain ones over

An immaculate little ship with mahogany toerail and teak pilothouse window mullions.

others as they have become more predictable in their behavior. In general, the entire line of Interlux products can always be counted on to deliver the finish I'm after, and among varnishes, their #96 Schooner Varnish and #95 Clipper Clear are two of the most satisfying products I've had the pleasure to use. In surveying those in my profession I find the same satisfaction with many other brands, and so I hesitate to declare any one varnish the absolute winner over all the rest. The key to finding a varnish that works is taking the time to get to know the var-

nish you choose. The more familiar you become with its idiosyncrasies, the more expert you will become at its application, and in turn the more you will come to regard it as the best.

Following are the names of some companies that make excellent varnishes. I put Interlux at the top of the list and name their best varnishes because I use these products almost exclusively, and because, all in all, I think this company makes the greatest effort to assist the user in getting the most from their products. If you ever have a question related to the use of Interlux products, the company has an easy to remember toll-free number that puts you in touch with the answers: 1-800-INTRLUX.

INTERLUX (made by International Paint Co.)

• #60 Rubbed Effect. For interiors only. A beautifully rich, pigmented varnish that gives you the soft sheen of a hand-rubbed finish without the hard labor. Very forgiving in application, dries to a hard, durable finish. I have used this on umpteen cabin soles (even on race boats!) with wonderful results.

• #90 Superspar. A high-solids, classic spar varnish that is great for high-gloss interior work; has no UVA, which in my book disqualifies it for exterior use.

• #95 Clipper Clear. The newest varnish in the Interlux line, this has the highest-grade UV technology of all their products. A polyurethane resin product, it is lighter in color than other varnishes in their line and touted to be the one that leaves all other varnishes in its wake. Although Clipper Clear is too new at this writing to have passed the judgment of time, it's a beauty to work with.

• #96 Schooner. This phenolic-resin varnish has been the mainstay in my refinishing business since it came out several years ago. It flows on beautifully without any adulteration whatsoever, but under difficult conditions responds handsomely to a little splash of brushing liquid. High in ultraviolet protection, durable, and an all-around joy to work with.

• #97 Inter-Poly Clear. This is a high-abrasion polyurethane resin varnish that is intended for use on areas destined to take a beating. I use this to build the first coats of a cabin sole before applying the #60 for a rubbed-looking finish. If you're looking for a glossy cabin sole, continue on up through all the coats with this varnish.

OTHERS

• Epifanes (also private labeled as Hinckley's)
• Z-Spar (Captain's and Flagship)
• McKloskey's (Bote-Kote)
• Woolsey

A note on some new "types" of varnish: There are many two-part varnish systems on the market these days that involve sealing the bare wood with epoxy-type base coats and then topcoating with a polyurethane formula, or sealing with a buildup of conventional spar varnish and then clear-coating over that with a polyurethane application. While the technology sounds fabulous, and looks wonderful when applied correctly with the requisite attention to detail (usually by a professional), such finishes become a liability when the time comes for patchwork or removal for a complete refinish. The promise of greater gloss retention and durability is negated by the complications attendant to their application and maintenance. If this type of finish is what you seek, I would encourage the use of a high-quality conventional polyurethane varnish such as Clipper Clear. All the varnishes I recommend are one-part.

GENERAL VARNISH TRIVIA

• Two thin coats are better than one thick coat. An excessively thick coat of varnish will never completely cure.

• Varnish is never to be given the Elvis Presley treatment (all shook up . . .). If you are adding thinners, don't "stir" those in, because the more stirring you do the more bubbles you introduce to the varnish: bubbles which are loathe to brush out as you work. To disperse thinners, add them to the varnish through the strainer (see below) and then gently "rock" the varnish bucket to swirl the varnish and thinner around and around. In very little time they will become one, and you will have introduced but one bubble to the mix.

• The exception to the no-stirring rule: If you are working with satin, rubbed-effect, or any other type of flattened or pigmented varnish, you *must* stir the varnish, not only before you pour it from the can but periodically as you apply it from the bucket. The pigments are heavier than the vehicle and continually settle out. If you do not stir it, you will end up with a very irregular sheen on the finished surface.

• Always strain varnish, even from a new can, to filter out debris and scum.

• Never varnish directly from the can. You not only introduce a great deal of grit to the varnish this way, but the open varnish loses solvent as it sits exposed to the air, rendering it less brushable by the time you get about a third of the way through the can.

• Don't use old tuna cans (or *any* recycled containers) for varnish pots. You run the likely risk of contaminating the varnish. Buy paper paint buckets in the pint size from a chandlery or paint store, and throw them away after each daily use.

• To reduce buildup of varnish in the rim of the original can, punch two or three holes in the bottom of the inside rim with an ice pick when you first open the can.

• When reclosing a varnish can, pound the lid down along the rim edge with a rubber mallet, *not* with a hammer, your shoe, or a winch handle. A rubber mallet allows you to give the lid a good whack, or eight, without maiming it, thereby ensuring an airtight seal and minimizing skinning of the remaining varnish. If there still happens to be a little varnish in the rim of the can, drape a clean diaper or cotton rag over the lid before you pound to absorb the backsplatting. Save the rag and keep it with your rubber mallet and ice pick as a can-closing "team."

• Don't play chemist with varnishes and solvents. When you purchase the varnish, read the label for recommended thinners. Most good varnish companies package as companion products to their varnishes a drying-retardant to aid brushing and an accelerating thinner for appli-

cation in cold climates and for spraying. If you add whatever you have lying around the shop as thinner, you run the very real risk of ruining the varnish. Companion thinners may cost a little more, but they are worth every cent when they eliminate the guesswork attendant to using solvents.

• Trust that a good varnish is formulated to perform beautifully in application without the addition of *anything*. The only time you should bother with thinning, other than as a way of getting your first couple of coats to really penetrate bare wood, is when you are *solving a problem*. The weather is so hot it's making the varnish unbrushable; the air is so moist you run the risk of having the varnish bloom before it dries: Such dilemmas are the impetus for thinning. If conditions are normal and you are opening a perfectly healthy can of varnish, it is ready to go *as is*. Adding thinner just for drill is a mistake.

• Realize that all varnishes dry more slowly as you build up the coats, so that by the time you've reached the fifth or sixth coat you will need to give the varnish at least a day between coatings to allow proper curing.

• A varnish accident antidote: If your brightwork resides on a fiberglass boat, and some sloppy person has left varnish drips that won't come up easily with a fresh razor blade—especially in nonskid areas—you can dispatch such eyesores in one easy application of Interlux Pintoff 299. Dab it on thickly, let it sit for about five minutes, and then wipe it and the varnish off. If you're cleaning nonskid, dislodge the dregs with a Pepsodent toothbrush. Wash the area with lacquer thinner when you're finished and then repolish with fiberglass polish if necessary.

• A couple of varnish problems may arise in storage. The first of these, skinning over, begins as not much more than a monomolecular film, but becomes, after time, thicker and thicker until ultimately a pelt-like covering is formed. Skinning is usually caused by insufficient closing of the container and is prevalent in partially empty cans. To minimize this problem, seal opened varnish cans *well* and store bottom up. If you do encounter skinning, you can rescue the remaining varnish by straining it into a clean container.

The second problem, thickening of the varnish or precipitation of its solids in the can, will cause difficult application and faulty drying. Thickening can result from storage in excessively cold areas, the ideal storage temperature for oleoresinous varnishes being 70 degrees Fahrenheit (20 degrees Centigrade). Containers should not be left outdoors, and in a variable-temperature storeroom they should be stored not on the floor but up on shelves or at least on boards. If thickening is still present when the varnish returns to room temperature, the condition is probably due to a poor sealing of the container, which necessitates thinning to proper viscosity before reuse. If precipitation seems evident upon reopening a can of varnish, it too is likely a result of storage in a cold area after poor sealing. Such a condition can only be dealt with by discarding the varnish and buying a fresh can.

VARNISHING ACCOUTREMENTS

Paper buckets. These disposable buckets range in size from one pint to one gallon. The pint size is ideal for use while varnishing because it forces you to work with no more than a cup and a half of varnish at a time, which is the maximum pour one can expect to apply under any conditions before the solvent content of the varnish begins to dissipate and cause brushing problems. Beginners should stay with a half-cup or one-quarter-bucket pour until they've mastered an efficient application time.

Keeping the level of varnish in the bucket at or below the halfway point also enables you to add thinners in the prescribed "rock the boat" manner (described above) without sloshing it all over the place.

Pint-sized paper buckets cost between 15 and 25 cents each, depending on where you purchase them. Buy a couple of dozen on your first shopping trip and store them in a clean, *closed* paper grocery bag to keep from having to throw them away before it is time to varnish.

Incidentally, I have heard people suggest that these buckets should be saved and reused after each coat. C'mon! The only reason for saving these *disposable* buckets is for later use as varnishing pedestals in the shop or for work on the dock, when you don't want your subjects resting flat on the workbench or ground. The incredibly small amount of money you may save by reusing them doesn't warrant the mess or danger of interim transport and storage of sticky buckets or the possibility of contamination of the next pour of varnish by debris that settles onto the sticky interior after its previous use. Don't be a cheapskate; it's not worth it.

Paper paint strainers. You can always tell when advice on refinishing has been written by a man. They invariably recommend straining varnish with a woman's stocking. Any woman—or Joe Namath—could tell you that conducting such a delicate operation with such an unwieldy garment is a one-way ticket to the funny farm. Besides, one of the ugliest things in life is a spent nylon stocking. Women would never keep them around just in case they might one day want to strain some varnish through them.

Treat yourself at the outset of a refinishing project to a couple of dozen clean, cone-shaped paper paint strainers. These are available at almost every chandlery or paint and hardware store. Take them to the boat or shop and put them into a Ziploc bag, where they will stay clean until you need them, and at 10 cents a pop, congratulate yourself on your intelligence in surrounding yourself with the right tools for the right job.

Tack cloths. A tack cloth is a piece of cheesecloth treated with resinous materials which, when wiped over a surface prepared for varnishing, picks up any particulate matter that has settled upon that surface. A good tack cloth will remain soft and tacky indefinitely, especially if kept in an airtight container between uses. There are two basic types, "antistatic" and "superactivated." The former is not sticky but slightly oily to the touch, is relatively ineffective for picking up grit, and itself often leaves behind a modicum of cheesecloth lint. I recommend leaving these on the shelf at the marine store. A superactivated tack cloth is incredibly sticky and does the job for which it was intended. The key to complete satisfaction, however, is opening up the cloth completely. Unfold it until it is only doubled over once, then wad it back up and it's ready to use. As you use it during your varnishing, turn it again and again, inside out, so you aren't depositing the grit you just picked up over the next area. Essentially, you are collecting all the grit, lint, and dust inside the cloth with the intention of throwing the cloth away as soon as it has stopped performing up to snuff. If it is still in usable shape after you are finished for the day, put it in a Ziploc bag and close tightly. It will remain soft as long as it is sealed, and should be good for several applications of varnish.

A good commercial tack cloth is relatively inexpensive —usually around one dollar at most —so there is absolutely no reason to waste time and money buying the materials to make your own. A homemade tack cloth usually causes more problems than it solves, so the effort is not only wasted but can be detrimental to the ensuing finish.

Best two brands: Gerson and Red Devil superactivated tack cloths.

Oils and Oil Formulas

TUNG OIL

Tung oil formulas constitute the best oils available for use on marine surfaces, especially interi-

ors. They are a higher-quality drying oil than linseed and do not darken. In "oil sealer" formulations they are usually blended with synthetic and natural resins, solvents for penetration, and occasionally (though not among the good ones) an added pigment for people who want absolute uniformity of wood color.

Daly's Seafin Teak Oil is my favorite Tung oil formula, and I use it for all oil finishes on interiors and as a wet-sanded sealer on teak before the first coat of varnish on exterior brightwork. Daly's is manufactured by a homegrown Seattle boy, Jim Daly, who had the good sense to bring into the business as his partner and head chemist his brilliant cousin, Herb Paulson. Between the two of them, they've managed to come up with some pretty wonderful wood refinishing products, and SeaFin Teak Oil is the jewel in their crown.

BOILED LINSEED OIL

When linseed oil is heated to a temperature of 300 to 500 degrees Fahrenheit, its drying properties are enhanced. Boiled linseed oil dries in 12 to 15 hours, as compared with four to six *days* for the oil in its raw state. In the old days, boiled oil was truly "kettled" or heat-treated oil in which driers were incorporated at high temperature. Heating the oil to such a high temperature darkens it very much, however, and since light-colored oil is often demanded, and high heat is wasteful of oil, time, and fuel, it has become the practice to make a "drier" using salts of lead or manganese. The metallic oxides are heated with a small portion of the oil until they dissolve, then this drier is added to the main body of the oil maintained at a much lower temperature, usually not much above the boiling point of water. The result is a lesser loss of oil during the boiling, and the oil obtained is lighter in color. Bunghole oil, passed off by its manufacturers as being equally effective as boiled linseed oil, is a simple mixture of raw linseed oil with driers, thinned with benzine or turpentine. Raw linseed oil after it has aged a bit is distinguished by its green color, which it derives from its content of chlorophyll. Boiled oil is medium to dark brown but can still have a slight greenish cast.

This "cooked" version of the raw oil has many uses in marine finishing, and in this book is used in combination with SeaFin and a little japan drier as a "sealing" option for exterior mahogany prior to the application of varnish.

TIPS ON HANDLING OIL

• Whenever possible, transfer oil to a bottle with a closeable squirt top (old Teak Wonder bottles are perfect if cleaned and dried thoroughly). This eliminates a vast number of accidents and makes for easier, more uniform application.

• Never attempt to apply oil with a bristle brush; always use foam brushes.

• Likewise, don't apply oil with a rag—you cheat the wood of a sufficient application.

• Read the safety considerations in this book's Appendix for information on disposal of the materials (rags especially) used in oiling projects.

• Clean oil drips immediately with lacquer thinner or mineral spirits. If they go undiscovered until they are dried and will not respond to the solvent, use Te-Ka A&B to spot-clean them.

TEAK DRESSINGS AND RELATED COATINGS

If a can of something calls out to you with claims of being a revolutionary breakthrough in wood finishing, and seductively swears never to chip, peel, or fade—for a year!—and promises complete ease of application ("you simply wipe it on"), it's a safe bet you're reading the label on a "teak dressing" of some type. I'm not sure where this term originated, but I think it translates to mean "a product that sounds fantastic to unsuspecting boatowners desperate to pay any amount of money for the possibility of effortlessly applying a finish that will never need to be retouched." Teak dressings run the gamut from oil formulas, to petroleum-based silicone formulas, to water-based co-polymerized resin formulas, and so forth and so on. The market is predicated on the average boatowner's lust for brown wood (especially decks) and feeds his misguided belief that the teak on his boat will not survive without such treatments. These products are such a farce in the grand scheme of serious brightwork care I have to wonder if they were invented by the Wizard of Oz. Personally, I think it's time for Toto to pull back the curtain.

I'll never forget the time I was accosted by a salesman in a Seattle chandlery who smugly announced that "of course teak decks will rot if left exposed in the Northwest for any but a short period of time, and if you were doing your homework you would know that, Rebecca!" He had no sooner uttered the words than he was reaching for the latest cure-all "dressing" that supported his claim, a product that I was duty-bound in his opinion to recommend to my readers. Try as I may, I still can't think of a single boat whose teak decks have rotted from unprotected exposure to the Northwest's rainy climate.

I can only feel pity for the unarmed neophyte who stands before this salesman, trusting that his word is the objective truth. This sort of diatribe is indeed what usually prefaces the sale of teak dressings or products that support the theory about decks that this guy espoused. If people take this approach with you at a chandlery, immediately consider the source. Is a person whose sole purpose in professional life is to push his latest moneymaker actually going to say you *don't* need his new bottle of snake oil? Learn to read between the lines of sales pitches and brochures with their fabulous claims and start taking responsibility for knowing some basic truths about your subject. There are too many companies out there cashing in on the average boatowner's ignorance of the facts about the

A beautiful hull of cedar strips with laminated stems, finished bright.

wood on his vessel. One of those facts is that teak can and will survive without the dubious protection of any of these miracle never-fade-chip-or-peel coatings, most of which are neither serious protection nor even very flattering to your wood. True protective finishes don't "go on in one easy application" or come packaged as a sealer, dressing, guard, or any of the other profusion of cute names assigned to the nostrums of the coatings industry. They come in cans marked "Varnish," and require the addition of that all-important additive, "Elbow Grease."

Solvents

TURPENTINE

The classic "paint thinner" used from early times in the production and thinning of oleoresinous paints and varnishes, turpentine is made by distilling the rosin or "gum" from the longleaf pine tree (hence the name "gum turpentine"). Used solely in combination with finishes made from natural resins and oils, it is a slow-evaporating solvent that facilitates brushing and flowing in such finishes. With the advent of coatings made from synthetic resins, turpentine has become more or less obsolete as a brushing additive, as most manufacturers have turned to mineral spirits in their formulations and therefore recommend using the same in thinning those products.

MINERAL SPIRITS

Known generically as paint thinner, this is a hydrocarbon distillate from petroleum products derived from the upper end of the gasoline range, which boasts a very high boiling point and therefore evaporates slowly, acting as an aid to the brushing and flowing of varnishes and paints. Often referred to as aliphatic (which is a Greek word, meaning "fat") hydrocarbons. Typically the highest quality mineral spirits are steam distilled to remove the greatest amount of impurities from the raw solvent material.

LACQUER THINNER

Every brand of lacquer thinner is a little different. No one in the industry can tell you exactly what their competitor is using for a lacquer thinner formulation, except that generically it is a combination of hot solvents. Most companies are proprietary about their lacquer thinner formulas —to the point of acting as though they'd been asked to divulge the Coca Cola formula. Suffice it to say, lacquer thinner is a solvent that will aid the brightwork refinisher in stripping residual dregs left behind on the wood by chemical stripping formulas, and help in cleaning errant oil-based finishes off surfaces before they have had a chance to dry. Lacquer thinner is not a solvent to be used as an additive in varnishes or paints. It is generally a utility solvent meant to clean up after accidents and remove contaminants from newly exposed wood that is slated for a finish.

ACETONE

A colorless, volatile liquid of the ketone family (whose members are closely related to alcohol), with a characteristic pleasant odor. Considered the most important ketone (after Alex P., that is), this solvent has a low flash point and evaporates rapidly without leaving any residue. It is used as a utility solvent, for washing unfinished surfaces of grease, pencil markings, etc. to prevent contamination of finishes later applied.

SHELLAC THINNER

This is the industry name for denatured alcohol, an ethyl alcohol rendered unfit for human consumption by the addition of a substance known as a denaturant, such as wood or methyl alcohol. For this reason, many state governments have dictated that it cannot be sold under the name "alcohol," since there is the possibility that certain humans—presumably ones on a pretty slim booze budget —might mistake it for party libations. Shellac thinner can assist in the drying of bare woods after they have been doused, for whatever reason, with water. It is often added in equal parts to water as a final wash after bleaching with oxalic acid and neutralizing with borax.

JAPAN DRIER

This solvent originated in antiquity as a resin-based liquid drier. Artists and craftsmen through the centuries have used it to make their paints and varnishes "kick" under difficult drying circumstances. Today, true japan drier is used as a "sizing" material for gold-leaf work, while modern "japan drier" formulations mimic the original by combining any of a number of metallic driers —cobalt, manganese, etc. —with oils and solvents—usually mineral spirits. Any good varnish manufacturer will recommend staying away from this type of solvent as an additive, since there is no way to control the behavior of a varnish once japan drier has been added to it. Even a slightly excessive amount of japan drier can imbalance the formulated drying mechanism in a varnish, and then it becomes unbrushable. Adding slower drying brushing thinners at that point to recapture the workability of the varnish is not unlike relaxing with a triple belt of Scotch after you've had too much espresso. The patient may seem fine for the short term, but the long-term effect is damaged goods. If you are concerned about your varnish drying under cold or moist conditions, use the recommended fast-drying thinner packaged by that varnish manufacturer. If they make or recommend no such thinner, buy a varnish that does. Odds are it will be a better varnish.

SILICONE REMOVERS

These are a must for cleaning areas slated for varnishing that have been "polished" with silicone waxes between recoatings. Failing to remove silicone from bare wood or a previously varnished surface can result in "fisheyes" (or cratering) or complete rejection of the new varnish. Usually xylol- or toluol-based solvent formulations will remove silicone from a wood or varnished surface, and should be wiped across the surface one pass at a time before turning the face of the rag, to avoid simply moving the silicone molecules around.

Do not think of solvents of any kind as a form of "after-finishing bathtime" for yourself. Solvents are absorbed through the skin and move directly through the bloodstream into the liver, where after frequent and prolonged exposure they can cause serious health problems. Take steps through all your refinishing projects to prevent petroleum materials from getting on your skin. When occasionally you do find you've dipped your fingers into the varnish pot, clean up with Goop or any of the other George Bush "shop hand cleaners" —kinder and gentler to your skin.

Many solvents are known or suspected carcinogens and can cause other health problems as well. Be sure you protect yourself adequately. Appendix 1 on Safety has some specific recommendations.

Stains

Stain is a solution of coloring material or pigment in some sort of vehicle. There are four basic types: water, oil, nongrain-raising, and spirit. Water-based stains exist only in formulations for certain kinds of furniture finishing and are inappropriate for use on boats. Nongrain-raising stains have a very short drying period and as a result do not penetrate the wood as deeply as oil stains. They are also difficult to brush evenly for the same reason. Spirit stains, which are composed of aniline dyes mixed with alcohol, fade drastically when exposed to the sun and are used primarily for touch-up work on furniture, as they will penetrate old finishing materials. For marine applications, all you need to know about are oil-based stains.

The best oil-based stains comprise some type or combination of oils (usually linseed and Tung), pigments, driers, and solvents such as mineral spirits and/or aromatics to aid penetration and promote drying. Some of the stains also contain resins that act as a binder to help hold the pigment in place when subsequent finishes are applied over them. Oil stains are commonly referred to as "pigmented" oil stains or "wiping" stains. They are easy to apply and produce a uniform color with minimum rubbing. Because of the opaque nature of the pigments, however, as opposed for example to aniline dyes, these stains can diminish the clarity of the grain they are covering, and overapplication—essentially more than one coating—can render the wood a rather muddy-looking color with a less descript grain than might be desirable. The important thing to remember in using stains is moderation and uniformity of application.

Metal Polishes

When you've pulled all the fittings off the boat for the brightwork project, make the cleanup and polishing of those fittings a project in itself while watching old movies on Saturday nights. The two best polishes I've found are Liberty Polish, for polishing bronze, brass, and stainless steel, and Brite Boy metal polish for stainless steel.

Before you begin polishing, make sure all old oil, or varnish, or paint is cleaned off (use chemical strippers and Pepsodent toothbrushes for this phase) and the fitting is free of bedding compound or other debris. Use clean, absorbent rags (baby diapers are perfect) and turn often when polishing.

I do not recommend coating polished fittings and other metal with plastic sealing products. Even though this may seem to promise an end to your metal-polishing career, in reality it does not. Such sealers eventually (and most within a year) begin to wear away, leaving mottled areas of oxidized metal wherever the sealer has vanished. Then you have the doubly irksome mess to contend with: stripping off the plastic sealer (a process akin to chemically stripping wood) and then repolishing the trim. Accept the fact that bronze or brass exterior appointments will either be verdigrised or need regular polishing.

Miscellaneous Materials

BRONZE WOOL
The ideal method of rubbing oil into wood, once a good oil foundation exists, is by way of the bronze wool pad. In standard furniture refinishing, you would be directed toward its cousin, steel wool, primarily for its lower cost, but in marine refinishing—even if the piece is being refinished at the shop—steel wool is verboten, because it will rust the minute any residual slivers are exposed to the marine environment. And there is no way to use a metal wool pad without leaving behind at least some slivering. Bronze wool does cost more than steel wool, usually running about a dollar a pad. The price is moot. There is just no substituting any other kind of pad for the bronze persuasion.

Long strands of bronze wool make a good pad; short strands break, shed, and wear out too quickly, leaving a mess in their wake. The best brand I have found over the years is Elephant, which comes in extra-fine, fine, medium, and coarse grades. For brightwork refinishing, especially oil rubbing, never use anything but fine or extra-fine bronze wool.

A bronze wool pad will harden once it has been soaked with oil. To extend the usable life of a pad that is not sufficiently worn out to merit tossing, seal it immediately after use in a clean mason jar, or for a short amount of time in a Ziploc storage bag.

Always wear gloves—the nitrile variety is best—when working with bronze wool. The slivers can cause infection if they become lodged in your skin.

COTTON BABY DIAPERS
Every metropolitan area in this day and age has

at least one baby-diaper service. You can usually call such a service and buy quantities of used, prefolded cotton diapers. These are the ones that have been retired from service because they've become just a little too ratty for their special customers, but they're still in excellent shape and are the best kind of rag for use on most refinishing projects on the boat. Baby diapers have become so popular as a cloth for marine application that many chandleries are now carrying them in one-pound bundles. They're terrific for waxing and sealing gelcoat and for use with metal cleaners, among a number of other uses. The best thing about the baby diaper is that it is incredibly absorbent but leaves next to no lint in its wake, unlike terry cloth.

PURPLE SHOP RAGS

If you have a friend who happens to be a professional mechanic, ask him to let you rent some of his commercial shop rags. It could cost you as little as a nickel apiece if he (or she) rents in large enough quantity from the supplier. These make excellent rags for buffing down wet-sanded oil sealers and finishes. They're not as absorbent as baby diapers, but for this application absorption is not vital, and the shop rags can be returned to be cleaned, whereas you have to throw away diapers that have become caked with wet-sanding residue.

HARDMAN'S DOUBLE BUBBLE EPOXY

For those little repairs during "intermediate prep" where the crack is too small to scarf in a new piece of wood but too wide to leave open for a varnish finish, this epoxy is handy. It comes in a small double packet with a wooden popsicle stick for stirring, and is a high-quality fast-setting epoxy that works well when mixed with teak dust for surface repairs. It is available in most full-service chandleries or hardware stores.

ZIPLOC STORAGE BAGS

These are the "poor man's Tupperware"; no toolkit should be without them! Protect your materials by getting into the habit of popping things immediately into a Ziploc sandwich or storage-sized bag. I can't imagine a grocery store that doesn't carry these; pick up a box next time you're out shopping for dinner.

CHAMOIS

Real chamois skins are the best means to clean brightwork, especially when out on sailing trips. Use a chamois first thing in the day to wipe up the dew; this gives you a natural source of fresh water for keeping brightwork clean and removing saltwater crystals that damage the finish. Always soak a dry chamois in fresh water before use; do not use it dry. After you're finished wiping for the day, the chamois should be washed in a very mild soap solution (Ivory Snow, for example) until all the dirt and grime have been removed. Then rinse *thoroughly* (very important, as the soap residue tends to stiffen the leather), wring out, stretch to original size, and hang up to dry. Store it where it will not collect soot or moisture (Ziploc bags are good). A good chamois should last a long time if properly cared for, and eliminates the presence of terry cloth rags or diapers, which never get quite clean enough to prevent scratching of the varnish and are a nuisance to dry when you're out at sea.

MURPHY'S OIL SOAP

This product is also widely available at the grocery store, and is a wonderful alternative to boat soap or any other cleaning agent you might use to either wash your boat (including teak decks) or clean brightwork surfaces in preparation for varnish refreshers. It is very mild, leaves no heavy film, and can be used on just about any surface on a boat.

If you use it on your brightwork, remember you must still rinse it off with clear, fresh water and wipe the varnished or oiled finish dry to prevent water spotting.

APPENDIX I

SAFETY FOR THE REFINISHER

*There was only one catch and that was Catch-22, which
specified that a concern for one's own safety in the face
of dangers that were real and immediate was the process
of a rational mind.*

—Joseph Heller

When you work on any phase of brightwork refinishing, you are destined to encounter some real and immediate dangers. Show that you are indeed in possession of a rational mind by taking steps to protect yourself from such dangers, not only out of consideration for your personal safety, but in the interest of making refinishing work something you'd be inclined to want to do again.

Protective Gear

EYE PROTECTION
If you are not bespectacled and you plan to work with any product that has the ability to splash, splatter, or spill, you absolutely must make provisions to protect your eyes. One little accident can mean a lifetime of impaired vision, which is too steep a price to pay for a momentary lapse of good judgment. Industrial safety supply houses carry a vast array of goggles, eye shields, and safety glasses for protection from everything under and up to the sun. When choosing tinted eyeshields for outside work —a deck-bleaching job, for example —choose a pair that is rated for 100% protection from ultraviolet rays, but also one that has a lighter tint, as too dark a tint can make it difficult to really see how your work is

coming out. For constant exposure to the sun's glare, a mirrored or gradient mirrored coating gives superior eye protection. Don't be cheap when it comes to buying proper sunglasses for work around the water —a good pair should be no less than $40.00, and that's without prescription. Also, protect your investment by buying a strap for your glasses or eyeshields, since eyewear can take an unplanned dive into the water whenever you lean over the rail. Another less obvious item for eye protection is a sun-visor, which eliminates half of the sun's direct exposure to your eyes and the early onset of the sailor's trademark: crow's feet.

Once you get into the habit of wearing a visor, you'll discover you squint a good deal less. Be aware of surroundings, though, when wearing a visor, as some of your peripheral vision is cut down along with the sun's glare, and as a result you can bean yourself pretty thoroughly on a forgotten boom.

3M DUST/MIST MASKS
These are also called "sanding respirators," depending on which 3M catalog you're consulting. To prevent your sinuses from becoming inoperative while there are still roses to smell, and to protect your lungs from toxic wood dusts

(yes, *toxic!*) as well as those powdery dusts that fly about when you sand varnish finishes, buy a *good* dust mask to wear while you do any sanding work. In the words of my favorite 3M rep, the fifty-cent particle mask is no better than your own nose hairs for protection against inhalation of these types of dusts. Buy the double-strapped, quilted "Dust & Mist" mask and breathe easier knowing you are protecting your sinuses and lungs as best you can.

3M CHARCOAL MASKS (#9913)
This is a mask that looks just like the quilted Dust/Mist mask described above, except that it is a charcoal gray color. There's a good reason for that color: it has a charcoal filter layer, and that layer protects you from the intoxicating fumes present when you work with certain oil and varnish formulas. This type of disposable mask does not supplant the more protective respirator type, but for varnishing and oiling in your shop, a boat's interior, or in any enclosed space, or for application of some more potent finishes on exteriors, this mask makes the difference between sober and drunken finishing adventures, between safety and danger to your health. When you buy these masks, seal them immediately in a Ziploc bag to keep the charcoal filter from using itself up during storage.

By the way, disposable masks are just that: disposable. Wearing a mask for several days to save money is dumb and unsanitary. Save money in some other way. In the case of the charcoal mask, one day's wearing is all you get before the charcoal layer loses its effectiveness, so wearing it more than one day defeats the purpose of using it for protection from toxic air.

VENTILATOR MASKS OR RESPIRATORS
Anytime you are doing any work in an enclosed environment that involves exposure to toxic chemicals—solvent strippers are a perfect example—you must protect your brain cells with a good respirator. A visit to an industrial safety supply house is a good place to start when choosing a respirator. The personnel in such places can help you determine exactly what sort of cartridge you need (there are different types for different chemicals), can help you get a mask that fits you properly (a mask that doesn't fit is nothing but a big hunk of junk hanging off your face), and sell you what you need rather than what just happens to be on the shelf (which is what you might get at the typical hardware store).

The replacement of spent cartridges is vital to the effectiveness of the respirator. Take cartridges off the mask between uses and store them in a sealed mason jar or Ziploc bag with a piece of paper taped to the container where you can keep a record of how long the cartridge was in use. This helps you know when it's time to replace the cartridge, since your sense of smell cannot always detect the toxic level of fumes from certain materials that get past a worn-out cartridge. If you leave the cartridge on the mask between uses, it will continue to absorb whatever fumes and vapors happen to be present in the air, and then the next time you go to use it the cartridges will be worthless; so make sure you take the cartridges off and seal them away from the air when not in use. If you have a beard, a half-mask respirator will do you no good, as it is impossible to get a proper seal over your whiskers. You will need to buy a full-face respirator.

AIR-SUPPLIED RESPIRATORS
When working with methylene chlorides and other such solvents, these give you a better margin of safety than charcoal-cartridge respirators. They are expensive, but they are good.

NITRILE GLOVES
Protect your hands from the ravages of sanding, bleaching, and oiling with something more tenacious than your average dishwashing glove.

Nitrile gloves are used by commercial fishermen who swear that a fishhook won't puncture the tough material, and I believe they're telling the truth. Other types of gloves fall apart from heavy-grit sanding or absorb the chemicals we usually encounter during brightwork projects. Nitrile gloves just stay in one piece for a long, long time. Distinguished by their mint green color, they come in all weights, lengths, and sizes, and the widest selection can be found at the average industrial supply house. Some chandleries carry an excellent commercial brand of nitrile gloves called "Granet" gloves.

NEOPRENE GLOVES

Usually a cloth glove inside, these coated gloves are a must when using chemical strippers. The neoprene coating will not melt from exposure to the solvents, and will not allow the solvent to absorb through the glove and reach your skin. Nitrile gloves are not appropriate for these circumstances, as the nitrile breaks down when exposed to the hot solvents in stripping products. Some of the best neoprene-coated gloves are made by Playtex and can be found in hardware stores and industrial supply houses. If neoprene gloves are unavailable, a rubber-coated glove can also work, but is usually less flexible and more cumbersome to work with.

LATEX EXAMINATION GLOVES

One of the wisest purchases you can make for your varnishing kit is a box of these light-weight gloves that are typically found in the doctor's office. They fit like a second skin, hold up through a full day's varnishing, and are inexpensive enough to justify throwing away at day's end. I never varnish—even a small trim—without donning my latex gloves first. And I never have to wash my hands in solvent when I'm through, either.

KNEEPADS

To prevent the onset of Catholic rheumatism (which plagued so many of us during those interminable High Masses of old), treat yourself to a good pair of kneepads. One of the nicest presents I've ever received was from a compatriot in the boat business who happened to be a sailmaker. They were skateboarding kneepads—but without the hard plastic guards. They were made of thick, firm foam rubber wrapped in nylon knit, and they fastened behind my knees with a Velcro elastic strap. I wore those pads every workday for six years before I had to replace the poor flattened things with new ones. The good thing about these pads, aside from their thickness, was the way they strapped on—not like sports kneepads, which slide up over your ankles and onto the knees, and then cut off your circulation when you kneel down. Visit your nearest skateboarding shop and pick up a pair of these beauties. They truly are the "Bee's Knees."

CONSTRUCTION RAIN SUIT

Don't ruin your skin by attempting to bleach your boat without protecting your whole body. And don't ruin your expensive foulies by wearing them for such a messy project. Go to that wonderful —yes, you guessed it—industrial supply house and choose something in a tasteful yellow construction rainsuit for such work. A two-piece suit (a good one that won't fall apart the first time you bend over) usually costs around $20.00 at most, and is lightweight and flexible for comfortable bleaching in any weather. Buy the overall-style pants and get them big enough to be able to wear sweaters underneath in the event you're bleaching in cold weather.

A GOOD FIRST-AID KIT

This is one of the most important items to have in your tool box, and yet people rarely have one anywhere around when they most need it. A first-aid kit is available in all kinds of places, from your neighborhood pharmacy to the safety supply houses. Do the right thing. Buy one today.

General Safety Considerations

Proper ventilation is the number one safety rule when using finishing materials. If you are working anywhere that is not the great out-of-doors, see to it that you have proper cross-ventilation —one open window is not the answer —and treat yourself to frequent trips out of and from the enclosed working environment for big gulps of clean air. (I'm always a little shocked to see people who take this break and use it as an opportunity to have a cigarette. . . .)

Never allow anyone —even if it's the boss — to smoke around an area where you are using any type of chemicals, even if it's just varnish. Virtually all finishes contain a solvent, and all solvents are either flammable or combustible. And while some stripping materials containing methylene chloride are considered inflammable, their vapors are toxic and harmful to any bystander not equipped with proper protection.

Proper storage of chemicals is a way to protect yourself from unexpected explosions. Make sure storage areas are below 80 degrees Fahrenheit (27 degrees Centigrade). Whenever you open any can of solvent or stripper or oil or anything that has a solvent base, "burp" the can slowly before removing the lid by just barely turning the lid to release the build-up of any vaporized pressure. Never stand nose down over a can that's being burped or you'll get a schnoz full of fumes; hold the can at arm's length from your face as you open it.

The responsible, thoughtful use of chemicals includes proper disposal. Most people do not realize that something as seemingly innocent as Tung oil becomes combustible when soaked into a rag that is then left in a heap. If the spoils of your day's work include oily or solvent-soaked rags, take those rags back to your shop or somewhere safe outdoors and hang them up to dry before discarding them. Do not rinse them in more solvents, as this only increases their flammability. *Definitely* do not pour spent solvents down storm drains or the shop sink; this is irresponsible pollution, and is illegal. If you have stripping dregs, don't dump them into the nearest dumpster or trash can; call your local waste disposal department and ask for the nearest toxic waste repository.

While most products come with instructions for "reactive measures" when accidents occur, the absolute best treatment is immediate medical attention. Don't play junior doctor at a time like this; your method of treatment beyond the stop-gap measures recommended could exacerbate the problem and turn a slight mishap into a permanent injury.

Have you ever almost fallen overboard when working on your boat while it is tied up to the dock? I have —almost, that is —in the middle of winter when I was doing a washdown during 35-degree weather, which prompted me to wonder whether I'd have had a difficult time getting back out of the water and up onto the dock, which was some distance above the water. I realized that it wouldn't have been so easy, and from then on got into the habit of checking my surroundings and, if appropriate, putting the stern ladder down in the event of any unplanned dips.

THE BRIGHTWORK REFINISHER'S DICTIONARY

Abrasive —A substance used for wearing away a surface by friction. Sandpaper and bronze wool are the two most commonly employed forms of abrasive material used in refinishing brightwork.

Acetone —Dimethyl ketone, a water white solvent that has a very low flash point and evaporates rapidly without leaving behind any residue.

Across grain —Not with the run or natural direction of the grain pattern.

Alkyd resin —A synthetic resin made from polyhydric alcohols and polybasic acids generally modified with resins, fatty oils, or fatty acids; used in the manufacture of some marine varnishes, often in combination with other natural or synthetic resins.

Alligatoring —The appearance of a deeply crinkled varnish surface, caused by application of too thick a coat over an existing hardened coat of varnish.

Amber —A yellow gum resin formerly used in the manufacture of varnish. No longer used in commercial manufacture because of scarceness of supply.

Anodized aluminum —Aluminum fittings or structures that sport a protective oxide film which has been created by an electrolytic process.

Application —Principally, the act of covering an entire surface with a finish; the application of a coat. Methods of application in brightwork refinishing include brushing, rolling, wet-sanding, and bronze-wooling.

Backache —A common ailment with yacht refinishers, not to be confused with "pain in the neck," which is someone who constantly interrupts a refinisher's work for the purpose of bragging about their own refinishing prowess.

Baseball —The only sport to listen to while refinishing a boat.

Beer —The wrong beverage to drink while refinishing a boat, even if the baseball game is on.

Belt sander —A power sanding machine that uses a cloth belt coated with grit, running in one direction, to plane surfaces down in a hurry. It is an inappropriate sander for use on brightwork projects.

Bleaching —The process of removing dirt, oil, water stains, and mildew from bare wood surfaces, by the application of oxalic acid, two-part commercial wood bleach products, or detergent systems with added enzymes.

Blistering —The formation of bubbles under the surface of a finish, usually after the finish is cured.

Blooming —The appearance of a milky or flat finish surface after a gloss varnish has dried, also known as clouding, fogging, or blushing.

Boatyard —Typically a place where you can haul your boat out of the water, for the purpose of doing or having done repairs to all areas of your boat; also known as "the yard."

Body —The combination of the density and viscosity of a finish, also known as its consistency; also the thickness of the dried film.

Boiled linseed oil —Linseed oil that has either been heated until partially oxidized or has had small amounts of liquid drier added, or both, for the purpose of faster drying.

Bonding —The adhering of varnish coats to the wood surface or to each other.

Bosun's chair —A specially designed sling-shaped chair, usually made of canvas, used in taking trips to the top of one's mast (a challenging point from which to varnish that mast).

Bottom painting —A nasty job one should take great pains to push off onto somebody else.

Brightwork —Often mistakenly thought to refer to the brass or bronze parts of a boat, but actually the catch-all term for any wood —interior or exterior —on a boat that has been varnished, oiled, sealed, or otherwise not covered with an opaque finish, thereby leaving exposed the natural grain of the wood.

Brilliance —A description of the luster or reflective quality of a dried varnish film.

Bristol —A term synonymous with perfection, which originated with the magnificent yachts designed and built by the Herreshoffs of Bristol, Rhode Island, around the turn of the century. If your boat is said to be "in Bristol condition," it has been accorded high praise, indeed.

Bronze wool —Spun strands of bronze formed into a pad, used as an abrasive in refinishing on boats. It is a good alternative to steel wool because of its resistance to rusting.

Brush —An instrument of finish application, usually comprised of bristles derived from a member of the animal kingdom. A variation on this device is the foam brush.

Brush marks —Bristle marks remaining in a dried film, caused by working the finish after it has begun to set. Can be prevented by proper thinning with solvents (also known as brushing liquids) designed to delay drying during application.

Brushing liquid —A slow-drying solvent, usually high-grade mineral spirits or a mineral spirits based formula. Added in small increments to varnish to facilitate ease of brushing and promote good leveling.

Brushing —The act of applying a finish with the aid of a brush, either of bristle or foam variety.

Bubbling —The appearance of small bubbles on the surface while a finish is being applied and after it has dried.

Building coats —Also known as buildup coats, the coats that represent the initial formation of the finish surface, applied with less an eye to perfection than to body. Usually the first six coats of varnish constitute buildup coats, with subsequent applications of the finish intended to be "finish coats."

Bungs —Tight-fitting wooden dowels used to fill the voids above countersunk fasteners.

Cabin sole —The floor of a boat's interior.

Canvas —The absolute best form of brightwork maintenance, specifically in the form of covers that protect finished woods from the exterior elements.

Carnauba wax —A hard wax that can be used to protect anodized aluminum trims when employing bleaching products to clean adjacent or nearby teak.

Caulking —A material, usually adhesive in nature, used in sealing voids on a boat's exterior, for the purpose of preventing the introduction of moisture in those areas.

Chamois, or chamois skins —Soft, pliable animal skins used for wiping fresh water or heavy dew from varnished brightwork.

Chandlery —The yachtsman's department store; a place to buy everything from sandpaper to screws to sextants.

Cheap —The wrong reason for choosing a particular varnish or finishing material or brightwork "professional."

Checking —A varnish failure similar to crazing; the surface of the finish is deteriorated into a network of moderately deep cracks. Checking is more severe than crazing, in that the cracks are deeper and usually extend down to the underlying surface.

Cheesecloth —The loosely woven fabric used in the making of tack cloths. See Tack cloth.

Chemical stripper —A finish remover that by virtue of its "hot solvent" content is able to dissolve or render liquid a previously dried varnish or paint finish. Usually contains methylene chloride as a solvent, methyl cellulose as a thickening agent, and some type of wax or paraffin to inhibit the early escape of the solvent into the air.

China wood oil —See Tung oil.

Chipping —Finish flaking off in small areas where the finishing material is too brittle or insufficiently adhered to the surface beneath, often caused by some sort of blow to the area.

Clear finish —A term sometimes used to denote varnish as opposed to paint.

Clouding —See Blooming.

Clouds —Portents of the weather to come; see Precipitation.

Coat —The maximum depth of a finishing material achievable in one application, without producing runs or sags. However, in buildup terminology, one "coating" is not to be confused with "one coat"; two coatings with a jet-speed varnish, for example, will dry to a thickness about equal to that of one coat of a full-bodied, full-strength varnish.

Compatibility —The ability to be mixed or used with others, as in the compatibility of a solvent with a particular varnish.

Construction rain suit —Lightweight plastic overalls used for protection during boat bleaching projects.

Crawling —The tendency of a finish material to creep away or retreat from the continuous coating after it has been applied, leaving certain spots uncoated.

Cured —The condition of a finish after it has dried and hardened so completely that it has released all its solvent content.

Cutting in —Stealing the other guy's dance partner by varnishing without benefit of a taped edge (this can be a very impressive talent to behold).

Deck boots —Rubber boots designed specifically for wearing on board a boat; equipped with non-slip soles and completely watertight up to the boottops.

Dehumidifier —A device, usually electric, designed to remove the moisture from the air in an enclosed space, such as boat cabin interiors, minimizing the growth of mildew in such areas.

Denatured alcohol —Also known as shellac thinner, this solvent is frequently added to water to speed its evaporation when used as a wash on bare woods.

Dew point —The temperature at which moisture begins to condense in the air; in refinishing, especially during varnishing, this is a cause of surface problems, such as blooming, on a newly applied coat.

Dip stripping —A commercial form of stripping finishes by soaking pieces in a solvent bath; not recommended for stripping of boat parts, such as helms or louvered doors, as it melts the glue and ruins the joints on these items.

Disc sander —A power sander with hard or foam discs, to which another grit-coated paper disc is attached and spun in a circular motion, to sand down surfaces quickly; not recommended for use on brightwork trims because of the inherent danger of misshaping wood surfaces.

Drag —The resistance experienced when brushing a material that is setting up too quickly.

Driers —The salts of certain metals (manganese, cobalt, calcium, zinc) or volatile solvents with or without added gum resins that hasten the drying action of varnish or paint. Driers act as catalytic agents, carrying oxygen from the air to the oil and thereby rendering the liquid film hard.

Drips —Small, inexcusable drops of coating material found dried in the vicinity of finishing work.

Dry —The state reached when varnish has completely solidified and is devoid of tackiness; the early stage of a finish's curing process.

Drying oils —Oils which are capable of drying to a relatively tough, varnish-like film upon exposure to air and sunlight. Linseed oil, Tung oil, and oiticica oil are three commonly used drying oils in the manufacture of varnish.

Drying time —The time interval required between the application of a finish and subsequent resanding or preparation for additional coats.

Durability —The life of a finishing material and its resistance to change in appearance, elasticity, hardness, and adhesion.

Dust/mist mask —A quilted, double-strapped disposable paper mask worn for protection from dusts produced during refinishing work such as sanding; not to be confused with "particle masks" and "nuisance dust masks," which are lightweight, single-strapped masks that afford little or no protection from toxic wood and varnish dusts.

Edger —A wooden or metal straight-edged device used in painting and varnishing, as a temporary means of "masking" an adjacent surface; a "quickie" alternative to masking with tape.

Elasticity —A film's capacity to withstand expansion and contraction, caused by the changes in air temperature, without breaking.

Elbow grease —A vital ingredient in all phases of yacht refinishing, the omission of which often nets one a less than satisfactory finish.

Epoxy —Popular synthetic resin that finds application in all areas of boat construction and finishing; a quick-set formulation mixed with certain wood dusts is offered in this book as a means of filling surface voids in preparation for varnish application.

Erosion —The gradual disappearance of a finish as it wears.

Essential oil —Any volatile oil that gives distinctive odor or flavor. Turpentine is the most familiar essential oil in the world of refinishing.

Exterior finish —A finishing material designed specifically to withstand the harsher outdoor elements. It usually contains some type of ultra-violet inhibitor and a higher proportion of oil to resin than interior varnishes. See Spar varnish.

Finish —What you should be able to apply to your boat with the help of this book.

Finishing sander —A power sander whose base moves in a very small circular or "orbital" direction, gradually cutting the surface beneath to a smooth plane; the most appropriate type of sander for brightwork application. Also known as an orbital sander.

Filler —A composition, usually of nitrocellulose and solvents, used in filling pores or irregularities in a surface in preparation for the sealer coat of a finish. Can be pigmented or natural in color.

Flammability —The measure of a material's propensity for catching fire; degrees of flammability are specified in a product's "flash point" designation.

Flash point —The temperature at which a material will catch fire or flash when exposed to a flame.

Flat finish —A finish that has no surface gloss or luster whatsoever, due to the addition of "flatteners" or pigments.

Flatting agent —A material added to paint or varnish for the purpose of reducing the gloss characteristics of that finish.

Flowing —A property that denotes a finish's ability to flow out onto a surface and level smoothly without showing brush marks; the first half of the leveling process.

Foam brush —An instrument of coatings application consisting of a solid polyfoam head shaped to a bevel at the edge, attached to a handle of wood or plastic.

Foam roller —A polyfoam-skinned variation on the standard paint roller theme.

Fogging —See Blooming.

Gelcoat —The smooth, usually pigmented "skin" applied over fiberglass surfaces.

Gloss —The shine or luster of a dried film; the ability of a surface to reflect an image or light.

Gloss retention —The ability of a finish to retain its original sheen.

Glossiness —The degree of surface reflection resultant upon the drying of a finish. Basic degrees of glossiness are: High gloss (completely sharp contrasts with strong reflective qualities); Semi-gloss (a lack of sharpness in contrasts and clouding of reflected images); Flat finish or Eggshell gloss (reflections are barely discernible and contrasts merge).

Grain —The visible pattern of markings in wood that corresponds to the direction of its fibers; to sand "with the grain" is to sand with the direction of such markings.

Grit —A grading system, usually numerical, that determines the coarseness of the abrasive material known as sandpaper.

Gum turpentine —The distilled solvent by-product of the resinous material, or "gum," obtained by tapping the living long-leaf pine tree.

Hand-sanding —Abrading a surface with sandpaper without the aid of a power sander.

Heat gun —Looks like a hairdryer, but the good ones put out 1,200 degrees of heat—enough to dry your hair for good. Used to soften old finishes to prepare them for removal by scraping.

Heat-stripping —Removing a paint or varnish finish by applying a high level of heat and then scraping the softened finish away from the wood. Can involve the use of propane torches, specially designed "heat guns," or the good ol' everyday iron.

Heat lamps —Excellent devices to use for the purpose of dehumidifying a boat's interior; when carefully used, can also serve as an aid to drying an interior finish during particularly cool weather; see Dehumidifier.

Heavy bodied —A varnish or similar material that has a thick consistency or high viscosity.

Heavy-bodied oil —Oil thickened by heat or oxidation.

Holiday —A classic brightwork term denoting skips in finish application. (Or what you may take when all your varnishing is completed.)

Humidity —The measure of the degree of water vapor in the air.

Inflammability —The same thing as flammability, though often mistakenly believed to be the opposite of that term.

Interior finish —A finish designed for use only indoors or on boat interiors; usually of a higher resin content than spar varnishes and not designed to withstand typical outside elements.

Japan drier —An older name for liquid driers that originally were made up of resin and oil and that have now have been replaced in modern additive use by solutions of metallic soaps in solvents; known more generically as "driers."

Kingplank —The central, often decorative-looking plank on a boat's deck; frequently celebrated with a varnish finish while surrounding planks are left bare.

Kneepads —Protection from Catholic rheumatism, worn during any refinishing work that entails long stretches on the prayer bones.

Lacquer —A finish usually mistakenly thought to be related to shellac and, surprisingly, even varnish by refinishing amateurs. Originally referred to all thin-bodied, quick-drying "spirit varnishes." The term today is used to denote a thin-bodied finish containing appreciable amounts of nitrocellulose, applicable by spraying. Lacquer has poor durability on exterior woods and does not adhere at all well to oily woods, is difficult to apply with a brush, and requires more coats than varnish because the solid content is appreciably less. For these reasons, lacquer is not an appropriate brightwork finish.

Lacquer thinner —A mixture of solvents with a low flash point, used as a utility solvent in refinishing. Used for a variety of chores, from washing bare woods after chemical stripping to cleaning up oil drips during oil application; never used as a thinner for oleoresinous finishes like varnish or paint.

Lap lines —A raised, set portion of finish that marks the boundary of the previous wet edge, caused by either unfavorable weather conditions, improperly thinned varnish, or simply by the partial setting of the earlier stroke before the subsequent one has had a chance to be brushed into it.

Latex gloves —Lightweight examining gloves normally found in your doctor's office; perfect protection when varnishing, they eliminate the toxic "solvent wash-up" after the job is done.

Leveling, or leveling out —The smooth flowing out of a finish, free from brush marks, lap lines, and other defects after it has been applied and before it dries.

Lifting —When one coat of finishing material, upon being applied over another coat, softens and raises the undercoat in irregular wrinkles, due to the solvent action of the freshly applied coat. The resultant defect has the appearance of a varnished surface to which a chemical stripper has been applied and allowed to dry.

Linseed oil —The oil derived from the seeds of the flax plant, *Linum usitatissimum*, obtained either by extraction with volatile solvents or by pressing, used to great extent in making paints and some varnishes.

Long-oil varnish —A term used to signify the amount of oil in a varnish, meaning that the proportion of oil to resin is great, averaging above 25 gallons of oil per 100 pounds of resin. A long-oil varnish is usually slower drying but tougher, more elastic and more durable than a short-oil varnish. Spar varnish is a typical long-oil varnish.

Low-tack masking tape —Any masking tape that has a glue backing formulated to stick lightly and pull up without harming the surface below.

Masking tape —Originally an adhesive-backed crepe paper used to mask off parts of a surface not intended to be coated; now signifies any number of varieties of adhesive-backed paper tape in addition to the original crepe paper tapes.

Mildew — The familiar term for a type of mold or fungus growth commonly found on wood surfaces where the finish has deteriorated or failed to adhere, and/or on bare wood surfaces, where moisture is incessantly present; black in color, it's often mistakenly observed to be simply dirt.

Mineral spirits —A solvent distilled from crude petroleum, it varies in its solvent qualities and is considered the modern replacement for turpentine. Used as a thinner for many paints and varnishes.

Miscibility —A material's capability of being mixed or blended uniformly with another.

Naphtha —A petroleum distillate, having a high flash point, which is used in certain types of varnishes; not recommended as a standard thinner for varnish unless specified by the manufacturer.

Natural resins —Resins which are derived from natural sources, such as the copols, shellac, sandarac, and amber; they are obtained as natural or stimulated exudations from trees, and are not modified in any way chemically.

Nondrying oils —Oils which do not of themselves possess the ability to take up oxygen and convert to nonliquid form.

Nonflammable —The opposite of flammable, which is to say that if it is nonflammable, it is not combustible or inclined to catch fire.

Nonskid —The quality of a surface that prevents persons from slipping under wet conditions; teak decks have, by nature, a nonskid quality; so does a waffle-patterned fiberglass deck.

Oil stains —Stains of two basic types: those made by dissolving oil-soluble colors in naphtha or similar solvents, usually called penetrating stains; and those which contain pigment colors mixed with a binder such as linseed oil and thinned with solvents such as turpentine or naphtha, usually called wiping stains because they are applied to the work, allowed to partially dry and then wiped off.

Oiticica oil —A drying oil of Brazilian origin, used in the manufacture of some varnishes, often in combination with Tung or linseed oils.

Oleoresinous varnish —In modern usage applied to varnish composed of drying oils cooked (or polymerized by heat reaction) with resins, and thinned to proper viscosity with hydrocarbon solvents.

Orbital sander —See Finishing sander.

Oxalic acid —A dicarboxylic acid often used as a bleaching agent for bare woods.

Oxidation —The process of absorbing or combining with oxygen to change the nature of a surface or the physical composition of a finishing material. The combining of a drying oil with oxygen from the air to form a solid film is an example of the process of oxidation; so is the reaction of a bronze fitting with the airs oxygen to form a verdigrised appearance.

Paint thinner —A generic term for mineral spirits.

Particle masks —A commercial term for single-thickness, one-strap dust masks which are disposable and, at the lowest end of the price scale, afford the least protection of all the types of disposable masks on the market.

Pastewood filler —A filling material in a paste or semipaste consistency designed to fill the open pores of wood before the application of varnish; see also Filler.

Peeling —The separation of the finish from a wood surface as a result of loss of adhesion.

Penetrating stain —See Oil stain.

Phenolic resins —Synthetic resins made by the interaction of phenols and aldehydes that when used in varnishes promote alkali, chemical and alcohol resistance of the film, and make the varnish fast-drying, tough, and water resistant.

Pigment —An opaque substance used to color or reduce the sheen of a finish.

Pine tar —A by-product of Southern yellow pine trees; its use as a marine wood finish dates back to the colonial era. In early times, the tar was obtained by burning the resin-soaked "light wood" that remained after the bark, sapwood, and smaller limbs from slash pine forests had rotted away. The products netted from the destructive distillation of this resinous heartwood included not only tar, but charcoal, turpentine, pine oil, tar oils, and pitch.

The pine tar was combined with solvents and oils to create a dark brown finish still found on many older vessels. The eventual depletion of highly resinous old-growth stumpwood in slash forests, along with the development of more efficient solvent-steam distillation processes for the extraction of what are known in the industry as "naval stores" —the term referring to pinetree by-products—has forced the demise of the destructive distillation industry, but pine tar continues to be produced, and used in marine wood-finish formulations by diehard fans of the finish. The typical reasons given by lovers of this almost unsightly, dark finish are that it is inexpensive and easy to apply. It usually looks it.

Pipkin —Small earthenware pot used in the Middle Ages in the manufacture of varnish.

Pitch —A black liquid substance left as a residue after distilling tar, oil, or similar materials: "When Noah built his ark and coated the seams with pitch he was doubtless following the most approved system of use of protective coatings on structural materials, which was then probably of remote antiquity and traditional origin, and which he may have learned when he was a boy, four or five hundred years before." (A.H. Sabin). We modern refinishers should live so long. . . .

Plugs —See Bungs.

Polishing varnish —A very hard-drying, short-oil varnish intended for interiors or furniture, capable of being polished by means of silica or other abrasive material and mineral oil, to give it a "rubbed" finish. Many varnish manufacturers are now packaging "rubbed effect" varnishes, which are similar in formulation to polishing varnishes but with added flatteners to give the look of the rubbed surface without having to do any actual rubbing.

Polyurethane —A synthetic resin used in modern varnish manufacture, superior to other synthetic resins for its resistance to abrasion and chemicals, as well as its ability to promote clarity and gloss; an aliphatic polyurethane resin is used in making the highest-quality varnishes on the market today.

Precipitation —The varnisher's impetus for a day off.

Preventive maintenance —The most intelligent approach to keeping up the finish (or lack thereof) on one's brightwork.

Raised grain —The standing up or raising of the short broken fibers on the surface of wood, as they absorb moisture, caused by the application of water or water-based substances to the wood.

Razor blade scraper —A device designed to hold a single-edged razor blade, for use in cutting or scraping with such blades.

Reduce —To thin the viscosity or consistency of a varnish by adding volatile materials. When a volume of reducer equal to 25 percent of the material being reduced is added, the material is said to be reduced 25 percent, or one part of reducer has been added to four parts varnish; similarly, 100 percent reduction is equal parts varnish and reducer.

Reducer —See Thinner.

Residual tack —The state reached in the drying of certain coatings where the film can be handled without damage but continues to retain a noticeable degree of surface stickiness.

Resin —A solid or semi-solid organic substance, natural or synthetic, which is soluble in ether, alcohol, or similar solvents, but not in water, which combined with oxidized oils forms the hardened film of dried varnish. See Natural resins and Synthetic resins.

Retarders —See Brushing liquid.

Retired diapers —The official designation given by diaper service companies to those diapers that are no longer good enough for their little customers; ideal for use in many different phases of brightwork refinishing, and usually sold by the pound at diaper services. Also becoming a popular retail item in chandleries.

Ribs —Raised ridges in the finish caused by heavy brush marks that were not sanded or rubbed from the underneath coats before subsequent finishing coats were applied; a compounded effect of brush marks. See Brush marks.

Rosin —The molten resin that remains after the distillation of turpentine from the gum of the pine tree.

Rottenstone —A siliceous limestone imported from England and Belgium, softer and able to be more finely ground than pumice, used with mineral oil in polishing varnished surfaces to a handrubbed finish. Derives its name from the offensive odor the original "lump rubble" gives off when broken up.

Rubrail —A bumper strip of hardwood or metal (or both) used to protect a boat's topsides.

Rubbed-effect varnish —An interior varnish, usually of higher resin content than spar varnishes, with added flatteners to give the look of a hand-rubbed or polished finish.

Rubber mallet —An appropriate tool for closing lids when resealing varnish cans; not to be confused with a hammer, which often renders the innocent cover a pathetic, deformed disc, too misshapen to provide an adequate seal.

Rubbing oil —A mineral oil used with rottenstone or pumice to rub the dried film of a finishing material; a neutral oil or parrafine oil can also be used for this purpose.

Runs —Fingered or curtained-looking defects in a varnish finish and on surrounding areas, caused by the application of an excess of varnish.

Safety glasses —Protective eyewear, clear or tinted, usually made of hard plastic; worn to guard against chemical splashing or the assault on one's eyes from any other type of substance that may fly up during refinishing work.

Sags —Thick "curtains" of varnish on a surface, usually vertical or sloping, caused by an excessively thick application of the finish, or by the collection of quantities of varnish in cracks, crevices, corners, etc. that continue to flow after the surrounding areas have begun to set.

Salt water —The wet stuff of the ocean; Mother Nature's bleach.

Sanding —The act of abrading or wearing away the surface of something by rubbing with grit-coated paper, known as sandpaper; sanding is done by "hand" or by "machine" and can be accomplished with or without the aid of wetting materials such as water or oil.

Sanding sponge —A commercially manufactured foam rubber sponge that is coated on all sides with a gritty material and intended to serve as an abrasive alternative to sandpaper.

Sanding swirls —Curly looking scratches in a wood or finish surface, created by sanding with an orbital finishing sander.

Sandpaper —A paper coated with an abrasive material, used to define the surface of wood, metal, or a finishing material. See section on Sandpapers in text.

Satin finish —A dried varnish film that has more luster than a flat or rubbed finish but less than a full-gloss type of varnish. Derives its name from the similarity to the finish of the textile satin.

Scraper —Any of a number of types of medium- to broad-bladed knives used in the removal of finishes, often beveled and varying in design from flat "pushing" scrapers to hook or "pulling" types with curved ends.

Scratches —Defects in a surface covered by a finish or on surrounding areas, caused by careless sanding or the use of abrasives that are too coarse.

Sealer —A finishing material is applied over bare wood or wood that has been stained and/or filled with paste filler, to seal the pores and stop suction of succeeding coats into soft or porous areas. Can be a very thinned down version of the varnish being used, or a specially formulated resinous material containing a high proportion of volatile solvents, or even an oil-based finish with added resins and solvents.

Semi-gloss —A varnish that dries to a sheen that is about halfway between full gloss and a flat finish, by virtue of its added "flatteners" or pigments.

Shelf life —The maximum time interval that a material, such as varnish, can be stored before it loses its effectiveness or ability to be applied.

Shellac varnish —What the people of the 17th century knew as "seedlac," a spirit varnish made by cutting lac, a gum resin produced by the secreting action of insects on the twigs of certain trees in India, with denatured alcohol. The name is derived from the Sanskrit word "laksha," meaning one hundred thousand, which originated when a native of India exclaimed "lakh" as he discovered hundreds of thousands of the tiny insects swarming on the twigs and branches of various trees. The insects, called *Tachardia* or *Coccus lacca*, suck the sap of the trees into their bodies and convert it into a resinous substance that they excrete though their body pores to form an incrustation on the trees. It takes 7,200 insects to produce enough resin for one gallon of liquid shellac. Shellac varnish produces a finish without much luster that unless very carefully applied and dried is easily prone to scratching. Shellac turns white permanently from contact with water, and is not a suitable type of finish for use on boats.

Shellac thinner —The legal trade name for ethyl alcohol to which has been added a denaturant, rendering it unfit for human consumption.

Short-oil varnishes —Oleoresinous varnishes containing oil and resin in the ratio of one-and-a-half parts oil or less to one part of resin; used as interior varnishes, gold-sizes, etc., where durability is not important. See Long-oil varnish.

Shrinking —The action of a piece of wood, whether veneer or solid, whereby loss of moisture from the wood after the application of a finish, due to natural aging processes or excessive exposure to heat, causes the finish to crack, lose gloss, or break at joints and begin delaminating.

Silica —A transparent pigment used extensively in the manufacture of pastewood fillers, consisting essentially of silicon dioxide. It is typically very unflattering to the grain markings of the wood.

Skinning —The change in the surface of varnish (whether as it sits in a poorly sealed or half-filled can or upon application to a wood surface) where through exposure to the air it forms a "skin" or partially dried barrier over the undried remainder of the varnish. Because most varnishes, once the can has been opened, have a tendency to skin over to some extent, straining is essential to obtaining a coat free of broken lumps of this skin. In the case of an applied coat of varnish, skinning is not representative of a dried condition, though such a conclusion is sometimes drawn upon initially touching a skinned-over surface.

Skips —If you're all alone in the world and varnishing your boat, and you wish you had some company, all you need do is leave a skip —or, as we say in the business, a "holiday" —and someone will quickly appear out of nowhere to say, "You missed a spot."

Slow tack —A term referring to any varnish that is slow to skin over or dry through to a tack-free state.

Snap shackle —The *wrong* thing to use —for reasons of safety alone —in attaching a bosun's chair to the lifting halyard; an appropriate alternative is a locking carabineer, the type used by mountain climbers.

Softwood —The pith of the grain of wood, that part which is softer and more easily excavated when scrubbed with bristle-type devices; also known as soft grain or summer grain.

Solvent —A liquid that is capable of dissolving any given material. Water is a solvent; so are turpentine, lacquer thinner, mineral spirits, and acetone.

Solvent drunk —Also known as a "varnish high." Intoxication caused by varnishing in a poorly ventilated area or at close range outside for many hours.

Spar varnish —Boat varnish (for *any* use on a boat, not just for spars), specifically formulated for outstanding water resistance. Typically has a higher oil content than other varnishes.

Speedbloc —The Porter Cable company's model name for its version of a quarter-sheet orbital sander, originally made by Rockwell.

Spontaneous combustion —Known in its early stages as "heating up," this term applies to the phenomenon in which a material generates heat without the application of any external source of heat. When a piece of cotton fabric, for example, is soaked with boiled linseed oil, and is rolled or wadded up before the oil has had a chance to completely dry, oxidation may continue as the fabric sits. This itself generates heat and stimulates further oxidation, until the process becomes cumulative and serious heating up occurs because the heat cannot escape. At its worst, such combustion can cause serious charring and even full-fledged fires in dock boxes, on boats, or in the shop where such carelessness has gone undetected.

Spreading rate —The amount of surface or area a given volume of varnish can be spread over by brushing, spraying, or other methods of application. Usually expressed in square feet covered per gallon.

Stain —See Oil stain.

Steel wool —Pads of spun steel available in varying degrees of coarseness, used as an abrasive, especially for rubbing finishes. Not appropriate for use around boats, as the shavings left behind leave rust stains on surfaces where they fall. See Bronze wool.

Strainer —A cone-shaped paper device with a mesh bottom used for straining particulate matter from varnish and paints just prior to use; a pair of women's denier stockings is *not* a strainer.

Stripping —The act of removing a finish completely from the varnished or painted surface.

Sunshine —Both friend and foe to the varnisher, sailor, and dermal organ of the human body.

Synthetic resins —Manmade substances physically similar to natural resins, used in modern production of finishing materials; created by chemical reaction of comparatively simple compounds in duplication of resins found in nature; some synthetic resins used in modern varnishes are phenolics, alkyds, epoxy resins, and polyurethanes.

Tack free —The state reached by a finish when it has dried to the extent that it is not sticky to the touch.

Tack cloth —A square of cheesecloth that has been coated with a sticky varnish-type mixture; used to pick up particulate matter that settles onto brightwork surfaces just before varnish is applied.

Tackiness —The stickiness of a film during the course of its drying.

Tarnish —To lessen the luster, usually of a metal, by oxidation.

Teak flour —Fine sawdust produced by power-sanding teak with a finishing grit sandpaper; used in mixture with quick-set epoxy for surface repairs during refinishing prepwork.

Teak —A wood known in botanical circles as *Tectona grandis* from the tree family *Verbenaceae*; grown primarily in Burma, southern India, and Southeast Asia; a leathery-feeling and leathery-smelling wood when freshly cut, teak is becoming the most ubiquitous of the hardwoods employed in commercial production of boats. Remarkable for its reserve of natural oil and ability to survive the ravages of Mother Nature without benefit of protective coatings.

Teak dressing —Any type of temporary coating designed to "protect" the one wood that least requires such dubious protection; the coating usually requires constant recoating to remain intact.

Teakwood —Redundant phraseology, similar in logic to salmonfish, beefmeat, windowglass, roseflower, or mahoganywood. The proper word is teak!

Thinner —The volatile constituents used to thin a finishing material to such an extent that it may be easily applied or more readily absorbed into the surface of bare wood. Can be a simple solvent, a mixture of solvents, or even a very dilute solution of the same medium as that used in the material to be thinned; also known as reducer.

Time —Something of which, if you don't have enough for doing a job correctly the first time, you'll never have for doing it over.

Tipping off —A light dragging with an empty brush over a freshly applied stroke of varnish or paint, to smooth and even out brush or roller marks and blend that area into previously applied strokes.

Tools —Things you should never lend; things you should never ask to borrow.

Tooth —A surface roughness, brought about usually by sanding or employing some other method of abrasion, that allows a succeeding coat of film to adhere readily to that surface.

Toxicity —The poisonous effect on a human being resulting from introduction of certain materials into the system; lacquer thinner is a toxic solvent, entering the bloodstream by the inhalation of the fumes or by absorption through the skin. Hardwood dusts have been found to be toxic in studies of certain populations (woodworking professionals, especially) subjected to continual inhaling of said dusts.

Trisodium phosphate —A salt used in bleaching and as a fungicide for woods.

TSP —See Trisodium phosphate.

Tung oil —Also known as Chinawood oil, a drying oil extracted from the nut of the tree *Aleurites cordata*, or Tung tree. Used extensively in the manufacture of quality varnish and marine wood finishes.

Turpentine —The commonly used term, also known as spirits of turpentine, denoting the volatile portion of the gum obtained from the pine tree. See also Gum turpentine and Rosin.

Unseasoned wood —Wood that is not thoroughly cured, which is to say that it has not given up its store of moisture; unseasoned wood is prone to later shrinking, which promotes failure of a finish on that wood.

Ultraviolet light —Non-visible light rays that occur just beyond the violet end of the spectrum, capable of stimulating chemical reactions and responsible, to a certain extent, for the breakdown of varnish films.

Ultraviolet absorbers —Varnish additives, refractive in nature, that retard the damaging effects of the sun's ultraviolet rays on a varnish finish. Also known as UVA or UV filters.

UV filters, or UVA —See Ultraviolet absorbers.

Varnish —A transparent finish usually consisting of resins, drying oils, and various solvents that dries in contact with air by evaporation of its volatile constituents, by the oxidation of its oil and resin ingredients, or by both methods, to a continuous protective coating. See also Spar varnish.

Vehicle —The liquid portion of a finish; oil is the vehicle for most varnishes. Anything dissolved in the liquid portion of a finish, a solid, for example (like a resin) then becomes part of the vehicle.

Veneer —Boards made by laminating thin sheets of wood together, the top or outside layers of which are often more expensive hardwoods, ultimately possessing more strength and better non-warping properties than solid planks of the same hardwoods.

Viscosity —The root of this word, viscous, is from the Latin "viscum" meaning "birdlime made from mistletoe," obviously very viscous stuff. . . . The viscosity of a material is its resistance to flow. Cold molasses has a high viscosity; cold water, very low.

Volatile thinner —A liquid that evaporates and that is used for thinning or reducing the consistency of finishing materials for ready absorption into the wood surface or ease of application.

Warping —A swerving or misshaping of the plane of a plank of wood or a thin veneer caused by the absorption or the loss of moisture.

Water white —A material is said to be water white when it is as colorless as water.

Water stain —A permanent black discoloration of the wood, found especially around exposed end-grain, around fasteners, and at joinery, caused by prolonged absorption of water; hardwoods lacking a high natural oil content, such as spruce, mahogany, and white oak, are particularly susceptible to such staining.

Waterline —The horizontal line, often marked with a painted stripe, at the point of water displacement on a boat's hull; the boundary, visually, between a boat's "bottom" and its "topsides."

Weather resisting —Finishes or finishing materials (such as extended-use masking tapes) capable of resisting deterioration from exposure to the weather.

Wet edge —The brushability of a stroke of varnish or paint that endures when speedy application is made of subsequent strokes of the material, resulting in a surface free of lap lines and brush marks.

Wet/Dry vacuum —An industrial type of vacuum designed for use in vacuuming liquids as well as dry materials.

Wet-sanding —Using water or oil to aid in the shaping or finishing of a wood or varnish surface with sandpaper; requires the use of specially designed wet-or-dry sandpapers, which will not disintegrate from the exposure to moisture.

Wind —The sailor's consort, the varnisher's enemy.

Wood oil —See Tung oil.

Wow —A slight depression in the plane of the wood; what you should hope to hear passersby saying about your varnish.

Wrinkling —An irregularity of the varnish surface in the form of puckered or wrinkled areas; also known as rivelling.

Yacht —The best definition of this term I've ever read is this paragraph from Bruce Bingham's *The Sailor's Sketchbook*: "A yacht is, indeed, a boat but a boat is not necessarily a yacht. . . . A boat is only a yacht when she has dignity, polish, and class. What a boat and yacht have in common, besides being able to float, is the unique ability to reflect their owner's attitudes and degrees of fortitude, patience, attention to detail, and the desire for beauty and respect for things produced through human effort. However large or small, old or new, a yacht tells who and what we are: caring owners and loving friends. She is the profound expression and extension of ourselves."

Ziploc storage bags —A brand of plastic storage bags, sold in various sizes, that close to an air-tight state by pressing a specially designed sealing strip together; the best means of protecting refinishing materials such as masking tape, varnish strainers, foam brushes, etc., from getting dirty and becoming unusable after their purchase and before one needs them.

CONCLUSION:
A BRIGHTWORK JUNKIE'S
PHILOSOPHY

*I*n all walks of life, we seek a foundation of knowledge that will direct us in our journeys. Ultimately we do best finding our way down those paths with the things we know best; the theories that work are the ones we believe in, regardless of how much they may differ from the next person's.

So it goes with brightwork. For every varnish made, there will always be an adherent and a detractor; the same for every type of brush, oil, grit of sandpaper, method of stripping, and varnish additive. Even the languages within this unique society differ from one camp to the next. One person's *tomahto* will always be another's *tomayto*. Efifons, Epifaynes, Epifanns; Deks Olje will forever be Decks Olyuh to some (those who read the front of the label), Decks Olgee to others, and Decks Olé to many. Never mind the correctness or the original intent behind any of these disparities. Our utterances of names, philosophies, and product success stories come from the place that supersedes the gray matter: our hearts.

Like languages, every person who speaks a certain brightwork tongue will defend to the death his right to speak it, because in that language he is able to do his best thinking. Don't argue with someone from Quebec over the propriety of French on his street signs. Likewise, don't engage a longtime lover of Penetrol in a battle over its place in his varnish. These people are moving through life communicating from that most valid of all platforms: their own interpretation of the truth.

This book is a collection of my brightwork truths. With luck, language barriers won't prevent its readers from grasping my intent, which is to simply share those interpretations.

> Thus, Courteous Reader, are we at length arriv'd at our desired Port: Our Performances have been no way inferior to our Promises. What we ingaged for in the beginning, we have punctually accomplisht; and nothing certainly remains, but that you convert our Precepts to Practice; for that will be the ready way to examin, and try, whether they are false or insufficient. We have all along been directed by an unerring Guide, Experience; and do therefore advise you, upon the least miscarriage, to make a diligent review, and doubt not but second thought will convince you of too slight an observance. We desire you'd be as exact and regular in your performances, as we have been in ours; for by these means, Satisfaction will attend both Parties, all our designs must succeed to our wish, and our Labours shall be crowned with success and reputation.

FINIS.

A reproduction of the last paragraph from *A Treatise of Japanning and Varnishing —1688*, by John Stalker and George Parker

BIBLIOGRAPHY

Beiser, Arthur. *The Proper Yacht.* 2nd ed. Camden, Maine: International Marine Publishing Company, 1978.

Bingham, Bruce. *The Sailor's Sketchbook.* Newport, Rhode Island: Seven Seas Press, 1983.

Burkill, I.H. *A Dictionary of the Economic Products of the Malay Peninsula.* Kuala Lumpur, Malaysia: Ministry of Agriculture and Cooperatives, 1966.

Chatfield, H.W. *Glossary of Terms Used in the Paint, Varnish and Allied Trades.* London: Scott Greenwood & Son, Ltd., 1951.

Edlin, Herbert. *What Wood Is That?* London: Thames and Hudson, Ltd., 1969.

Feller, Stolow, and Jones. *On Picture Varnishes and Their Solvents.* Washington, D.C.: National Gallery of Art, 1985.

Fisher, E.M. "What You Should Know About Paint," *National Painters Magazine.* New York: Schnell Publishing Company, Inc., 1952.

Gibbia, S.W. *Wood Finishing and Refinishing,* 3rd ed. New York: Van Nostrand Reinhold Company, 1981.

Hess, Manfred. *Paint Film Defects — Their Causes and Cures.* New York: Reinhold Publishing Company, 1931.

Holley, C.D. and E.F. Ladd. *Analysis of Mixed Paints, Color Pigments, and Varnishes.* New York: John Wiley & Sons, Publishers, 1908.

Joachim, Benjamin. *Allied Paint and Varnish Chemistry.* St. Louis: American Paint Journal Company, 1934.

Mantell, C.L., C.W. Kopf, J.L. Curtis, and E.M. Rigers, *The Technology of Natural Resins.* New York: John Wiley & Sons, Publishers, 1942.

Martin, Ray C. *Glossary of Paint, Varnish, Lacquer, and Allied Terms.* St. Louis: American Paint Journal Company, 1937.

O'Neil, Isabel. *The Art of the Painted Finish.* New York: William Morrow & Company, 1971.

Pardey, Larry. "Bare Wood —The Salty, Scrubbed Look," *Sail* magazine. Boston: November, 1986.

Parker, Dean H. *Principles of Surface Coating Technology.* New York: Interscience Publishers, John Wiley & Sons, Publishers, 1965.

Sabin, Alvah Horton. *The Industrial and Artistic Technology of Paint and Varnish.* New York: John Wiley & Sons, Publishers, 1905.

Soderberg, George. *Finishing Materials and Methods.* Bloomington, Illinois: McKnight & McKnight Publishing Company, 1959.

Toch, Maximilian. *The Chemistry and Technology of Paints.* New York: Van Nostrand and Company, 1916.

von Fisher, William, ed. *Paint and Varnish Technology.* New York: Reinhold Publishing Company, 1948.

INDEX

Acetone, 162
Acid bleach stripping: of oil finishes, 50, 59-63
Adhesive, tape: removal, 152-153
Alkyd resins, 27
Alligatoring, of varnish, 95
Anodized aluminum: protecting when bleaching, 121

Bare wood: as finish option, 16; maintenance of, 6, 16; seasoning finish for, 9
Bleaching: accoutrements, 149; products, 148; to clean teak decks, 120-124; to remove oil finishes, 59-63; to remove weathered spots, 68
Blistering, of varnish, 94
Blooming, of varnish, 95
Blushing, of varnish, 95
Brightwork: definition of, 5; essentials in, 144; finishes, choosing, 13, comprising, 15; first-aid kit, 105; organizing projects around, 43-45; qualifiers to options, 10-11
Brushes, 153-154
Brushing liquids, 34, 157. *See also* Mineral spirits
Bubbling, of varnish, 94
Buckets, disposable: for varnishing, 158
Bungs: replacing, 72; tendency to "wow," 69; waterstains surrounding, 70

Cabin soles: refinishing, 115-117
Canvas covers, 11, 100
Chamois skins: 165; using to clean varnish, 99-100, 127, 128
Checking, of varnish, 96
Chemical stripping, 50, 54-58
Chemical strippers: 146-147; tips on using, 147-148
Chipping, of varnish, 96

Clouding, of varnish, 95
Coatings: general types of, 49
Cocabola: finishes for, 20-21
Commissioning: finish options, 8, 10
Crawling, of varnish, 96

Decks, teak: bleaching, 120-124; maintaining, 127-128; oiling, 128-129; sanding, 124-127; trimming bloated seams, 124-125
Detailing: after varnishing, 94; preparatory to finish, 72-73
Deterioration, of varnish: assessing levels, 104-105
Diapers, cotton: using for brightwork, 164-165
Dockside etiquette, 131-132
Dry-scraping: to strip wood, 50, 58
Dutchman's pants: as weather barometer, 46-47

Epoxy: finish, removal of, 54; Hardman's five-minute, 165; filling voids with sawdust mixture, 71-72; resins in varnish 28
Etiquette, dockside, 131-132
Extended-use masking tapes, 150

Fillers, pastewood, 75
First-aid kit: for brightwork, 105; for personal safety, 168-169
Fish-eyes, in varnish, 96
Fittings: cleaning, 73, 164
Foam rollers: varnishing with, 154
Foam brushes. *See* Poly-foam brushes
Fogging, of varnish, 95

Gelcoat, fiberglass: cleaning off oil, 160; cleaning off varnish, 147

Gloves: latex, 168; neoprene-coated, 168; nitrile, 167-168

Hardwood scrapers, 56
Heat stripping, 49, 50-54
Heat guns: 135-136; stripping with, 50-54
Holidays, in varnishwork, 91
Hot-weather varnishing, 91

Interior finishes, 16, 81-84
Interlux: recommended varnishes, 155-156
Ironbark (*or* Ironwood): finishes for, 20

Japan drier: 163; adding to linseed oil sealer, 79

Kneepads, choosing proper, 168

Lacquer thinner, 162
Lifting, of varnish, 96
Linseed oil: 30-31; sealing mahogany with boiled, 78, 160; stabilizing unseasoned wood with, 10
Louvered doors: stripping, 54

Mahogany: 19; finishes for, 20
Maintenance, finish: oil, 84; planning, 11; varnish, 99-105
Masking tape. *See* Tape, masking
Masts. *See* Spars
Materials: general brightwork, 143-165; shopping for, 46
Methylene chloride: protection from, 55, 147; strippers containing, 147
Mineral spirits, 162

New boats: finish options for, 8, 11
Nitrile gloves. *See* gloves

PHOTO CREDITS

The author and publisher wish to thank the following, without whose contributions this book would have been like a yacht without brightwork. The page numbers on which their photos may be found appear after their names.

Neil Rabinowitz: 4, 12, 29, 68, 80, 82, 85, 113, 130, 142
Marty Loken: 38, 42, 57, 64, 71, 86, 133, 149, 161
Chris Eden: 1, 48, 61, 90, 134
Greg L'Esperance: Dedication page

All other photographs were taken by the author.